The Study of World Politics

The Study of World Politics, Volume 2: globalization and governance is the final volume of a collection of essays by James N. Rosenau.

James N. Rosenau's work is known for originality and clarity and the seventeen articles in this volume are no exception. The aim of this volume is to address the specific challenge posed by globalization and governance. The issues covered in this book include:

- the challenge – tensions, contradictions, outcomes and global affairs
- the profession – community, globalized space and international relations
- globalization – complexities, contradictions, and theory
- governance – understanding and future

The Study of World Politics is the product of one of the most innovative scholars in the last half century and the subjects addressed provide the big picture whilst also being meticulous in detail. This volume gives the reader an unparalleled understanding of globalization and governance and is an invaluable tool to students and scholars alike.

James N. Rosenau is University Professor of International Affairs at The George Washington University, USA, having previously been affiliated with three other universities. He is a former President of the International Studies Association (1984–5) and a holder of a Guggenheim Fellowship (1987–8). His books include *Turbulence in World Politics: A theory of change and continuity* (1990), *Along the Domestic–Foreign Frontier: Exploring governance in a turbulent world* (1997), and *Distant Proximities: Dynamics beyond globalization* (2003).

The Study of World Politics

Volume 2: globilization
and governance

James N. Rosenau

Routledge
Taylor & Francis Group

LONDON AND NEW YORK

First published 2006
by Routledge
2 Park Square, Milton Park, Abingdon, Oxon OX14 4RN

Simultaneously published in the USA and Canada
by Routledge
711 Third Avenue, New York, NY 10017

Routledge is an imprint of the Taylor & Francis Group

Transferred to Digital Printing 2006

Typeset in Baskerville by
RefineCatch Ltd, Bungay, Suffolk

British Library Cataloguing in Publication Data
A catalogue record for this book is available from the British Library

Library of Congress Cataloging in Publication Data
A catalog record for this book has been requested

ISBN13: 978-0-415-38549-7 (hbk)
ISBN13: 978-0-415-38548-0 (pbk)
ISBN13: 978-0-415-40462-4 (set)

Contents

PART III
Methods   79

PART IV
Concepts and theories   95

PART V
The analysis of foreign policy   169

Volume 2

Illustrations

Tables

Acknowledgments

Needless to say, a long career of writing incurs a number of intellectual and administrative debts. In addition to assistants in four universities and my invisible college – those colleagues and students in the field who have provided suggestions and criticisms on panels and in correspondence and who are too numerous to list – I am especially grateful to Hongying Wang for her advice and support in the process of completing this two-volume project.

*   *   *

Several chapters of this volume were previously published, and I am grateful to the publishers of those works for permission to reprint them here.

Chapter 2, "The new global order: underpinnings and outcomes," was excerpted from a chapter written for Armand Clesse, Richard Cooper, and Yoshikazu Sakamoto (eds.), *The International System After the Collapse of the East–West Order* (Dordrecht, Netherlands; Martinus Nijhoff, 1994), pp 106–26, and is reprinted here with permission of Brill Academic Publishers.

Chapter 4, "Aging agendas and ambiguous anomalies," was originally published in Stephanie Lawson (ed.), *New Agenda for International Relations* (Cambridge: Polity Press, 2002), pp. 19–34, and is reprinted here with permission of Polity Press.

Chapter 5, "Global affairs in an epochal transformation," first appeared in Edward Peartree and Ryan Henry (eds.), *The Information Revolution and International Security* (Washington, DC: CSIS, 1998), and is reprinted here by permission of the CSIS Press.

Chapter 6, "Material and imagined communities in globalized Space," was originally published in Donald H. McMillen (ed.), *Globalization and Regional Communities: Geoeconomic, Sociocultural and Security Implications for Australia* (Toowomba, Australia: USQ Press, 1997), pp. 24–40, and is reprinted here by permission of Donald McMillen.

Chapter 7, "Many globalizations, one international relations," was originally published in the inaugural issue of *Globalizations* (No. 1, 2004), and is reprinted here with permission of Taylor and Francis Ltd, http://www.tandf.co.uk/journals.

Chapter 8, "The globalization of globalization," was originally published in Michael Breecher and Frank Harvey (eds.), *Millennium Reflections on International*

Studies (Ann Arbor, MI: University of Michigan Press, 2002), pp. 271–90, © The University of Michigan, and is reprinted here by permission.

Chapter 9, "The complexities and contradictions of globalization," incorporates excerpts from two articles which originally appeared in *Security Dialogue*: "New Dimensions of Security: The Interaction of Globalizing and Localizing Dynamics", Vol. 25 (September 1994), pp. 255–81, © International Peace Research Institute, Oslo (PRIO), 1994, and "The Dynamics of Globalization: Toward an Operational Formulation," Vol. 27 (September 1996), pp. 247–62, © International Peace Research Institute, Oslo (PRIO), 1996. Those articles are reused here with permission from SAGE Publications Ltd.

Chapter 13, "Toward an ontology for global governance," is reprinted by permission from *Approaches to Global Governance Theory* edited by Martin Hewson and Timothy J. Sinclair, the State University of New York Press. © 1999 State University of New York. All Rights Reserved. The chapter appeared as pages 287–301 in that volume.

Chapter 14, "Governance in the twenty-first century," is reprinted from *Global Governance: A Review of Multilateralism and International Organizations*, Vol. 1, No. 1. Copyright © 1995 by Lynne Rienner Publishers Inc. Used with permission.

Chapter 15, "Global governance as disaggregated complexity," was originally published in Alice D. Ba and Matthew J. Hoffmann (eds.), *Contending Perspectives on Global Governance: Coherence, Contestation and World Order* (London: Routledge, 2005), pp. 131–53.

Chapter 16, "Change, complexity, and governance in globalizing space," was originally published in Jan Pierre (ed.), *Debating Governance* (Oxford: Oxford University Press, 2000), pp. 167–200, and is reprinted here by permission of Oxford University Press, www.oup.com.

Chapter 17, "Strong demand, huge supply: governance in an emergent epoch" was originally published in Ian Bache and Matthew Flinders (eds.), *Multi-Level Governance* (New York: Oxford University Press, 2004), pp. 31–48, and is reprinted here by permission of Oxford University Press, www.oup.com.

Again, I must acknowledge the hard work and editorial skill of my research assistant, Miles Townes, to whom fell the tasks of acquiring these permissions and otherwise assisting in the preparation of the manuscript. I am very grateful for his help. I am also grateful to my publisher, Craig Fowlie, for his support in generating and supporting this project.

1 Introduction

In contrast to the first volume of this two-volume selection of my essays on *The Study of World Politics*, those included here focus on two substantive phenomena. The first volume is subtitled *Theoretical and Methodological Challenges* and spans a wide range of conceptual problems confronted across nearly five decades of probing why world affairs unfold as they do. Here, on the other hand, the essays were all written since the end of the Cold War, a landmark event in the sense that it resulted in the surfacing of new structures and processes through which the affairs of polities, societies, and economies are conducted. The termination of the US–Soviet rivalry permitted a rapid and vast acceleration of the dynamics of globalization in every realm of human endeavor, an acceleration that, in turn, highlighted the question of whether and how world affairs could be governed. Hence this volume is subtitled *Globalization and Governance* since these two complex phenomena have constituted the core of my writing since 1989.

To describe the two central phenomena as complex is to understate the enigmas they pose. Globalization has a number of dimensions that are so loosely linked that one is tempted to cling to a narrow formulation that focuses on trade, finance, and other economic structures and processes rather than allowing for the diversity of the interactions which have and continue to undergo globalizing dynamics. Indeed, much of the literature on the subject is framed in this narrow context and, as such, offers clear-cut, though contentious, perspectives on the nature and underpinnings of globalization. While in no way dismissing the importance of the economic dimension, I prefer to confront the complexities of a broad conception of globalizing processes and to treat them as having a common characteristic: namely, expansion across long-established national and societal boundaries. As can be seen in Table 8.1, this broad formulation has led to the identification of innumerable foci worthy of systematic inquiry.

The transformations of world affairs that followed the end of the Cold War and their implications for the study of globalization are probed in the chapters of Parts 1 and 2, while some of the dynamics of globalization itself are analyzed in Part 3. Relatively speaking, these chapters are straightforward in the sense that they are rooted in my conviction that globalization consists of boundary-spanning ideas and activities. Taken together, they contend that the new, post-Cold War arrangements have lessened the role of the state, that a central feature of the arrangements is a continuing disaggregation of authority in all parts of the world and all walks of life, and that consequently the salience of local phenomena has been heightened. Put differently, the global–local nexus underlies tensions between worldwide forces pressing for integration and those fostering fragmentation, an interaction that I have sought to capture in a label ("fragmegration") that combines the two forces.

These themes in the first eleven chapters are straightforward compared to those that permeate Part 4. The latter consists of five chapters that focus on the nature of governance on a global scale. While a vast literature has long existed on the structures and processes of governance, it has been largely concerned with governance and government at the local and national levels. The advent of pervasive globalization, however, has led to considerable speculation as to the ways in which governance can be and has been recast in a global context – what has come to be called "global governance."[1] Perforce, therefore, the analysis of these chapters is murky, with some overlap and duplication, and with a restless ambivalence weaving through them as I sought to identify reasons why the future of global governance is not bleak even as I point to several severe obstacles that may prevent the emergence of an effective set of institutions that would, in effect, amount to global governance. A measure of ambivalence can be discerned in a tendency to give new labels to the phenomena deemed to be reflective of the emergent trends toward global governance. As will be seen, for example, the most complex designation involves what I call "mobius-web governance," which is elsewhere described as

> Rooted in the impetus to employ rule systems that steer issues through both hierarchical and networked interactions across levels of aggregation that may encompass all the diverse collectivities and individuals who participate in the processes of governance. These interactions constitute a hybrid structure in which the dynamics of governance are so intricate and overlapping among the several levels as to form a singular weblike process that, like a mobius, neither begins nor culminates at any level or at any point in time. Mobius-web governance does not culminate with the passage of a law or compliance with its regulations. Rather, it is operative as long as the issues subjected to governance continue to be of concern.[2]

In order to retain the original context in which the essays were written I did not revise them with a view to rendering them consistent with the structures and processes that evolved in subsequent years. It is tempting to display one's wisdom by retrospectively indicating the accuracy of one's earlier writings. Such a display, however, is profoundly misleading, if not essentially disingenuous and deceitful. So here the reader will find all the misreadings and miscalculations to which analysts of world affairs are prone. Some expected outcomes proved to be sound, but others were erroneous. For the most part, however, the expected developments were cast at a level of abstraction high enough to avoid being dead wrong.

The temptation to up-date the citations was especially acute because some of the cited materials were encompassed in subsequent books. Yet, again it seemed prudent to present the essays as they were originally written in order to convey a sense of how the various ideas evolved and fluctuated. This process can be discerned in the way my preoccupation with the global–local nexus is articulated in several essays even as it ultimately culminated in my 2003 book quoted above.

In short, the collective goal of the essays turns out to be that of provoking thought about the complexities and dynamics that presently sustain world politics. At the very least it is hoped that the ensuing analysis will contribute to an appreciation of the difficulties that attach to comprehending the sources and consequences of globalization and global governance.

Part I
The challenge

2 The new global order

Underpinnings and outcomes[1]

What heady years these have been! In 1988 six wars came to an end.[2] In 1989 the Berlin wall came down and the Cold War came to an end. In 1990 a 32-nation coalition formed to contest and reverse a despot's naked aggression in the Middle East. In 1991 that aggression, under authority granted by the United Nations, was quickly ended and reversed.

So swiftly and so extensively did these events follow on each other that hopes soared, allowing people to dare to believe that the world had shaken the shackles of the past and was moving onto something new and, presumably, better. Yes, uncertainty was pervasive and, yes, problems remain; but now it was possible to imagine that humankind was on a different track, a saner, gentler track that offered the potential for righting wrongs and ameliorating distortions. History, it seemed, had ended,[3] or at least its "very texture . . . was changing before our very eyes."[4] Nothing less than a new global order was in the making. Presidents proclaimed it, pundits affirmed it, and people sensed it.

And then came the aftermath. Instead of the arms trade dwindling to a trickle, its flow expanded. Instead of the European Community opening its doors to new states clamoring for membership, it reverted to old hesitations and squabbles. Instead of evolving a new set of arrangements for the Middle East, the states of that region reverted to old patterns and historic enmities. Israel remained stubbornly opposed to change. Saudi Arabia retreated behind its long-standing cultural barriers. Saddam Hussein still controlled Iraq and continued to oppress its minorities. Instead of thriving on greater independence, Czechoslovakia split in two and Yugoslavia collapsed into a brutal civil war. By mid-1993 nothing seemed new. The emergent global order appeared to be no more than a mirage, a momentary fantasy of what might have been, proof that hopes should be contained and aspirations narrowed. History, it could be argued, was deceptive. Rather than tracing new paths into the sunset, it offered a dizzying ride on a roller coaster.[5]

Global orders as outcomes

The ensuing analysis suggests that this ups-and-downs approach to the turbulence of our time is an erroneous reading of history. It suffers from a failure to distinguish between global orders and global underpinnings, between outcomes and sources, between hopes and fears on the one hand and dynamic forces on the other.

Although much of the discussion about an emergent global order focuses on empirical changes – the collapse of Communism, the splintering of the Soviet Union, the UN resolutions and the 32-nation coalition – its conclusions invariably concern the way in which the changes portend new value hierarchies, new arrangements whereby self-serving actions in the international arena are sub-ordinated to collective interests that allow for the promotion and preservation of democratic values, a more equitable distribution of resources, and a wider set of opportunities for people and states to participate in the decisions that shape their fates. And most of all, the emergent order is conceived to embody new ways of establishing and maintaining peace on a regional and global scale.

Although there is no inherent reason why dialogues over the structures and vulnerabilities of the prevailing global order should give way to debates about its prospect for improving the human condition, somehow they always do. Perhaps this is because the word "order" is itself loaded with value dimensions. To estab-lish and maintain collective order is to achieve a measure of harmony among groups and between them and nature. To be plagued or threatened with collective disorder is to suffer conflict among groups and asymmetries between them and nature. With few exceptions, no one favors disorder; most aspire to an under-lying order so that they can get on with their tasks and move toward their goals. Yet, one person's order is another's disorder, and herein lies the incentive to recast, knowingly or otherwise, any analytic discussion of global order into a value context.

Another powerful inducement to ponder the prevailing order in value terms derives from the relevance of power and hierarchy to the conduct of world affairs. The most immediately visible activities on the international scene all involve collectivities – governments, organizations, groups – at all levels of aggregation seeking to get other collectivities to comply with their demands. In so doing they exercise power in various forms and their successes and failures in this regard manifest a hierarchical pattern, what is perhaps best described as the international pecking order. This power-derived hierarchical dimension of the prevailing global order evokes value perspectives because it can serve as an easy explanation for why things happen the way they do: noxious outcomes are seen by those lacking power to be the work of those who have power, just as the resistance of the Have-nots is explained by the Haves as stemming from long-standing grievances or efforts to break free of severe constraints imposed by the existing pecking order.

From this reasoning it is a short step to the presumption that the roots of the prevailing order are to be found in the distribution of global power, the hierarchy to which it gives rise, and the superior–subordinate relationships it sustains. Thus it is that students of world politics speak of hegemonic orders, balance-of-power orders, and a variety of other arrangements which depict who gets whom to get things done in the way they are done. From this reasoning it also follows that when the distribution of power among states remains stable across long stretches of time, uncertainty is at a minimum and order is at a maximum. The stable order may be noxious or it may be praiseworthy, but in any event it is a hierarchy which describes the arrangements through which world politics unfold.

Thus it is that wars, the collapse of ideologies, and the breakdown of governments, fostering as they do vast uncertainties and extensive speculation as to how key actors will adapt to the new circumstances, can give rise to visions of a new global order emerging out of the one that collapsed with the outbreak of hostilities, the bankruptcy of ideologies, and the changes in officialdom. Surely, the reasoning goes, such conditions constitute a propitious moment, a time to be seized for the establishment of a new, more equitable pecking order and for the encouragement of innovative patterns that bring fresh thought and resolve to bear on old conflicts.

And thus too can hopes for a new order be dashed as the terms of peace, the expression of post-ideological aspirations, and the fragility of newly installed governments fail to live up to the expectations engendered by the collapse of the old patterns. Never mind that planning never moved beyond the presumption that profound change would alter the way things are done, that little thought was given to the nature of the emergent order and the new arrangements that would replace the old hierarchies and conflict resolution processes. Surely, at such a propitious moment things are bound to get better!

That is why hopes soared through 1990 and into the first three months of 1991: the moment had arrived, with George Bush leading the way in voicing the conviction that the old order collapsed with the Cold War and that the Gulf War was the first great incident of a new, emergent order. And that is why, too, the hopes came crashing down as history moved into and beyond the remaining quarters of 1991, when it became increasingly clear that sovereign states were bent upon clinging protectively to their self-interests and that the remaining superpower was neither able nor willing to exercise the power necessary to get all concerned to break with past patterns and adopt new security arrangements.

Global order as underpinnings

But there is another way to conceive of global order. If the existing hierarchy and the relational patterns it sustains are viewed as outcomes, as the result of complex dynamics which reach deep into societies and only slowly come to their surfaces, then these underlying dynamics can be treated as a form of order. As the arrangements from which outcomes derive, these underpinnings include the viability of the sovereignty principle, the emergence of new types of actors and the capacity of states to manage them, the basic orientations which publics and governments have toward the nature of authority, and the skills through which citizens and officials exercise their responsibilities and participate in world affairs. If such dynamics undergo transformation, then a new order, an underlying order that will eventually surface to reshape the conduct of governments and the structure of the international pecking order, can be said to have moved into place.

It is the contention of the remainder of this paper that the underpinnings of world politics have undergone a profound transformation and that signs of it have already surfaced even if much of the current scene appears very much yet another replay of history. What follows, in other words, asserts that a new global order has emerged! It is not the kind of order that people have been looking for and, indeed, it remains only dimly, if at all, recognized. Nor does it rest on values having to do with the certainties of a predictable hierarchy or the uncertainties of prevailing conflict patterns. It is, rather, an empirical order, one that can still evolve in either desirable or noxious directions.

The distinction between global orders as underpinnings and as outcomes is important because the former are not readily observable and their impact is not easily assessed. The origins and sustenance of a social order are to be found largely in minds and hearts – in ideas, orientations, predispositions, habits, and belief systems – and their existence thus has to be inferred from behavior rather than being the behavior itself. If these ideational sources take a long time to mature, however, the outcomes that are observed in world politics can, for a long time, continue to seem like the same old way of conducting business. The manifest behavior, in other words, reflects long-standing habits that still get acted upon even as they are steadily being undermined by the transformation of the deeper underpinnings from which they originally sprung. Thus a time lag exists between the time when underpinnings change and the reflection of those changes in the outcomes that comprise the daily routines and crises of world politics.

Viewed in this way, the Cold War and the order on which it rested did not collapse suddenly in 1989. Rather, it began its long downhill slide well before the Berlin Wall came down and the people of Eastern Europe threw off the yoke of their Communist regimes. These latter developments were only the last stage in a complex process whereby the ideational foundations of the post-World War II order underwent transformation. To be sure, pundits, politicians, academics, and people everywhere were taken by surprise when the governments in Prague, Budapest, Sofia, and other East European capitals were, suddenly, replaced. But the pervasiveness of the surprise is not so much a measure of the rapidity with which history changed course as it was a measure of how fully people tend to focus on outcomes rather than underpinnings when they respond to the course of events. Had they been sensitive to underpinnings, to the deeper sources of the events that caught their eyes, they would have appreciated well before 1989 that a new global order was in the process of evolving.

At the heart of this new global order are new ideational constructs that value autonomy over compliance and interdependence over independence. Autonomy can mean a variety of things, depending on the context in which it is assessed, but in all contexts it involves a readiness to contest authority whenever the alternative involves yielding to tradition and unthinking acceptance of unwanted directives issued by those higher in the pecking order. This underlying ideational premise applies to the individual in the group, the group in the province, the province in the state, the state in the international organization, and so on. The scopes of these contexts differ, but the same readiness to seek autonomy by founding legitimacy on performance rather than convention obtains for all of them. Examples of it surfacing in these diverse contexts are abundant once one begins to think in terms of the underpinnings of global order: in the mass defections from

Communist parties, through the intifada, around the Berlin Wall and the squares of East European cities, in the demands of various Soviet republics in 1990, in the actions of the US in UNESCO during the 1980s, and so on.

But to aspire to autonomy is not necessarily to seek independence. Rather achieving autonomy means being free to select the ways in which interdependence with other individuals, groups, provinces, states, and international organizations is established. The world has become too complex and dynamic for independence to satisfy needs and wants. Instead there is widespread recognition at the ideational level that needs and wants have to be sought through reciprocal arrangements with others, that it is not contradictory to maintain both autonomous and interdependent relationships in the global system. Thus concerned individuals have spawned large and unwieldy social movements, ecological groups have formed regional consortia, nine republics in the Soviet Union have sought to pursue some form of federation, the states of Europe have pooled their efforts to establish a greater degree of union, and the US and Canada have reached out to Mexico in an effort to widen their free trade agreement.

The transformation of three parameters

If the dominant outcomes of the emergent global order derive from a stress on autonomy in the context of interdependence, as distinguished from the old order's emphasis upon compliance in the context of independence, what are its underpinnings? What has undergone transformation such that the new ideational premises are fostering new outcomes even as long-standing patterns seem to be still in place?

My answer to these questions involves the basic parameters of world politics. If the parameters of any system are conceived as the boundaries beyond which lie the environment of the system – those recurrent patterns that may impact upon but are not a part of the system's functioning – and within which the variables of the system undergo their ceaseless processes of variation, then it follows that the parameters are normally fixed features of the system. They provide its continuities in the sense that they remain constant even as fluctuations occur in its variables. Thus they are, in effect, the foundations of global order – those values, premises, resources, and enduring institutions that underlie and limit the nature of the international pecking order, that accord legitimacy to alliances, that underpin orientations toward war, that justify concern for human rights, that shape predispositions toward authority and authorities, and so on through all the sources out of which variation occurs within the system.

If the parameters of world politics form the bases of the prevailing global order, then a new global order is bound to emerge if and when its parameters undergo profound transformation. And that is exactly what has happened in recent decades. For the first time since the period that culminated in the Treaty of Westphalia in 1648, the basic parameters of world politics have undergone extensive and rapid alteration, with the result that the underpinnings of a new world order have been laid.[6]

Table 2.1 Transformation of three global parameters

	from	*to*
micro parameter	individuals less analytically skill-ful and cathectically competent	individuals more analytically skillful and cathetically competent
macro-micro parameter	authority structures in place as people rely on traditional and/or constitutional sources of legitim-acy to comply with directives emanating from appropriate macro institutions	authority structures in crisis as people evolve performance cri-teria for legitimacy and compli-ance with the directives issued by macro officials
macro parameter	anarchic system of nation-states	bifurcation of anarchic system into state- and multi-centric subsystems

Elsewhere I have identified three parameters that are central to any prevailing global order: the overall structure of global politics (a macro parameter), the authority structures that link macro collectivities to citizens (a macro-micro parameter), and the skills of citizens (a micro parameter).[7] Each of these param-eters is judged to have undergone transformation in the current era, and the relative simultaneity of the transformations is considered a major reason why signs of an emergent global order – of deep underpinnings fostering unexpected outcomes – took politicians, journalists, academics, and others so utterly by surprise when the collapse of Communism rendered them unmistakably manifest late in 1989.

Table 2.1 summarizes the changes in the three parameters, but the order of their listing should not be interpreted as implying causal sequences in which the actions of individuals are conceived to precede the behavior of collectivities. On the contrary, incisive insights into the emergent world order are crucially dependent on an appreciation of the profoundly interactive nature of the three parameters – on recognizing that even as individuals shape the actions and orien-tations of the collectivities to which they belong, so do the goals, policies, and laws of the latter shape the actions and orientations of individuals. Out of such inter-action a network of causation is fashioned that is so thoroughly intermeshed as to render impossible the separation of causes from effects. Indeed, much of the rapidity of the transformations at work in world politics can be traced to the ways in which the changes in each parameter stimulate and reinforce the changes in the other two.

3 Ominous tensions in a globalizing world[1]

I prepared these remarks at a time (May 2002) when, from one American's perspective, the prospects for improving the security of peoples everywhere seem quite dim. At the micro level of individuals, insecurity is rampant and on the increase. In the words of one observer,

> There is so much fear in us today. There is fear of crime, but there is also fear of a more general nature. It used to be that people worked all their lives for the same company. Now, they change all the time. Companies fold, factories close. Life seems more and more precarious . . .[2]

And these insecurities are fully reflected on the global agenda at the macro level of collectivities and states. At this level security concerns have broadened well beyond military and strategic considerations to include restless publics, shaky economies, and fragile governments. The stalemated Israeli–Palestine conflict, the readiness of many Middle Eastern youth to become suicide bombers, the emergence of anti-immigrant sentiment and politicians in several European countries, and the inability of the Bush Administration to exercise the required leadership, underlie a pervasive foreboding as to the future of world affairs.

In short, we live in a very messy world, messier I think than was the case in earlier decades. Granted that every generation thinks it has more problems than its predecessors, but a case can readily be made that the present era is far messier than any other, that today's insecurities are more pervasive, its uncertainties more elusive, its ambiguities more perplexing, and its complexities more extensive. Let me briefly make that case by stressing that the central differentiation between the present epoch and previous ones involves the acceleration of personal, community, national, and international life. Due to innovative electronic technologies, to jet aircraft that move hundreds of thousands of people every year from one part of the world to another, and to the resulting shrinkage of time and distance, people and societies today have become substantially more interdependent than was the case in earlier eras. What is distant today is also proximate, and the prevalence of these distant proximities is what sets our time apart from previous generations.[3]

One major consequence of the accelerated pace of life in our time is the breakdown of long-standing boundaries – those boundaries that differentiate the public from the private, the domestic from the foreign, the local from the global, the political from the economic, to mention only a few of the distinctions that had become commonplace and that are today so obscure as to be the source of the widespread insecurities, uncertainties, ambiguities, and complexities that prevail throughout the world. The September 11 attacks did not initiate the insecurities, uncertainties, ambiguities, and complexities; rather, the attacks aggravated dynamics that were already deeply rooted in the social, political, and economic life of people, communities, and societies.

Until now I have always been an optimist about the probabilities of globalization fostering long-term processes of reconciliation among those groups caught up in seemingly intractable tensions. But my optimism is under severe challenge today. The repercussions of the Middle Eastern and India–Pakistan crises as well as the war on terrorism strike me as being on an order of magnitude far beyond any that have been experienced since the end of the Cold War. Indeed, the Cold War was at least marked by a form of stability, but today instability, even chaos, seems to mark the prevailing order. And it does so in such a way as to cast doubt on whether the liberating dimensions of globalization are sufficient to reverse the descent toward worldwide chaos and thereby achieve a modicum of security for both peoples and collectivities.

One way to probe future likelihoods is to distinguish between order and fragmentation in and among societies on the one hand and between the desirability and undesirability of these conditions on the other. And one way to probe the likelihood of globalization fostering long-term processes of reconciliation is to focus on how its underlying dynamics play out at several levels of aggregation. Let me explore briefly each of these paths of inquiry by way of trying to salvage my optimism in the face of pervasive forebodings.

Order and fragmentation

Order and fragmentation have always been integral features of world affairs, but due to technological developments that have shrunk time and distance, today they are considerably more interactive than ever before. The tempo of global life within and among countries has accelerated to the point where it is plausible to assert that each increment of order gives rise to an increment of fragmentation, and vice versa. So as to stress and capture the extent of this interaction, I have long argued that its centrality to the course of events justifies a special label, one that highlights the ways in which the tensions between order and fragmentation are inextricably linked to each other. My label for this linkage is "fragmegration," a term that derives in part from fragmentation and in part from integration and that has the virtue, despite its grating and contrived nature, of capturing in a single word these contrary tendencies and thus serving as a reminder of how closely they are interwoven. Indeed, I would argue that the best way to grasp global life today is to view it through fragmegrative lenses, to treat every circumstance and every process as an instance of fragmegrative dynamics.[4]

To appreciate the links between order and fragmentation it is important to recognize that both concepts are loaded with values, that one person's order is another's disorder and that what is fragmentation for some is coherence for others. Both order and fragmentation, in other words, can be desirable or undesirable, depending on the value perspective through which they are assessed. Put more specifically, order can suggest group or societal arrangements that process issues peacefully and creatively, allowing diverse groups to participate freely in how the issues are handled; or it can connote a deadly stagnation and tyrannical hierarchy that inhibits free participation by those encompassed by the issues. Likewise, fragmentation can highlight the breakdown of coherence and the onset of chaos; or it can point to a pluralism that affords opportunities for various groups to pursue their goals. Table 3.1 depicts four different societal conditions and political forms that may prevail when the value dimensions of order and fragmentation are taken into consideration.

Once the analytic concepts of order and fragmentation are pondered in the context of value perspectives in this way, and irrespective of whether they are approached with the war on terrorism and the other foreboding situations in mind, the question arises as to whether any of the four conditions constitute the central tendency at work in the twenty-first century. Quite aside from our prefer- ence for either of the two desirable conditions, are they likely to succumb in the long run to either of the two undesirable arrangements? Is the world headed for pervasive tyrannies and endless chaos? Or does humankind have the will, the resources, the imagination, and the perseverance to sustain and expand some form of democratic order? In short, are fragmegrative dynamics likely to render the future insufferable or manageable?

In good part the answers to these questions must rest on empirical assessments, but they are equally rooted in our temperaments, our inclinations toward opti- mistic or pessimistic conceptions of the human condition. It is a mistake, I think, to resort to our professional training and treat the questions as simply a matter of gathering data and sifting them for evidence. Inevitably our responses are rooted in either coherent value schemes or uncoordinated impressions and, as such, they amount to huge judgments about elusive phenomena. In an intensely fragmegra- tive era neither limited judgments nor clear-cut phenomena can yield an adequate understanding of where humankind is headed. Perforce we must engage in nuanced analysis even as we give voice to our underlying impulses and intuitive feelings.

Table 3.1 Desirable and undesirable order and fragmentation

	ORDER	FRAGMENTATION
DESIRABLE	centralized democracy	decentralized pluralism
UNDESIRABLE	tyranny	chaos

Furthermore, our nuanced analyses have to confront the reality that they have to be developed in what elsewhere I have described as conceptual jails.[5] All of us are ensconced in one or another such jail, in theoretical frameworks that organize our responses to events and that tend to be so thorough as to prevent us from discerning possible responses not encompassed by our frameworks. For example, despite the profound ways in which the September 11 attacks demonstrated the porosity and weaknesses of states and the high salience of nongovernmental actors, most of us continue to think in terms of national sovereignty and a state-centric world in which the interactions of national governments determine the course of events. It is a powerful jail, so solidly constructed and so lacking in exits that we quickly dismiss as "radical" any ideas that posit transnational institutions as the route to a new and more secure world order. Such institutions are not neglected, but neither are they viewed as alternatives to the state system. In the words of one analyst, we are blissfully unaware of "how mired we all are in the mud of nationalism, unable to devise a genuine transnational policy that will let us begin to function as citizens of the world."[6] Similarly, even as we acknowledge that national sovereignty has undergone diminution and is caught up in profound transformative dynamics, so do we continue to respect and protest it.

The dynamics of globalization

In order to clarify the question of whether the future will be insufferable or manageable and thereby possibly point the way to a jailbreak from our all-encompassing conceptual prisons, I turn now to a path of inquiry that highlights the possibility of globalizing dynamics fostering long-term processes of reconciliation in this fragmegrative era. It must first be noted that none of the issues that mark the present world scene are sealed off from the global system. Thus all of them are incrementally shaped by the dynamics of fragmegration. I refer here not to pressures emanating from the interstate system, such as the policies pursued by the US or the parties to the Middle Eastern crisis – though such pressures are not irrelevant – but rather I have in mind even more fundamental external dynamics: those worldwide socio-economic and political influences that underlie the structures of states and derive from the orientations of publics, the precepts of cultures, the proliferation of organizations, and the nature of economies (see Table 8.1).

Many of these dynamics reflect the ever-growing role played by individuals at the micro level in world affairs. A vast number of nongovernmental micro roles have evolved – combatants, innocent victims, commanders, strategists, suppliers, narcotraffickers, reformers, urbanites, peasants, fundamentalists, merchants, suicide bombers, insurgents, land owners, conglomerate executives, sharecroppers, radicals, money launderers, unionists, protectionists, leftists, paramilitarists, guerrillas, aid workers, to mention but the more obvious ones – that enable men and women to engage in actions that have extensive macro consequences.

Put differently, it becomes increasingly difficult to probe world politics without taking into account the ways in which ordinary people shape the course of events. States and other macro collectivities are still crucial actors on the global stage, but numerous others have joined them. Our conceptual jails may impede our capacity to appreciate and assess the ever-greater role that people at the micro level are playing, but one can begin to grasp their greater roles by taking note of how suicide bombers, who lie outside the control of states, can take matters into their own hands and undermine negotiations designed to resolve some of the key conflicts that are high on the global agenda.

But are the interactive combinations of the eight sources of fragmegration set forth in Table 8.1 likely to contribute to a manageable future marked by security for individuals and collectively for the international system? Or, put more cautiously, is there any reason to believe that the forces underlying fragmegration can have salutary effects? One basis for an affirmative answer is that none of the societies and situations marked by intense conflict is immune to the fragmegrative dynamics. None can be oblivious to the pervasive impact of microelectronic technologies, the vast potential of the skill revolution, the power of the organizational explosion, the extensive consequences of the mobility upheaval, the continued institutionalization of global bifurcated structures, or the relentless globalization of national economies. And being parties to deep authority crises, all of them know this dynamic intimately as well as the extent to which states, sovereignty, and territoriality are weakening. In subtle and crucial ways, in short, situations everywhere are caught up in the forces that are transforming the course of events.

However, to be exposed to these forces is not necessarily to be acquiescent to their power. Conceivably the situations wracked with tensions and conflict can continue for several more decades without let up. With scenarios that trace a descent into chaos continuing to be viable, perhaps even probable if the momentum against globalization continues to mount without being addressed, it is possible that conflicted societies and situations will prove to be immune to the various fragmegrative dynamics. Put differently, it is hard to imagine advances toward collective security in the international system if such advances lack the support of the many types of aforementioned individuals who now occupy key roles on the global stage.

Can optimism be justified?

Thus one is faced with this question, and responding to it is not easy for me. My temperament is pervasively optimistic, but my analytic antennae tell me that on a global scale the central tendencies may well unfold more toward tyranny and chaos than democracy and pluralism. I can readily construct scenarios in which global governance proves insufficient to cope with the potential for chaos that prevails in most parts of the world. Such a perspective derives not so much from the implications of September 11 (though that is not a trivial aspect of the possible disarray), but more from the seemingly low, even very low, probability that global governance can effectively reduce the rich–poor gap, control the squalor of ever more crowded urban areas, fashion a modicum of worldwide consensus around a set of core values necessary to the predominance of democracy and pluralism, diminish environmental pollution, replenish the world's supplies of water, raise the income of the more than two billion people who presently earn less than $2 a day, bring a modicum of peace to the Middle East, moderate the conflict over Kashmir, re-orient the US in the direction of sharing its wealth more fully, enable the peoples of Africa to lift themselves out of poverty and sickness – to mention only the more obvious problems that seem intractable and enduring.

Yet, an optimistic temperament will not yield readily to a parade of horribles. Further reflection allows for the nuanced possibility that the four conditions set forth in Table 3.1 are not necessarily mutually exclusive. Elsewhere I have argued that a prime characteristic of our fragmegrative circumstances is a widespread and persistent trend toward the disaggregation of authority. The potential for disaggregation is implicit in the dynamics outlined in Table 2.1 of the previous chapter – as people everywhere become more skillful, as authority crises become more pervasive, and as global structures undergo bifurcation. Viewed optimistic-ally, at least parts of the disaggregated, networked world can amount as much to an order marked by constructive pluralism as to one mired in deleterious chaos. Indeed, the more disaggregated global governance becomes, the less will be the scope for tyrannies to operate effectively.

In short, a modicum of optimism is salvaged by viewing the long-run future as likely to consist of pockets of democracy and pluralism managing to function and flourish in the face of widespread and pervasive tyrannies and chaos. Nor can one ignore the democratic and pluralistic institutions committed to overcoming tyr-anny and minimizing chaos. The power and competence of such institutions, both INGOs and NGOs, is limited, to be sure, but they can draw on an endless reservoir of good will to achieve global governance that is both effective and ennobling. There is, moreover, a dialectic relationship between democratic or pluralistic order and tyrannical or chaotic fragmentation. As instances of the latter become more salient they trigger renewed efforts to establish the former. One is reminded of the age-old dilemma of the liberal: oft-times things need to get worse so as to unleash forces that strive to make them better.

Conclusion

In sum, despite a host of value and empirical obstacles, we cannot shy away from assessing where the world is headed. The prospects for order and fragmentation are too crucial to ignore. Collective perspectives voiced from an ivory tower may not always be accurate or informed, but they will be thoughtful and explicit, allowing for reconsideration and revision. My present view is that the long-term future is not likely to consist of new transformations. Rather I envision islands of desirable order and fragmentation surrounded by oceans of undesirable tyranny and chaos, with neither capable of encroaching on the other – a prolonged stalemate that is unlikely to yield to efforts at alteration in either direction.

4 Aging agendas and ambiguous anomalies

Tensions and contradictions of an emergent epoch[1]

> In the next century I believe most states will begin to change from cultlike entities charged with emotion into far simpler and more civilized entities, into less powerful and more rational administrative units that will represent only one of the many complex and multileveled ways in which our planetary society is organized.
>
> (Václav Havel[2])

There is both alliteration and causation embedded in the title of this paper. It bends unduly in the direction of alliteration because, in many cases, the anomalies that pervade world affairs are ambiguous and the agendas that guide our inquiries are aging. It has a causal dimension in the sense that the anomalies are rendering our agendas obsolete.

Put differently, we need to update our research agendas because the proliferating anomalies are indicative of a transforming world, a world that can no longer be adequately grasped by the research priorities that have guided us in the last few decades. To be sure, some items on the aging agendas will persist on the new ones. Doubtless the world will have to continue to be alert to the problems of nuclear proliferation, civil strife, population trends, Russia, global warming, and the growing gap between the rich and poor. Still, I believe the transformations at work in the world are so extensive that we can no longer confine our inquiries to these long-standing staples of our profession. If we do, if our research priorities are not updated to account for the new agenda items that lie just across the horizon, we'll be spinning our wheels while the world moves on without our input.

The updating task is not as easy as it may seem at first glance. The aging agendas are founded on a deep-seated habit that prevents us from pondering the implications of new empirical data, that does not readily yield to new conceptualizations, and that inhibits us from treating the anomalies as signifying new and persistent patterns. Shackled by this habit – which I shall discuss at length shortly – we are likely to dismiss startling new data as merely more of the same, as easily interpreted by presently available conceptual equipment, rather than as anomalous indicators of emergent and significant trends.

Before examining the conceptual habit that diverts us, let us look first at some data and anomalies that ought to give us pause and that suggest challenges which should find a place high on our reinvigorated research agendas. Consider these three bits of data that I regard as startling:

1   It is estimated that today 1.4 billion e-mail messages cross national boundaries every day.[3] Quite possibly, moreover, these dynamics are poised for another step-level leap forward with the advent of the Internet (which is growing by one million web pages a day[4]) and new computer technologies which include the prospect of a chip 100 billion (repeat 100 billion) times faster than those available today.[5] Future generations might look back to the latter part of the 1990s and the widening scope of the Internet as the historical starting point for a new phase of modern globalization.
2   It has been calculated that Indonesia had only one independent environmental organization twenty years ago, whereas now there are more than 20,000 linked to an environmental organization network based in Jakarta. Likewise, registered nonprofit organizations in the Philippines grew from 18,000 to 58,000 between 1989 and 1996; in Slovakia the figure went from a handful in the 1980s to more than 10,000 today; and in the US 70 percent of the nonprofit organizations – not counting religious groups and private foundations – filing tax returns with the Treasury Department are less than thirty years old and a third are less than fifteen years old.[6]
3   The movement of people – everyone from the tourist to the terrorist and the migrant to the jet-setter – has been so extensive that around five percent of the people alive today are estimated to be living in a country other than the one where they were born.[7] Indeed, every day a half million airline passengers cross national boundaries.[8]

What do we do with data like these? Treat them as simply an extension of past patterns? Or are they so extraordinary that we need to pause and ponder what they signify about the underpinnings of world politics? My response is that they point to the likelihood of political dynamics with which we have little familiarity and, consequently, we may lack the conceptual tools to comprehend their underlying import. Indeed, I would argue that they reflect but a few of the new and powerful patterns around which political systems are going to have to develop new agendas and policies if they are to exercise even a modicum of control over the needs and demands inherent in the emergent patterns. And if the political world evolves new agendas, surely we academics need to do the same.

This need seems even more compelling as one ponders the anomalies that pervade the current scene. The anomalies are at a much higher level of abstraction than the foregoing data, and as such they constitute even more of a challenge to our research agendas. Here are five anomalies that I view as inexplicable by our current conceptual equipment:

1   One involves the widespread idea that one of the US's major military adversaries, China, is also among its biggest trading partners. That is surely an

ambiguous anomaly in terms of the way we conventionally understand global politics.

2   Another consists of the contradiction between the widespread presumption that states are rational actors and the accepted understanding that at the same time they are internally divided, pursue a multiplicity of inconsistent goals, lack effective means for adapting to rapid change, never have sufficient information, and depend on unwieldy bureaucracies for innovative policies.

3   Furthermore if states are rational actors, why do the powerful ones provide aid to the poor ones and why do they accord small and weak states the same voting rights as they have in international governmental organizations (IGOs)?

4   And of what use is the rational-actor model when "highly disparate states of varied capabilities, following unique historical trajectories and responding to immensely variable local circumstances, 'decide' all at once (i.e. in a very brief historical period)" to pursue the same policies such as initiating nation-wide pension systems or protecting threatened species from extinction?[9]

5   Then there is the "paradox ... that while the governments of established states ... are suffering this progressive loss of real authority, the queue of societies that want their own state is lengthening."[10] Put differently, the present era is marked by a simultaneity of "the crisis of the nation-state and the explosion of nationalisms."[11]

Implicit in both the foregoing data and anomalies are at least four interrelated items that I think should be located high on our new research agendas. Unfortunately time and space constraints prevent elaboration of them. Here I can only take note of them by casting them as questions that I find puzzling and are illustrative of possible foci on our new agendas.[12] The four questions are:

1   What are the implications and consequences of the deterritorialization that accompanies the accelerating collapse of time and space in response to a continuing wave of technological innovations?

2   What are the consequences for culture and identity of the enormous proliferation of organizations and the vast movement of people around the world?

3   Is a global elite emerging?

4   As the competence of states wanes, will new spheres of authority (SOAs), even new terminal entities, emerge to capture the loyalties and refocus the orientations of people?

In addition to these substantive agenda items, there is one methodological dilemma that will have to be faced, namely, how do we empirically assess phenomena in a nonlinear ever more complex world pervaded with endless feedback loops. The long-standing empirical procedure of positing independent, intervening, and dependent variables is a linear method and it is no longer viable because under conditions of complexity and globalization every dependent variable is an independent variable in the next millisecond. Put differently, the agenda items that lie ahead will focus essentially on nonlinear processes and not linear outcomes. One could avoid this serious methodological challenge by resorting to critical theory and other non-empirical approaches, but avoidance will not do for those who are empirically oriented. Rather, they may have to tool up in computer sciences in order to evolve nonlinear models with which to identify the data they need for simulations and data analysis.

The states-are-forever habit

Given startling new data, ambiguous anomalies, and hints of new questions to investigate, it seems clear to me that our research agendas have become hostage to convention, to habitual modes of inquiry that are increasingly removed from the dynamics and statics of world affairs at the outset of a new century. Perhaps the most clear-cut indicator of this discrepancy between the emergent world and our tools for analyzing it are the innumerable research agendas still rooted deeply in a conception of the world as crisscrossed by boundaries that divide the international from the domestic and that accord to nation-states the role of presiding over these boundaries. Such a conception of world affairs is, I am convinced, profoundly flawed. The institutions, structures, and processes that sustain economic, political, and social life today are undergoing extensive transformations that are rendering the international–domestic dichotomy obsolete and, even worse, severely distorting our grasp of how the world works. Today what is foreign is also domestic, and what is domestic is also foreign. The two domains overlap and in some respects they are even one and the same. They form a new frontier where politics unfolds, a frontier that is marked by an endless flow of new technologies, by an endless proliferation of new organizations, and by an endless movement of people across borders, not to mention the endless flow of polluted air and water, crime, drugs, and diseases.[13]

Earlier I suggested that there is a prime habit that inhibits our coming to grips with the pervasive dynamics of transformation. I call it the states-are-forever habit. The widely shared beliefs as to what states represent, what they can accomplish, and what they can prevent are virtually innate. Most people simply assume that the terminal entity for loyalties, policy decisions, and moral authority is, for better or worse, the state. Those familiar with history know that the state is of relatively recent origin, that for millennia it was preceded by other terminal entities; but even history-minded observers seem unable to envision a future world in which states are not the terminal entity. Indeed, despite myriad evidence that states, even the long-established and coherent ones, are less and less capable of coping with the twin challenges of globalization and localization, the inclination to assume that states are the terminal entities through which authority is exercised and order maintained remains undiminished, unquestioned, and unexplored. We are so accustomed to assuming states are *the* terminal collectivity that we lack any inclination to ask whether ongoing changes might be the first traces of newly emerging terminal entities. There are exceptions (noted briefly below), but for many analysts the diminution of state competencies is neither ambiguous nor anomalous; for them, it is a misreading of the role states play in the course of events, a vast underestimate of their power and influence.

I share the notion that the state's decline is neither ambiguous nor anomalous; but in my view the diminution is a clear-cut central tendency, an accurate portrayal of a major trend line unfolding in the current era. Yes, state institutions still have a modicum of authority, but their capacity to exercise it has lessened considerably. States cannot prevent ideas from moving across their borders. They cannot control the flow of money, jobs, and production facilities in and out of their country. They have only minimal control over the flow of people and, to repeat, virtually no control over the flow of drugs or the drift of polluted air and water. Their capacity to promote and maintain cohesion among the groups that comprise their society is at an all-time low as crime, corruption, and ethnic sensitivities undermine any larger sense of national community they may have had. Cynicism toward politicians and major institutions is widespread and people increasingly perceive no connection between their own welfare and that of their communities. Selfishness and greed have replaced more encompassing loyalties. Thus many states are unable to enforce laws, prevent widespread corruption, collect taxes, or mobilize their armed forces for battle. They cannot collectively bring order to war-torn societies. In short, landscapes have been supplemented and – in many instances – replaced by ethnoscapes, financescapes, ideoscapes, mediascapes, technoscapes, and identiscapes.[14]

This listing of the weaknesses of states could be enumerated at length, but it is sufficient for the purpose of emphasizing that the central institution of modern society is no longer suitable as the organizing focus of our research agendas. Rather than divide up the world in terms of clear-cut boundaries that separate the domestic from the international, it needs to be seen as consisting of indeterminate and shifting boundaries that differentiate the local from the global. Put in terms of our research agendas, we need to cease thinking of ourselves as students of international relations and begin to view our inquiries as devoted to the study of global affairs, a reorientation that makes it easier to remove the state from the center of our concerns and that allows for unfettered probing of the relations that link the local and the global, the regional and the provincial, the social and the political, the private and the public, the multinational corporation and the nongovernmental organization (NGO), the US's cultural artifacts and their adaptation into non-American settings, the social movement and its disparate supporters, and a host of other connections that tend to be obscured by the imposition of state-based conceptions. Stated in an even more general way, students of politics need to approach political processes as unfolding in decentralized, often nebulous institutional contexts.

Such an orientation might not be difficult: other disciplines have accomplished it. Anthropologists, for example, "have now acquired the habit of contrasting the local and the global, and tend to take for granted that the local is to the global more or less as continuity is to change."[15] Yet, it is a measure of the degree to which specialists in world affairs are entrapped in the states-are-forever habit that I immediately need to intrude a caveat and emphasize that I am not anticipating the demise of the state as a political entity. It ought to be unnecessary to make this disclaimer, but states are so deeply ensconced in our paradigms that I feel compelled to stress what I am not saying. The state will surely be around for the foreseeable future and I am not saying otherwise. Rather, I think it is probable, as will be seen, that other SOAs designed to cope with the links and overlaps between localizing and globalizing dynamics will evolve and render the global stage ever more dense. Some SOAs will prove to be rivals of states, while others will become their partners, but in either event SOAs – or whatever they come to be labeled – ought to be moving to the top of our research agendas. They may seem anomalous today, but they strike me as destined to be patterned regularities in our future inquiries.

While the states-are-forever habit is widely shared, it is perhaps significant that some thoughtful analysts have broken away from this conventional mode and recently published lengthy, serious, responsible, and impressive inquiries that explore ways in which the authority of states may be undergoing relocation. Although coming from different research traditions, for example, three distinguished scholars have come to the shared conclusion that the economic, social, and cultural dynamics transforming modernity are also enveloping the political realm and its centerpiece, the state. Castells, Held and his colleagues, and Strange have all authored lengthy and major analyses of currently unfolding trends[16] and each has found that, as Castells puts it,

> ... the nation-state is increasingly submitted to a more subtle, and more troubling, competition from sources of power that are undefined, and, sometimes, undefinable. These are networks of capital, production, communication, crime, international institutions, supranational military apparatuses, non-governmental organizations, transnational religious, and public opinion movements. And below the state, there are communities, tribes, localities, cults, and gangs. So, while nation-states do continue to exist, and they will continue to do so in the foreseeable future, there are, and there will increasingly be, *nodes of a broader network of power*. They will often be confronted by other flows of power in the network, which directly contradict the exercise of their authority . . .[17]

To repeat, however, such formulations are the exception. They may be a portent of intellectual changes that lie ahead – especially if it is the case, as one observer contends, that younger generations of scholars are both weary and wary of state-based assumptions[18] – but for now the states-are-forever habit continues to have a hold on many analysts and virtually all policy makers. It is a deeply engrained impulse, a given, a cast of mind, an article of faith so embedded in our organizing premises as to be beyond questioning. And even the weary, while they may be ready to move beyond a state-based conception, offer no alternative formulation that enables them to do so.

Rebuilding the state in war-torn societies

Lest there be any doubt that I have overstated the strength of the states-are-forever habit, one need only note how brilliantly visible and evident it is in efforts to rebuild war-torn societies. Even as practitioners and academics alike ponder the challenge of governance in the context of war-torn societies, they do so by falling back on the well-worn and long-standing presumption that the state is the repository of governance, that it is the only effective institution available for managing the affairs of large aggregates of people and their societies. This presumption is so fully engrained in the culture of modernity that it is not treated as problematic. The idea that a collapsed state might be replaced by widespread disarray is so widely shared that any state teetering on extinction is considered worth propping up rather than permitting the disorder that might result if its various subgroups go their own way. Thus, for example, one of the reasons the 32-nation coalition that won the Gulf War did not carry the battle to Baghdad was a fear that Iraq would break up, that the Kurds and Shiites would go their own way, and that a level of disorder would then set in that could lead to unforeseen consequences. The certainties that attached to Saddam Hussein remaining in power were viewed as preferable to the uncertainties that might follow from his and his country's political demise or truncation.

Likewise, to cite a more recent example, NATO's aspiration to prevent Serbs from leaving Kosovo and thereby maintaining a semblance of multiculturality would appear to be rooted in treating the preservation of states and their bound-aries as a given. Rarely, if ever, do voices get heard that say, in effect, "Okay, the Serbs are fleeing Kosovo and only the Kosovar Albanians remain. So be it. Why try to force the two highly antagonistic groups to live together?"[19] Put very differently, allowing history to follow a fragmenting course is roughly the sociological equivalent of Darwinian processes whereby the fittest survive. The Darwinian analogy would be that some groups will survive by being members of a multicultural state while others will survive by forming their own terminal entity.

The states-are-forever habit opposes partition and favors forcing antagonistic groups to remain together on the grounds that a rebuilt society and state will lead to degrees of stability and progress such that the antagonisms and hatreds will give way as conditions improve, as if hatred derives from rational calculations as to what is in the best interest of those who hate. To be sure, if the resources are available, the material destruction accompanying war can be cleared away and roads, bridges, homes, and factories rebuilt. But the logic of hatred is not readily amenable to alteration by the advent of new infrastructures. Nor is it necessarily susceptible to reduction by the presence of outsiders who can keep hateful enemies from acting out their animosities. It is as much wishful thinking as sound analysis to presume that a firm, humane, and prolonged external intervention can diminish hate.

Another indicator of the strength of the state as a deeply entrenched habit is the aforementioned anomaly wherein many subgroups around the world are pressing for the establishment of states of their own despite the evidence that such entities are increasingly ineffective. It would seem that the diverse pressures for statehood validate the state as the terminal entity. Even as leaders of established states welcome these validations of their basic premises, moreover, so do they often seek to preserve their interstate system by resisting any pressures that might lead to the evolution of new types of terminal entities. Consequently, when an internal war ravages a society and leads to a collapse of its state, the unquestioned impulse in the halls of government everywhere is to "rebuild" the state. Fragmentation along ethnic, economic, political, and cultural lines is considered such a dire threat to global stability that rebuilding the state is, to repeat, considered preferable to letting the fragmenting dynamics unfold in whatever ways history may dictate. It is as if the poverty, pain, and violence that accompany the rebuilding process are but temporary conditions and bound to be less costly than the price of not undertaking the effort to rebuild.

Framing a new research agenda

Given a readiness to treat the new technologies, the proliferation of organizations, and the massive movement of people as reflective of patterns that impel a struggle to free ourselves of the states-are-forever habit, how do we proceed beyond the aging agendas? What terminal entities should be the focal point of our inquiries? I think the answer involves a two-stage process. The first is to view the world as entering a new epoch dominated by the tensions and contradictions generated by the clash of globalizing and localizing dynamics. The second is to follow Hável's lead set forth in the epigraph and focus on the diffusion and relocation of authority to which these tensions have given rise.

Freed from the shackles of state-based models, it seems clear that the emergent epoch is defined by the interaction between globalization and localization, between those dynamics that promote an expansion of activities and attitudes beyond their existing confines and those that generate a contraction of activities and attitudes from their prior limits. In other words, I conceive of globalization not as referring to developments and orientations that are global in scope, but rather as denoting expansivity which may or may not eventuate in global phenomena, as "processes whereby social relations acquire relatively placeless, distanceless and borderless qualities."[20] Similarly, localization does not refer to events that culminate in what is conventionally known as the local community; rather, it depicts processes of devolution that may or may not converge on local communities. Thus, for example, a state can be viewed as a local entity when nationalistic forces take it over and press for a cancellation of treaty obligations, just as a city can be treated as globalizing when it paves the way for investors from abroad.

As the world shrinks, as communications technologies render the distant ever more proximate and vice versa, as more and more people move around the world, as money in the trillions is transferred in milliseconds from and to accounts everywhere, as goods and services are increasingly produced far from where they are consumed, as drugs, diseases, and weapons move readily from continent to continent, so do the interactions between globalization and localization intensify. And the more they intensify, the more do the interactions subsume the phenomena conventionally known as diplomatic relations, international political economy, Americanization, cultural exchanges, institutional isomorphism, transnational ties, and so on across all the processes and structures usually grouped under the heading of "international relations."

The outlines of a new research agenda can be discerned in the subordination of the diverse subfields of our discipline to the intensified interactions between global and local phenomena. In effect, the agenda is framed by the contradictory interactions that pervade the course of events. Each day brings word of a world inching slowly toward sanity even as it moves toward breakdown. And not only do these integrative and disintegrative events occur simultaneously, but more often than not they are causally related. More than that, the causal links tend to cumulate and generate a momentum such that integrative increments tend to give rise to disintegrative increments, and vice versa. The simultaneity of the good and the bad, the global and the local, the coherent and the incoherent, the centralizing and the decentralizing, the integrating and the fragmenting – to mention only a few of the interactive polarities that dominate world affairs – underlies the emergence of the new epoch in human affairs and the differences in kind that distinguish it.

These polarities amount to an endless series of tensions in which the forces pressing for greater globalization and those inducing greater localization interactively play themselves out. Such dynamics can be discerned in the tensions between core and periphery, between national and transnational systems, between communitarianism and cosmopolitanism, between cultures and subcultures, between states and markets, between patriots and urbanites, between decentralization and centralization, between universalism and particularism, between pace and space,[21] between self and other, between the distant and the proximate – to note only the more conspicuous links between opposites that presently underlie the course of events. And each of these tensions is marked by numerous variants; they take different forms in different parts of the world, in different countries, in different markets, in different communities, in different professions, and in different cyberspaces, with the result that there is enormous diversity in the way people experience the tensions that beset their lives.

It is important to stress the interactive foundations of these tensions. To disaggregate them for analytic purposes, to confine inquiry only to globalizing dynamics or only to localizing dynamics, is to risk overlooking what makes events unfold as they do. As one observer puts it, ". . . the distinction between the global and the local is becoming very complex and problematic."[22]

As noted in the previous chapter, I use the concept of fragmegration that some regard as an awkward label but that serves to capture the tensions and polarities that mark the emergent epoch. The concept juxtaposes the processes of fragmentation and integration occurring within and among organizations, communities, countries, regions, and transnational systems such that it is virtually impossible not to treat them as interactive and causally linked. To be sure, the label is probably too grating ever to catch on as the prime descriptor of the epoch[23] – to speak of the Westphalian system as having given way to the fragmegrative system runs counter to the need for historic landmarks as a basis for thinking about global structures – but it is nonetheless the case that fragmegrative processes are so pervasive and generic that the emergent epoch seems likely to acquire a label reflective of them.[24] In the absence of a widely accepted label, however, for the present I argue that we live, not in an age of globalization, but in a fragmegrative age.

Given its many causal factors, each of which reinforces the others, the fragmegrative epoch defies reduction to an overarching theory. There is no easy or overriding answer to the question of what drives the course of events. Power is too disaggregated, and feedback loops are too pervasive, to assert that global affairs are now driven by the United States, or by globalization, or by capitalism, or by whatever grand scheme may seem most compelling. No, what drives the emergent epoch consists of complex dynamics that spring, in turn, from numerous sources and cannot be traced to a singular origin.

It is reasonable to presume that the numerous causal factors and the fragmegrative tensions they generate are no less operative at the level of individuals than they are in the agendas of political systems. That is, the forces of fragmentation are rooted in the psychic comfort people derive from the familiar and close-at-hand values and practices of their neighborhoods and communities. Contrariwise, the forces of integration stem from the aspiration to share in the distant products of the global economy, to benefit from the efficiencies of regional unity, to avoid the dangers of environmental degradation, and/or to yield to the implications of the pictures taken from outer space that depict the earth as a solitary entity in a huge universe. Stated more generally, and in the succinct words of one astute observer, "There is a constant struggle between the collectivist and individualist elements within each human."[25]

Spheres of authority

The prevalence of fragmegrative tensions at every level of community raises a number of crucial questions that could well serve as the basis for new research agendas: how are both individuals and collectivities going to adapt to the tensions? How can they manage the simultaneous pull toward the local and the global? How well, that is, will societies, groups, and individuals be able to keep their essential structures intact and move toward their goals in the face of dynamic changes that are giving birth to a new epoch? In a decentralizing global system undergoing continual processes wherein authority is undermined and relocated, how can publics be mobilized and problems addressed? If territorial landscapes are giving way to ethnoscapes, technoscapes, financescapes, mediascapes, ideoscapes, and identiscapes, what is likely to happen to the loyalties, commitments, and orientations of individuals and groups? Is it possible, as some contend, that global markets "increase the incentives and wherewithal for organizing" new social contracts because they liberate "social, political, and cultural intentions from spatial constraints, and from economic domination"?[26] If the ability of states to control the flow of ideas, money, goods, and people across their boundaries has been substantially diminished, are new political structures likely to evolve, or is the world descending into an ever-greater disarray?

My point of departure in responding to such questions is to focus on the diverse spheres of authority – the SOAs – which are proliferating at an exponential rate. The proliferation is a consequence of the processes whereby the loci of authority are undergoing continuous disaggregation as the clash of global and local dynamics have weakened states and led to the evolution of new and myriad SOAs. Many of the new SOAs are the product of the inordinate complexities inherent in fragmegrative dynamics, while others result from the negotiation of new identities that are filling the social and psychological spaces vacated by weakening states and fragmenting societies, spaces that may have the capacity to siphon off the commitments and orientations that states are no longer able to serve. Some are loosely organized networks in which authority rarely needs to be exercised, while others are hierarchical and tightly structured. Some are transitory, while others are enduring. Some of the SOAs have long histories, but most derive from fragmegrative dynamics and are thus of recent origin.

Many observers are inclined to view the continuous devolution of authority away from states as amounting to the emergence of civil society. But this concept carries so much baggage and is the focus of so many different formulations that I prefer to speak of the world stage as simply becoming ever more dense with collective actors, with SOAs. The population of SOAs includes states as well as a wide range of other types of collectivities, from corporations to professional associations, from neighborhoods to epistemic communities, from nongovernmental organizations to social movements, from professional societies to truth commissions, from Davos elites to trade unions, from subnational governments to transnational advocacy groups, from networks of the like-minded to diaspora, from gated communities to vigilante gangs, from credit-rating agencies to strategic partnerships, from issue regimes to markets, and so on across a wide range of entities that have little in common other than being repositories of authority that evokes compliance on the part of others.

All the SOAs are founded on rules designed to serve their purposes and retain the involvement and commitment of their members. In effect, the old Westphalian social contracts on which states are founded are being supplemented – and in some instances supplanted – by new social contracts that are based on new and diverse forms of authority. And it is here, in the framing and promotion of new social contracts, that the aging of agendas and their replacements become extremely relevant: for it is in the interaction of global and local dynamics that the nature and direction of new agendas organized around new social contracts will be shaped and solidified. In the absence of interactions that help form new contracts founded on values that enable collectivities to remain intact and move toward their goals, it is reasonable to anticipate that the world is indeed headed for ever-greater disarray – for circumstances in which, in effect, there is no social contract or, put even more negatively, social contracts do evolve but they are founded on the principle that every individual is beholden only to himself or herself.

But what might be the bases of new social contracts? Leaving aside self-beholden contracts and the fact that contracts involving aggregates of people cannot be simply imposed from the top, or at least that they must resonate broadly with the affected publics, on what values should the new contracts rest such that localizing and globalizing forces can be reconciled and the tensions between them ameliorated? Whatever contractual variations may derive from local circumstances, are there a core set of values on which all the contracts can be founded? What, then, might be the essential terms of the new contracts? And, no less important, who shall be the parties to the new contracts? Clearly, full answers to these questions require a lengthy treatise that would far exceed the time and space available here. Elsewhere I have made a first pass at identifying and elaborating the circumstances under which the new social contracts will evolve, the identity of the signatories to them, and the key terms likely to be found in all the contracts.[27]

Conclusion

From the perspective of the turn of the century, a focus on the new social contracts generated by fragmegrative dynamics may seem idealistic and unrealistic. My efforts to spell out the new contracts have thus far been short of clauses that allow for the reconciliation of fragmegrative tensions or otherwise assure the effectiveness of SOAs in wielding their authority and achieving compliance. Nor have I managed to specify contractual clauses that allow for the handling of the troubled spots in the world where localizing dynamics are such as to have fostered violence and resistance to new sources of authority. On the contrary, there is no basis for believing that the emergent epoch will not be as marred by difficult and intractable trouble spots as the expiring epoch has been; indeed, such situations may never achieve that level of shared confidence that permits the drawing up of meaningful social contracts. And surely it is also the case that any new contracts will be slow to develop and that the habits necessary to support them may require generations to become fully implanted.

But such qualifications derive from the states-are-forever habit and the reasoning that has sustained the aging agendas. It ignores the transformative dynamics at work in the world and presumes that the future is bound to emulate the past. Thus it is equally reasonable to presume that the uncertainties inherent in the multiplicity of fragmegrative tensions are so pervasive that today's ambiguous anomalies may unfold into patterns consistent with the items seemingly destined to comprise the world's agenda in the future. Viewed in this way, it may not be idealistic to conclude that the acceleration of technological innovations, the organizational explosion, and the vast movements of people render the probability of new institutions expressive of new social contracts evolving no less than the likelihood of the old contracts perpetuating a state-dominated world. Havel's conception of the organization of the future of our planetary society may well prove sound.

5   Global affairs in an epochal transformation[1]

It sounds and seems arrogant (as if I know all the answers), but in this paper I dare to proceed from the presumption that the world is undergoing profound trans-formations that are so deep and pervasive as to amount to a seismic ontological shift. While the common sense of our epoch – those fundamental premises by which people understand the nature of their circumstances, or what philosophers call our ontology – is new and still emerging,[2] it is articulated in a variety of ways, some explicitly but many obscurely, and increasingly it is spreading everywhere – in every country through every walk of life and across all the layers of class and community that comprise global affairs. Among elites it is intuitively understood in some detail; among masses it is grasped in bare outline; but whatever the level of comprehension, the ontology is widely and intersubjectively shared across cultures and all the other boundaries that differentiate communities and peoples.

At the core of the emergent epoch

Before giving a label to the emergent ontology, let me try to identify some of its main components. At its root lies the premise that the order which sustains families, communities, countries, and the world through time rests on contradic-tions, ambiguities, and uncertainties. Where earlier epochs had their central tendencies and orderly patterns, the present epoch derives its order from contrary trends and episodic patterns. People now understand, emotionally as well as intellectually, that unexpected events are commonplace, that anomalies are normal occurrences, that minor incidents can mushroom into major outcomes, and that fundamental processes trigger opposing forces even as they expand their scope.

This is not to say that people have adjusted comfortably to these new circum-stances. On the contrary, a high level of disquiet and uncertainty persists and will doubtless continue until a new common sense emerges with a new, presently unforeseeable epoch. Rather, it is only to assert that what once seemed transitional is now accepted as enduring and that the complexities of modern life are so deeply rooted as to infuse ordinariness into the surprising development and the ambiguities and anxieties that attach to it.

Being complex, the new conditions that have evolved in recent decades cannot be explained by a single source.[3] Technological dynamics are major stimulants, but so is the breakdown of trust, the shrinking of distances, the globalization of economies, the explosive proliferation of organizations, the information revolution, the fragmentation of groups and the integration of regions, the surge of democratic practices and the spread of fundamentalism, the cessation of intense enmities and the revival of historic animosities – all of which in turn provoke further reactions that add to the complexity.

Cast in terms of contradictions that have become customary, the emergent ontology is marked by a pervasive multiplicity of opposites. The international system is less commanding, but it is still powerful. States are changing, but they are not disappearing. State sovereignty has eroded, but it is still vigorously asserted. Governments are weaker, but they still possess considerable resources and they can still throw their weight around. Company profits are soaring and wages are stagnant. Scenes of unspeakable horror and genocide flicker on our TV screens even as humanitarian organizations mobilize and undertake heroic remedial actions. The United Nations is asked to take on more assignments and not supplied with the funds to carry them out. Defense establishments acknowledge that their roles have drastically altered and continue to adhere to traditional strategies. At times publics are more demanding, but at other times they are more pliable. Citizens are both more active and more cynical. Borders still keep out intruders, but they are also more porous. In sum, we have come to know that we live in a world that is deteriorating in some areas, remaining fixed in others, and thriving in still others.

Given all the changes and contradictions, it might well be asked, where do tradition and history fit? The answer seems obvious: they are being redefined to accommodate to the contradictory realities of the new epoch. Traditions are serving as baselines for reactions against the transformative dynamics and the lessons of history are less compelling and increasingly irrelevant in a world sustained by the simultaneity of events rather than by their sequential cumulation.

The need for a new lexicon

Attaching a label to the new ontology is no simple matter. In good part the huge gap between our sense of profound transformations and our ability to grasp them stems from a huge shortage of the tools needed to narrow the gap. A new lexicon is needed for this purpose. Notwithstanding the widespread recognition that vast changes have spawned a new epoch based on new specifications of the way things are, our vocabulary and conceptual equipment for understanding the emergent world lag well behind the changes themselves. We still do not have ways of talking about the diminished role of states without at the same time privileging them as superior to all the other actors in the global arena.[4] We lack a means for treating the various contradictions as part and parcel of a more coherent order.[5] We are experiencing considerable difficulty in expanding the concept of security beyond the military realm.[6] Aside from vague uses of the concept of interdependence, we are deficient in our capacity to work around and through the overlap between domestic and foreign affairs.[7] We are short on incisive understandings of the nature of transformative dynamics and ways of differentiating between transitory changes and those that are profound and enduring. We are bereft of analytic equipment that allows us to treat the US as both the world's most powerful country and one that shut down its government twice in 1995. We do not have techniques for analyzing the nonlinearity and simultaneity of events such that the full array of their interconnections are identified.

In short, the need for a new vocabulary derived from new conceptual equipment is not trivial. Labels matter. They signify more elaborate content and, as such, they can serve as conceptual jails in which we become very comfortable and from which we are disinclined to escape. Without the rudiments of a new vocabulary, our descriptors reinforce our long-standing ways of thinking. They confirm our understanding of who the key actors are, what motivates them, and the processes that sustain their interactions. They impel us to privilege states by taking a stand on whether states are primary or secondary actors, to insist that the international system is anarchical or that it is marked by an underlying order, to affirm the importance of sovereignty by presuming that it still reigns supreme or that it has eroded somewhat, and so on across a number of long-standing presumptions that reinforce our conceptual jails. It is difficult to accord status to new actors, motives, and processes unless one has a way of capturing their essential qualities through words that differentiate them from the prevailing conceptions.

There are a few indicators that this need for new conceptual equipment has begun to be felt on the part of those who analyze the course of world affairs. Or at least a vocabulary is evolving that departs from past practice as people seek new terms to account for phenomena that are no longer readily accommodated by the existing lexicon. Some professional students of world politics, for example, have expressed restlessness over the lack of fit between balance-of-power conceptions of overall structures and the decentralization of the global system by offering new labels such as "polyarchy,"[8] "panarchy,"[9] "plurilateralism,"[10] and "collibration."[11] All of these formulations, however, imply that the emergent structures rest on static hierarchies and downplay the dynamics of globalization to which the decentralizing tendencies are a response.

But there are also signs that a vocabulary is also evolving to account for new global structures founded on cooperative tendencies. Three terms are particularly noteworthy in this regard. They all involve the need to analyze collective actions across national boundaries that are organized but not formalized, amorphous but not ineffectual, imaginary but not inconsequential. As powerful forces shrink the world, erode boundaries, and shift loci of authority, observers now refer as much to the "international community" as to the United Nations, as much to "global governance" as to the leadership of great powers, and as much to "coalitions of the willing" as to formal alliances, when discussing actions that governmental and nongovernmental organizations take or contemplate in concert with each other. These terms seem destined to become established ways of designating the considerable normative convergence and cooperative actions that now mark the global scene for which the lexicon of legal and political precedents makes no room.[12]

On the other hand, none of these efforts to make up for the lag between changing practices and our descriptors for them hint at the mushrooming tensions between the fragmenting consequences of conflict and the integrative effects of cooperation. Accordingly, emboldened by these signs of terminological adaptation, what follows carries the practice a step further by relying on several labels that may seem awkward at first, but that have the virtue of calling attention to the transformative dynamics that have given rise to a new common sense of a new epoch. Two of these terms, *fragmegration* and *spheres of authority* (SOA), were noted in the two previous chapters. From a fragmegrative perspective, the world is seen as short on clear-cut distinctions between domestic and foreign affairs, with the result that local problems can become transnational in scope even as global challenges can have repercussions for small communities. Viewed in this way, in other words, the global system is so disaggregated that it lacks overall patterns and, instead, is marked by various structures of systemic cooperation and subsystemic conflict in different regions, countries, and issue areas. Likewise, SOAs call attention to the various arenas in which diverse actors hierarchically interact and collectively undertake to pursue goals and implement policies while at the same time not privileging one actor as more primary than others. In some SOAs states and their intergovernmental organizations (IGOs) will be the prime actors, while in others states will be secondary to one or another of the numerous nongovernmental organizations (NGOs), transnational corporations, professional societies, ethnic minorities, epistemic communities, and other diverse agents of change that populate the global stage.

So as to make it even more difficult to fall back into the habit of privileging states, two additional terms are used to differentiate them from other actors: emphasizing the legal and political obligations that attach to statehood, such actors are labeled "sovereignty-bound" actors while all others are referred to as "sovereignty-free" actors.[13] (One analyst would go even further and treats the former as having yielded political space to the latter by relabeling IGOs as "Insufficient-for-Governance Organizations" and NGOs as "Necessary-to-Governance Organizations."[14]) Finally, in order to stress that the new epoch has roots in the past as well as in the dynamics of transformation, that the actions of people and organizations spring from long-standing habits as well as an ability to adapt to changing circumstances, the term "habdaptive" actor is used at those points when reference is made to the generic role of individuals and collectivities.[15]

Of course, new labels do not insure that the transformations presently at work in the world will be revealed, but they do allow us to begin to probe more incisively some of the major dimensions along which transformative dynamics are operating. The concept of fragmegration specifies, in effect, that the central processes of world affairs are neither unwavering nor unidirectional, that they create their own negation even as they foster change, that outcomes are fragile and ever vulnerable to reversal, and that the age-old struggle between tradition and innovation has collapsed into a singular dynamic. The concept of SOAs specifies that the identity of primary and secondary actors is not the key to understanding the course of events, that what counts is the exercise of authority that generates compliance with respect to any dynamic, and that the loci of authority can vary among numerous actors, many of whom are not legally empowered but who are nonetheless influential and able to command thought, opinion, or behavior. Elites and masses alike, in other words, respond to a world they accept as both coming together and coming apart under the control of diverse authorities in a wide range of issue arenas.

The dynamics of fragmegration

Sensitivity to the inextricably close links between the integrative and disintegrative forces at work in communities at all levels of aggregation is perhaps the primary consequence of those aspects of the information revolution that have collapsed time and expanded the visibility of underlying socio-economic and political processes. Until recently, the importance of fragmegrative processes could not be readily grasped in a short time frame. Such a perspective tends to highlight globalization and localization as separate and unrelated dynamics. Only as the time frame was lengthened to allow for a full array of the impacts and consequences of each dynamic could the interactions between them be discerned. And even then it was difficult to draw the connections. Their consequences for each other were obscured in the twentieth century by world wars and the Cold War (which focused attention on national concerns) and in earlier centuries by the slower pace at which life unfolded (thus making globalizing and localizing events seem independent of each other). But today, with the superpower rivalry over and with a wide array of technologies quickening the pace at which people and communities are becoming ever more interdependent, the interactions of globalizing and localizing dynamics and the tensions they foster are increasingly manifest.

This is another way of saying that the large degree to which fragmegrative dynamics have become recognizable is a measure of the extent to which the information revolution has intruded complexity and interdependence into the course of events. In earlier times – i.e. during that long stretch of history when the boundaries between national and international systems were less permeable and when it took weeks and months for ideas, people, and goods to move around the world – the occurrence of integrative developments such as the formation of states, the industrialization of societies, the evolution of empires, or the opening of new trade routes were not readily apparent as sources of fragmenting consequences. Nor did the onset of fragmenting processes such as civil wars or class conflicts lend themselves easily to tracing their integrative consequences. Doubtless both sets of causal links did exist and could be discerned in retrospect if a decadal context was used. But only as technologies of communication fostered extensive overlaps among local, national, and international systems did the simultaneity and interaction of fragmegrative dynamics became so readily evident, so widely pervasive, and so fully operative as immediate stimuli to tensions that careen back and forth through systems at all levels of economic, social, and political organization.[16]

Indeed, so interwoven are these contradictory processes that it is not far-fetched to conclude that every increment of fragmentation tends to give rise to a comparable increment of integration, that localizing and globalizing forces are products of each other. Viewed in this way, it is hardly surprising that fragmegration constitutes the core of the emergent common sense of the epoch. However they may articulate their understanding, people have come to expect, to take for granted, that the advance of globalization poses threats to the long-standing ties of local and national communities, that some groups will contest, even violently fight, the intrusion of global norms even as others will seek to obtain goods or increased market shares beyond their communities. The tensions inherent in these conflicting impulses dominate the agendas of SOAs and they also pervade the lives of habdaptive actors, be they persons or collectivities.

The pervasiveness of fragmegrative tensions is especially consequential in those SOAs that are highly disaggregated. The greater the number and diversity of sovereignty-free actors who exercise authority in a particular sphere, the more are both globalizing and localizing dynamics likely to clash and play off each other. SOAs that preside over environmental issues are illustrative in this regard. As developers propose new projects, so do environmentalists resist, and vice versa; and in good part the outcome of these tensions is shaped by the extent to which the information revolution highlights new findings that accord legitimacy to one or the other side of the conflict.

But this is not to suggest that SOAs in which the authority to act is concentrated among relatively few actors are free of fragmegrative tensions. On the contrary, it could be argued that such SOAs are especially vulnerable to the onset of crises when those who enjoy the concentration of authority – usually sovereignty-bound actors – employ their predominant position to initiate new globalizing or localizing policies. Clear-cut initiatives in either direction are likely to lead to a dispersion of the sphere's authority inasmuch as they alter the prior balance between the opposing forces. The recent history of the European Union is a case in point. Each proposal for taking major steps toward further unity was followed by intense efforts on the part of some of the affected governments or communities to adopt policies designed to preserve local prerogatives and practices.

Complex humanitarian emergencies

Perhaps no circumstances better exemplify the dynamics of fragmegration – as well as the emergence of a widely shared common sense of the new epoch fostered by the dynamics – than the proliferation of complex humanitarian emergencies (CHEs).[17] In the sudden elimination of the control mechanisms embedded in the superpower rivalry of the Cold War, all too many societies have collapsed into ethnic and genocidal warfare (the fragmenting dimension of fragmegration) that has evoked the consciences of publics in the more stable regions of the world and thus induced diverse coalitions of the willing comprised of NGOs as well as IGOs to ignore sovereign boundaries in an effort to alleviate the suffering and end the warfare (the integrative dimension). Putting aside policy considerations for the moment, the scale of humanitarian interventions is part and parcel of the transformation of world politics. They are expressive of a shrinking world that both cares and resists change, that both overcomes long-standing precedents to intervene collectively in domestic affairs and that is not lacking in voices claiming sovereign prerogatives, that fosters a readiness both to confront complexity no matter the odds against successfully alleviating historic enmities and to resort to violence to preserve subgroup autonomy, that encourages impulses toward decency as well as dawdling politicians and hesitant foreign offices fearful of involvement in fragmenting situations. The humanitarian interventions undertaken to date have been too late with too little, but they are nonetheless instances of a larger trend wherein the rights and well-being of people everywhere are increasingly the business of people everywhere.

Among those who have to deal with CHEs most directly, moreover, the convergence around the emergent ontology is especially thoroughgoing. Both those in military platoons and doctors or aid workers in the field share a closeness to the complexity that occurs on the ground when multi-ethnic communities break down. Being on the scene, they know the limits to planning and the virtues of adaptation. They understand from their daily tasks that long-range strategies are of little value in the day-to-day struggle to adjust to the latest upheavals or shifts that humanitarian situations endlessly spawn. They know first-hand that small events can lead to large outcomes, that slight changes in initial conditions can have very different consequences, and that people can quickly organize to offset the most recent unexpected turn in events. Their experience leads them to grasp when situations give rise to their own further development and thus acquire emergent properties. In short, both the military units and the humanitarian NGOs in the field learn quickly that they are faced with nonlinear and not linear situations, and in doing so they also come to appreciate that their first-hand experience cannot be fully grasped by their superiors back at headquarters and that therefore they cannot always count on the kinds of support which are most suitable to their tasks.

If this is so, if those in the field who address micro problems have a firmer grasp on the nature of CHEs than those who work on their macro dimensions from a headquarters perspective, and if it is also the case that the two groups need to share their understandings if effective policies are to be framed, it clearly follows that comparable sharings are needed among scholars who seek to uncover the underlying dynamics of CHEs. Perhaps most notably, this means that dialogues and collaborations are needed between anthropologists who proceed from the perspective of ground level and political scientists, economists, and sociologists who focus on states and international systems from, so to speak, a headquarters' viewpoint. Both groups have a lot to say on the conditions wherein small events can cumulate to large outcomes. Both are knowledgeable about the circumstances under which situations lead to adaptive, self-organizing responses and emergent properties. One can only presume that the more these micro and macro perspectives can be integrated, the greater will be the flow of policy relevant materials that can be usefully applied by governments and nongovernmental organizations alike.

Nor need the collaborative efforts be confined to those of us who labor in disciplinary vineyards. Since both micro- and macro-oriented scholars have come to grasp that small events can lead to large outcomes, that slight changes in initial conditions can produce very different effects, and that systems are capable of acquiring emergent properties through adaptive, self-organizing responses, they can both benefit from exchanges with complexity theorists, whose disciplines include mathematics, computer sciences, and biology and whose nonlinear attempts to integrate knowledge are founded precisely on assumptions about the consequences of small events and the adaptive and self-organizing capabilities of systems. As stressed in Chapter 13 of Volume I, there is no magic in complexity theory – indeed, to date it has posed more puzzles than it has solved – but its fundamentals are highly consistent with the dynamics of CHEs.

The sources of fragmegration

So as to grasp the underpinnings of the transformative dynamics and the insufficiencies of our conceptual equipment to explain them, it is useful to recur to the three prime parameters that are outlined in Table 2.1 and that have long served as boundary conditions for the conduct of global affairs even as in recent decades they have undergone profound transformations. It will be recalled that the three parameters involve the overall structure of global politics (a macro parameter), the authority structures that link macro collectivities to citizens (a macro-micro parameter), and the skills of citizens (a micro parameter).

The micro parameter: a skill revolution

The transformation of the micro parameter is to be found in the shifting capabilities of citizens everywhere. Individuals have undergone what can properly be termed a skill revolution. For a variety of reasons ranging from the advance of communications technology to the greater intricacies of life in an ever more interdependent world, people have become increasingly more competent in assessing where they fit in world affairs and how their behavior can be aggregated into significant collective outcomes. Included among these newly refined skills, moreover, is an expanded capacity to focus emotion as well as to analyze the causal sequences that sustain the course of events.[18]

Put differently, it is a grievous error to assume that citizenries are a constant in politics, that the world has rapidly changed and complexity greatly increased without consequences for the individuals who comprise the collectivities that interact on the global stage. As long as people were uninvolved in and apathetic about world affairs, it made sense to treat them as a constant parameter and to look to variabilities at the macro level for explanations of the course of events. Today, however, the skill revolution has expanded the learning capacity of individuals, enriched their cognitive maps, and elaborated the scenarios with which they anticipate the future. It is no accident that the squares of the world's cities have lately been filled with large crowds demanding change.

It is tempting to affirm the impact of the skill revolution by pointing to the many restless publics that have protested authoritarian rule and clamored for more democratic forms of governance. While the worldwide thrust toward an expansion of political liberties and a diminution in the central control of economies is certainly linked to citizens and publics having greater appreciation of their circumstances, there is nothing inherent in the skill revolution that leads people in more democratic directions. The change in the micro parameter is not so much one of new orientations as it is an evolution of new capacities for cogent analysis. The world's peoples are not so much converging around the same values as they are sharing a greater ability to recognize and articulate their values. Thus this parametric change is global in scope because it has enabled Islamic fundamentalists, Asian peasants, and Western sophisticates alike to serve better their respective orientations. And thus, too, the commotion in public squares has not been confined to cities in any particular region of the world. From Seoul to Prague, from Soweto to Beijing, from Paris to the West Bank, from Belgrade to Rangoon – to mention only a few of the places where collective demands have recently been voiced – the transformation of the micro parameter has been unmistakably evident.

Equally important, evidence of the skill revolution can be readily discerned in trend data for education, television viewing, computer usage, travel, and a host of other situations in which people are able to extend their analytic and emotional skills. And hardly less relevant, in a number of local circumstances – from traffic jams to water shortages, from budget crises to racial conflicts, from flows of refugees to threats of terrorism – people are relentlessly confronted with social, economic, and political complexities that impel them to forego their rudimentary premises and replace them with more elaborate conceptions of how to respond to the challenges of daily life.

This is not say that people everywhere are now equal in the skills they bring to bear upon world politics. Obviously, the analytically rich continue to be more skillful than the analytically poor.[19] But while the gap between the two ends of the skill continuum may be no narrower than in the past, the advance in the competencies of those at every point on the continuum is sufficient to contribute to a major transformation in the conduct of world affairs. Elites continue to retain control over resources, communications, and policy-making processes, but they are also increasingly constrained by publics who follow their activities, who are more skilled at knowing when to engage in collective action, and who are ever ready to demand appropriate performances in exchange for support.

The macro-micro parameter: a relocation of authority

This parameter-turned-variable consists of the recurrent orientations, practices, and patterns through which citizens at the micro level are linked to their collectivities at the macro level. In effect, it encompasses the authority structures whereby large aggregations, private organizations as well as public agencies, achieve and sustain the cooperation and compliance of their memberships.

Historically, these authority structures have been founded on traditional criteria of legitimacy derived from constitutional and legal sources. Under these circumstances individuals were habituated to compliance with the directives issued by higher authorities. They did what they were told to do because, well, because that is what one did. As a consequence, authority structures remained in place for decades, even centuries, as people unquestioningly yielded to the dictates of governments or the leadership of any other organizations with which they were affiliated. For a variety of reasons, including the expanded analytic skills of citizens, the foundations of this parameter have also undergone erosion. Throughout the world today, in both public and private settings, the sources of authority have shifted from traditional to performance criteria of legitimacy. Where the structures of authority were once in place, in other words, now they are in crisis, with the readiness of individuals to comply with governing directives being very much a function of their assessment of the performances of the authorities. The more the performance record is considered appropriate – in terms of satisfying needs, moving toward goals, and providing stability – the more are they likely to cooperate and comply. The less they approve the performance record, the more are they likely to withhold their compliance or otherwise complicate the efforts of macro authorities.

As a consequence of the pervasive authority crises, states and governments have become less effective in confronting challenges and implementing policies. They can still maintain public order through their police powers, but their ability to address substantive issues and solve substantive problems is declining as people find fault with their performances and thus question their authority, redefine the bases of their legitimacy, and withhold their cooperation. Such a transformation is being played out dramatically today in the former Soviet Union, as it did earlier within the countries of Eastern Europe. But authority crises in the former Communist world are only the more obvious instances of this newly emergent pattern. It is equally evident in every other part of the world, albeit the crises take different forms in different countries and different types of private organizations. In Canada the authority crisis is rooted in linguistic, cultural, and constitutional issues as Quebec seeks to secede or otherwise redefine its relationship to the central government. In France the devolution of authority was legally sanctioned through legislation that privatized several governmental activities and relocated authority away from Paris and toward greater jurisdiction for the provinces. In China the provinces enjoy a wider jurisdiction by, in effect, ignoring or defying Beijing. In Yugoslavia the crisis led to violence and civil war. In some crisis-ridden countries of Latin America the challenge to traditional authority originates with insurgent movements or the drug trade. And in those parts of the world where the shift to performance criteria of legitimacy has not resulted in the relocation of authority – such as the United States, Israel, Argentina, the Philippines, and South Korea – uneasy stalemates prevail in the policy-making process as governments have proven incapable of bridging societal divisions sufficiently to undertake the decisive actions necessary to address and resolve intractable problems.

Nor is the global authority crisis confined to states and governments. They are also manifest in subnational jurisdictions, international organizations, and transnational entities. Indeed, in some cases the crises unfold simultaneously at different levels: just as Moldavia rejected Moscow's authority, for example, so did several ethnic groups within Moldavia seek to establish their own autonomy by rejecting Moldavia's authority. Similarly, to cite but a few conspicuous examples of crises in international and transnational organizations, UNESCO, the PLO, the Mafia, and the Catholic Church have all experienced decentralizing dynamics that are at least partly rooted in the replacement of traditional with performance criteria of legitimacy.

The relocating of authority precipitated by the structural crises of states and governments at the national level occurs in several directions, depending in good part on the scope of the enterprises people perceive as more receptive to their concerns and thus more capable of meeting their increased preoccupation with the adequacy of performances. In many instances this has involved "inward" relocation toward subnational groups – toward ethnic minorities, local governments, single-issue organizations, religious and linguistic groupings, political factions, trade unions, and the like. In some instances the relocating process has moved in the opposite direction toward more encompassing collectivities that transcend national boundaries. The beneficiaries of this "outward" reallocation of authority range from supranational organizations like the European Union to intergovernmental organizations like the International Labor Organization, from nongovernmental organizations like Greenpeace to professional groups such as the *Medecin Sans Frontiers*, from multinational corporations to inchoate social movements that join together environmentalists or women in different countries, from informal international regimes like those active in different industries to formal associations of political parties like those that share conservative or socialist ideologies – to mention but a few types of larger-than-national entities that have become the focus of legitimacy sentiments. Needless to say, these multiple directions in which authority is being relocated serve to undermine the principle of national sovereignty and to reinforce the tensions between the centralizing and decentralizing dynamics that underlie the turbulence presently at work in world affairs.

The macro parameter: a bifurcation of global structures

For more than three centuries the overall structure of world politics has been founded on an anarchic system of sovereign nation-states that did not have to answer to any higher authority and that managed their conflicts through accommodation or war. States were not the only actors on the world stage, but traditionally they were the dominant collectivities who set the rules by which the others had to live. The resulting state-centric world evolved its own hierarchy based on the way in which military, economic, and political power was distributed. Depending on how many states had the greatest concentration of power, at different historical moments the overall system was varyingly marked by hegemonic, bi-polar, or multi-polar structures.

Today, however, the state-centric world is no longer predominant. Due to the skill revolution, the worldwide spread of authority crises, and the many other dynamics of fragmegration, it has undergone bifurcation. A complex multi-centric world of diverse, relatively autonomous actors has emerged, replete with structures, processes, and decision rules of its own. The sovereignty-free actors of the multi-centric world consist of multinational corporations, ethnic minorities, subnational governments and bureaucracies, professional societies, political parties, transnational organizations, and the like. Individually, and sometimes jointly, they compete, conflict, cooperate, or otherwise interact with the sovereignty-bound actors of the state-centric world.

While the bifurcation of world politics has not pushed states to the edge of the global stage, they are no longer the only key actors. Now they are faced with the new task of coping with disparate rivals from another world as well as the challenges posed by counterparts in their own world. A major outcome of this transformation of macro structures is, obviously, a further confounding of the arrangements through which global order is sustained. Not only have authority crises within states rendered the international pecking order more fluid, but the advent of bifurcation and the autonomy of actors in the multi-centric world have so swollen the population of entities that occupy significant roles on the world stage that their hierarchical differences were scrambled virtually beyond recognition well before the end of the Cold War intensified the struggle for global status. Or at least there are only a few issue areas – such as nuclear proliferation – where the outlines of hierarchy are unequivocal.

Good insights into the sometimes-conflict-sometimes-cooperate interactions of the state-centric and multi-centric worlds are readily available when the United Nations convenes summit meetings on one or another issue high on the global agenda and the multi-centric world organizes simultaneous deliberations on the same issues in or around the same city. A Rio de Janeiro meeting on the environment in 1992, a Vienna meeting on human rights in 1993, and a Beijing meeting on the rights of women in 1995 are illustrative in this regard. Indeed, such parallel conferences have become institutionalized and serve as main channels through which the two worlds interact in both formal and informal settings.

These three parametric transformations are conceived as having been underway for some four decades and as likely to continue for the foreseeable future. And they are also seen as both sources and consequences of the processes of fragmegration. The processes are posited as tapping into the skill revolution by sensitizing people to the possibility that the identity and bases of their citizenship may be changing, as tapping into many authority crises by redirecting loyalties and legitimacy sentiments which, in turn, are altering the allegiances collectivities can command, and as tapping into the bifurcation of global structures by weakening the sovereignty and competence of states and hastening the formation or consolidation of collectivities in the multi-centric world.

Despite these consequences, however, it must be reiterated that fragmegrative dynamics are rooted in contradiction and may move the course of events in opposite directions. Some of the enhanced analytic skills of people serve to expand their horizons to include transnational foci, while for other people the skill revolution has facilitated a retreat to local concerns. Likewise, some authority crises have enlarged the scope and authority of IGOs and NGOs, while others have contracted the range of national jurisdictions and extended that of local institutions. Globalization and localization, in short, are uneven and not linear processes, and this is a major reason why world affairs continue to be murky and elusive.

Fragmegration and the capacity to govern

Among the many consequences of a fragmegrative ontology, few are more telling than the insights it provides into the capacities of sovereignty-bound actors as they competitively seek to advance their interests in the face of dynamic technologies that are eroding national boundaries, intensifying the necessity of transnational cooperation, and consolidating subnational groups. In effect, national govern-ments are becoming weaker and increasingly less relevant to the course of events because globalization is generating new SOAs in which governments can play only limited roles. As products of changes created and driven by sovereignty-free actors and their markets, the new SOAs are marked by increasing structural differentiation – that is, by deeply embedded and decentralized constraints – that have diversified authority among numerous actors and thereby reduced the con-trol governments can exercise. Governments are not excluded from the new SOAs, but neither are they necessarily the central players. As one observer puts it,

> In recent decades . . . an accelerating divergence has taken place between the structure of the state and the structure of industrial and financial markets in the complex, globalizing world of the third industrial revolution. There is a new disjuncture between the institutional capacity to provide public goods and the structural characteristics of a much larger-scale, global economy . . . [The result is an] increasing predominance of political and economic struc-tures and processes that (1) are frequently (although not always) more trans-national and multinational in scale (i.e., are in significant ways more inclusive) than the state, (2) potentially have a greater impact on outcomes in critical issue-areas than does the state (i.e., may in effect be more "sovereign"), and (3) may permit actors to be decisionally autonomous of the state.[20]

And what are the implications for global governance and world order of these new SOAs anchored in the dynamics of fragmegration? Perhaps the most obvious concerns the likelihood of continued contradiction. Given the premise that profound transformations are at work in world affairs and that they are sustained by fundamental parametric shifts, it is reasonable to anticipate that CHEs and numerous other, less thoroughgoing and immediate authority crises – such as those associated with terrorism, currency collapses, environmental pollution, AIDS, the drug trade, crime syndicates – will continue to climb high on the global agenda and to occur with increasing frequency. At the same time the international community is likely to evolve new institutions and forms of cross-border cooperation designed to cope with the diverse challenges. National governments and their state-centric world may be weakened by fragmegrative dynamics, but the advent and urgings of the multi-centric world are likely to facilitate widely shared efforts to address common problems. To be sure, the bifurcation of global structures has rendered ever more complex the conduct of public affairs; yet, there is more than a little evidence that the new SOAs will evolve the capacity to form coalitions of the willing that, in one way or another, undertake to confront problems that make it onto the global agenda. Already discernible, for example, are new institutions, practices, and/or regimes designed to cope with threats to the health, rights, and well-being of peoples and communities posed by terrorists, currency weaknesses, pollution, disease, drugs, and the many other challenges to which the new epoch is heir.

As for CHEs, opposition groups in troubled states – equipped with greater emotional and analytic skills, readier to question and challenge authority – are increasingly willing and able to obtain both moral and material support from counterparts in the multi-centric world and to fight for what they regard as their just rights. Likewise, citizens in developed states are more cognizant of the circumstances that divide troubled states and give rise to appalling circumstances in their countries. This greater sensitivity has been significantly reinforced by a deepening awareness of disasters, both those brought on by nature as well as those fostered by technology and terrorism. Thus an earthquake in Kobe, floods in Bangladesh, famines in Africa, explosions of a nuclear plant at Chernobyl and a federal building in Oklahoma City, and numerous other disasters have been, like Somalia, Rwanda, and Bosnia, subjected to the CNN effect and heightened sensitivities to those moments when the circumstances of one's fellow human beings are unacceptable. As a consequence of greater awareness of such situations on the part of Western publics, and despite some evidence of disaster fatigue and a lessening of the CNN effect, there has been a spreading of shared norms relative to human rights and the well-being of people, thus further intensifying pressures on the international community to treat deep cleavages within societies as necessitating humanitarian interventions.

To some degree, of course, the heightened sensitivities to natural and human-made disasters derives from self-interest, from a greater awareness in industrial countries that their interests may be substantially harmed by disasters anywhere in the world. Whatever the extent to which moral or self-interest considerations are at work, however, the "international community" is now more likely than ever to act through coalitions of the willing to reverse the deterioration of the human condition. The politics of undertaking such actions will surely be convoluted and often mired in paralysis, but in this era of fragmegration the alternative of avoiding proactive responses to CHEs no longer appears viable.

Fragmegration and the information revolution

Some might argue that the microelectronic revolution which has made information so readily available to people everywhere adds to, rather than detracts from, the capacities of governments. Through a variety of technologies, it is reasoned, authorities are able to maintain more effective surveillance of their citizens, and it also facilitates their ability to observe from afar (usually from high altitudes) major developments within other societies. In addition, governments can employ these technologies to amass and swiftly process increasingly huge amounts of information that facilitates ever more incisive and decisive responses to any challenges that arise at home or abroad. Such reasoning is of course sound, but it ignores the many ways in which the very same benefits accrue to citizenries and their non-governmental organizations. Just as governments can penetrate more than ever into the conduct of groups at home and abroad, so can their deliberations be more easily observed than ever. Due to global television, events are simultaneously observed and experienced by allies and adversaries alike, thus depriving governments of the advantages of surprise they once had with respect to publics and nongovernmental organizations.

In short, as fragmegrative dynamics devolve authority in diverse directions, the ability of national governments to use the information revolution to control the course of events seems bound to decline. There are, so to speak, too many channels on television, too many conversations that can be sustained simultaneously by a single fiber optic wire, too many fax machines needed to conduct business and capable of mobilizing opposition, and too many sites on the Internet for governments to exercise the degrees of control they could wield in earlier epochs. In effect, the information revolution is neutral with respect to its impact on the various actors and institutions of global life. It can serve as both an aid and an obstacle to progress toward a more coherent world, as a source of both creative and malevolent adaptations to fragmegrative dynamics.

Part II
The profession

6   Material and imagined communities in globalized space[1]

More than a few observers have come to recognize that in a rapidly changing, interdependent world the separation of national and international affairs is problematic.[2] In some cases their concerns give voice to a desire for stability, to a longing for certitude as to what organizes and governs the course of events, to a sense that logically boundaries should divide domestic and foreign affairs. But many analysts also acknowledge that such boundaries may continuously elude our grasp because the phenomena, problems, and processes of greatest interest are not confined by them. From this perspective – which is also my own – it is clear that to separately analyze domestic and foreign affairs is more than arbitrary: it is downright erroneous. The two have always been a seamless web and the need to treat them as such is urgent in this time of enormous transformation. We can no longer allow the domestic–foreign boundary to confound our understanding of politics, that the boundary is best problematized by those who seek a deeper grasp of why events unfold as they do. Border guards may check passports and customs officials may impose duties, but to conceive of the foreign–domestic distinction in this simple way is to mislead, to mistake surface appearances for underlying patterns and to underplay the powerful dynamics that are accelerating the pervasive transformations of even the most routine dimensions of daily life. Individuals, groups, and communities are contending with the challenges of expanded horizons, with the ambiguities of transnationalization, with the realities of internationalization (or, as I prefer to put it, globalization, a term that does not presume the dominance of the international system).

To fully capture the overlap of domestic and foreign affairs, here it is referred to as Globalized Space, with its first letters being capitalized in order to stress its centrality and with the ensuing pages converging on the problem of how and when communities form, persist, change, or dissolve in Globalized Space. The problem of community formation has long been pondered, but in this time of transforming boundaries it seems ever more challenging. Questions of identity have climbed to the top of personal agendas and questions of shared norms have climbed to the top of community agendas, and the problem of how to mesh personal identities with shared community norms seems to climb ever higher on political agendas at all levels of organization. And the tensions embedded in these questions are closely linked to a multiplicity of contradictions that pervade Globalized Space:

the international system is less commanding, but it is still influential. States are changing, but they are not disappearing. Some communities are breaking up and others are consolidating. Governments are weaker, but they can still throw their weight around. Politicians run for office, but they border on becoming irrelevant even when they win.[3] At times publics are more demanding, but they are also more pliable at other times. People are more skillful, but huge numbers also feel more vulnerable to the vicissitudes of globalization. "Home" is no longer so much a place as it is a sense of connectedness, but it remains the center of daily life. Boundaries still keep out intruders, but they are also more porous. Landscapes are giving way to ethnoscapes, mediascapes, ideoscapes, technoscapes, and financescapes, but territoriality is still a central preoccupation for many people.[4]

Sorting out contradictions such as these poses a number of difficult questions: how do we assess a world in which Globalized Space is continuously shifting and widening, simultaneously undergoing erosion with respect to some issues and cohering with respect to others? In what ways are the concepts of local, national, regional, or international still meaningful? How do we reconceptualize territoriality so that it connotes identity and affiliation as well as geography? How long can an ever more interdependent and transnational world organize its affairs in terms of elusive boundaries? How do we trace the bonds of emergent communities and networks that are developing in cyberspace or evolving in issue areas that are founded on mental constructions? And since networks are founded on horizontal rather than vertical relationships, how can authority be exercised and decisions made on behalf of communities? To what extent are communities at any level imagined and to what degree are they material? In short, how do we go about understanding how communities at all levels – towns, cities, societies – are adapting to a globalizing world?

Various responses to such questions are possible. One, the most rigid, is to treat the indicators of change as superficial and to assert that the fundamentals of global life are no different today from what they were in the past. A second is to regard the changes as newly recognized rather than as new phenomena. A third is to perceive the changes as real and powerful, but to assert that they have not altered the basic parameters of world affairs. A fourth response, and the one that guides the ensuing analysis, presumes that the basic parameters which have long underlay world affairs are caught up in deep and pervasive changes. It treats Globalized Space as becoming ever more expansive and, thus, as a widening field of action, as the realm in which world affairs unfold, as the locale to which communities must either adapt or give way to new forms of organization, as the arena in which domestic and foreign issues converge, intermesh, or otherwise become indistinguishable as a seamless web. In effect, it is in Globalized Space and not the nation-state system where people sort and play out the many contradictions presently at work on the world stage.[5]

Such a perspective is not easily addressed. We are so accustomed to thinking of domestic and international politics as separate playing fields that it is difficult to conceptualize any structures and processes that may be superseding them as a new field of play. It is easier to assert what Globalized Space is not than to enumerate its diverse characteristics. It is not a vacuum to which the homeless in the nation-state system have fled. Nor is it a residual category for actors whose missions are not consonant with those of the nation-state system. Rather, it is populated by groups and organizations whose activities transgress the nation-state system and who have thus become increasingly independent of the nation-state system. In effect, Globalized Space has replaced the international system because all the world's public and private actors are being drawn, some eagerly and others reluctantly, into its confines. The processes of Globalized Space involve the intensification of either boundary-spanning or boundary-contracting activities in response to the multifaceted dynamics of globalization – to the emergence of a world economy, to the communications revolution and the rapid flow of information, to the ease of travel and the vast movements of people, and to the emergence of norms widely shared across traditional boundaries. Put more challengingly, Globalized Space is a terra incognito that sometimes takes the form of a market, sometimes appears as a civil society, sometimes seems to be a fledgling community, often looks like a regional network, sometimes resembles a legislative chamber, periodically is a crowded town square, occasionally is a battlefield, increasingly is traversed by an information highway, and usually looks like a multi-ring circus in which all these – and many other – activities are unfolding simultaneously.

Given this diversity, it is not so much a single political space as it is a host of diverse spheres (even though here it is referred to generically in the singular) that are so new as to confound established patterns and long-standing expectations, with the result that background often becomes foreground, time becomes disjointed, nonlinear patterns predominate, structures bifurcate, societies implode, regions unify, and politics swirl about issues of identity, territoriality, and the interface between long-established institutions and emergent orientations. Globalized Space is thus marked by complex and unfamiliar patterns which fluctuate erratically as different issues widen or alter its terrain and foster corresponding shifts in the distinction between "us" and "them" or – to use a less combative distinction – between Self and Other.

It follows that Globalized Space is conceived to be quite different from Internationalized Space. The latter is centuries old and is populated by nation-states and their organizations, whereas the former is just beginning to emerge and encompasses a wide array of actors whose common characteristic is that their activities are not confined to the territory of a single state.

In short, Globalized Space points to an epochal transformation, a new worldview as to the essential nature of human affairs, a new way of thinking about how politics unfold. At the center of the emergent worldview lies an understanding that the order which sustains families, communities, countries, regions, and the world through time rests on contradictions, ambiguities, and uncertainties. Where earlier epochs had their central tendencies and orderly patterns, the present epoch is conceived to derive its order from contrary trends and episodic patterns. The long-standing inclination to think in either/or terms has given way to framing challenges as both/and problems. People have begun to understand, emotionally as well as intellectually, that unexpected events are commonplace, that anomalies are normal occurrences, that minor incidents can mushroom into major outcomes, that fundamental processes trigger opposing forces even as they expand their scope, that what was once enduring may now be transitional, and that the complexities of modern life are so deeply rooted as to infuse ordinariness into the surprising development and the anxieties that attach to it.

Being complex, the new conditions that have widened Globalized Space cannot be explained by a single source.[6] The information revolution and other technological dynamics are major stimulants, but so is the breakdown of trust, the shrinking of distances, the globalization of economies, the greater skills of citizens, the explosive proliferation of organizations, the fragmentation of groups and the integration of regions, the surge of democratic practices and the spread of fundamentalism, the cessation of intense enmities and the revival of historic animosities – all of which in turn provoke further reactions that add to the complexity.

Not only does grasping this complexity call on us to locate Globalizing Space at the center of the political agenda, but it also requires us to back off from established conceptual premises and be ready to think afresh. It asks that we accept the possibility that the core of political units have shrunk as effective authority has shifted toward and beyond their peripheries. And, not least, it invites us to appreciate that *both* the dynamics of global change and the resistances to them are part and parcel of the human condition as one millennium ends and another begins.

Thinking afresh

To break with conventional approaches to any subject demands considerable effort. One must be continuously alert to the danger of slipping back into old analytic habits and, even more, to doing so unknowingly. Even if they are no longer functional, the old habits are comfortable. They worked earlier, one tends to reason, so why abandon them when thinking afresh can as readily lead to dead ends as down paths to greater understanding. Yet, if we do not confront our ways of thinking, talking, and writing about governance in a turbulent world, our analysis will suffer from a reliance on artifacts of the very past beyond which it seeks to move. It will remain plagued by a lack of conceptual tools appropriate to the task of sorting out the underpinnings of political processes sustained by the altered borders, redirected legitimacy sentiments, impaired or paralyzed governments, and new identities that underlie the emergence of new spheres of authority in Globalized Space.

A depleted toolshed suggests that understanding is no longer served by clinging to the notion that boundaries do indeed bind. We have become so accustomed to treating states and national governments as the foundations of politics that we fall back on them when contemplating the dynamics of global change, thereby relegating the shifting boundaries, relocated authorities, and proliferating NGOs to the status of new but secondary dimensions of the processes through which communities allocate values and frame policies. To be sure, few observers would dismiss the impact of these dimensions as peripheral. Nonetheless, the predominant tendency is to cling to old ways of thought that accord primacy to states and national governments. Table 6.1 conveys this conventional conception of how politics works. Its vertical domains call attention to the firmness of the boundaries that differentiate the various types of territorial communities, ranging from the least to the most encompassing. Each column represents a governance entity that has responsibility for the issues and qualities of life within its jurisdiction. Likewise, the rows in Tables 6.1 depict some of the diverse issues encompassed by any community in the waning epoch. Each row represents an issue-area and the concerns that set apart the groups active within it.

If it is accepted, however, that Globalized Space has widened and eroded the boundaries separating domestic and foreign affairs, then Table 6.2 is a more accurate portrayal of the underlying structure of world affairs in the emerging

Table 6.1 Governance sustained by territorial units and issue areas

Issue areas	*Levels of political organization*				
	Towns	*Cities*	*Provinces*	*Nation-states*	*International agencies*
Science and technology					
Commerce and trade					
Conservation vs development					
Labor					
Agriculture					
Immigration					
Education					
Human rights					
Religion					
Environment					
Health and welfare					
Housing					
Employment					
Constitutional issues					
Elections					
etc.					

Table 6.2 Governance along the domestic–foreign frontier

Levels of political organization

Issue-areas	Towns	Cities	Provinces	Nation-states	International agencies
Science and technology					
Commerce and trade					
Conservation vs development					
Labor					
Agriculture					
Immigration					
Education					
Human rights					
Religion					
Environment					
Health and welfare					
Housing					
Employment					
Constitutional issues					
Elections					
etc.					

Diagonal labels: arms trade, the Internet, international regimes, market forces, subnational governments, transnational corporations, multinational organizations, ethnic minorities, social movements, professional societies, humanitarian associations, church groups, terrorist organizations, coalitions of the willing, miscellaneous NGOs, political parties, crime networks, drug trade, labor unions, epistemic communities, etc.

epoch. It suggests that while the same political issues and territorial units are still part of the political scene, they are no longer constrained by firm boundaries. Instead, the table's diagonal spaces highlight some of the nonterritorial actors and networks active in Global Space that interdependently link the issues and units. To be sure, in various parts of the world the long-established boundaries remain fully intact, and it may also be the case that the structure implied in Table 6.2 has yet to surface fully; but here the analysis proceeds from the presumption that, indeed, the diagonal spaces represent common threads sufficiently woven into the fabric of global life to form the foundations of an emergent epoch. The essential argument is that the overlaps among communities depicted by the diagonal spaces have become increasingly salient precisely because they subsume numerous problems that cannot be accounted for, much less managed by, established collectivities. The enormous complexities and interdependencies that have been fostered by a multiplicity of postindustrial dynamics are simply too extensive for the diverse problems of territorial communities not to meld into a larger set of challenges which, in turn, foster the evolution of new arrangements for politics in a turbulent world. Among the new arrangements, perhaps none is more crucial than the advent of networks as organizational forms no less central to the conduct of world affairs than are hierarchical structures.[7] It follows that if the interactions of sovereign states in an anarchical world constitute the theoretical core of the waning epoch, the theoretical center of the emergent one consists of interactions among a diversity of globalizing and localizing forces, of tendencies toward integration and fragmentation that are so simultaneous and interactive as to collapse into erratic but discernible processes.

This is not to imply that long-standing approaches employed in the waning epoch fail to recognize that the expansion of Globalized Space or that actors other than states are active on the world stage. Quite to the contrary, most adherents of these approaches do appreciate the enormous complexities of world affairs. For them, however, such complexities are not considered so powerful as to yield understandings that justify moving beyond the presumption that attaches paramount relevance to the goals and actions of states. But here it is argued that the analytic clarity achieved by focusing on states is misleading, that paying attention to the epochal transformations which are widening Globalized Space and populating it with diverse actors and salient networks has an analytic potential that is likely to yield more powerful and fruitful insights.

But how to proceed? How to think afresh with respect to the map of the world depicted in Table 6.2? How to comprehend the responses of individuals and communities to the new epoch? Three conceptual clusters strike me as adequate to the task. One involves a focus on the dynamics that are transforming three of the basic parameters of world affairs, a focus that I have developed into a turbulence model of world politics. The second cluster focuses on the tensions between the boundary-spanning and boundary-contracting responses to the evolution of Globalized Space – tensions that I have sought to capture through the label of fragmegration, a label that highlights the close, continuous, and causal interactions between globalizing and localizing processes, between the forces fragmenting

communities and those integrating communities. The third focuses on the distinction between imagined and material communities and the likelihood of their
convergence. Since the first two foci have been addressed in other chapters, here
the analysis is confined to the third cluster.

Material and imagined communities

For communities to survive successfully in Globalized Space, they must expand or
contract through a convergence of their material resources and the bonds they
imagine to hold them together. Whether they be nation-states, natural economic
regions, cosmopolitan cities, or like-minded persons linked through the Internet,
communities cannot adapt to Globalized Space unless their members share an
imagined unity and have the material wherewithal to give concrete meaning to
the ties they imagine to bind them. Thus the boundaries of any community are
shaped, undermined, or extinguished as the material and imagined ties that bind
their members solidify, attentuate, or otherwise undergo change. To the extent
these two types of ties are reinforcing, then to that extent does the community
flourish; to the extent they are imbalanced, then to that extent the community is
likely to falter. Communities are imagined in the sense that they consist of cognitively developed values and practices that the members of such a group intersubjectively share and regard as binding them together into a single and coherent
collectivity.[8] Historically, these intersubjective sharings have often led to the writing and adoption of constitutions, to the passing and implementation of laws, to
the specifying and guarding of boundaries, to the claiming and development of
resources within the boundaries, and to many other material features of the
community that acquire their materiality by virtue of the intersubjective agreement
wherein they are treated as tangible community property.

In other words, the evolution of fledgling communities in Globalized Space
may well parallel the history of nation-states. Just as Australia is both an imagined
community (in the sense that a certain 20 million people intersubjectively regard
themselves, their history, laws, and traditions as Australian) and a material community (in the sense that the same 20 million people conduct themselves in terms
of the history, laws, traditions, resources, and other concrete realities they perceive
to unite them as a community), so may new communities other than states begin
to occupy Globalized Space. And with the passage of time, the imagined and
material dimensions of these once nascent communities may meld ever more
securely together, each shaping the other into a coherent whole that reinforces
both the cognitively imagined ties and the material expressions of them. Eventually the question of whether the imagined or material bases of an established
community came first becomes as unanswerable as the proverbial chicken-and-
egg problem.

Implicit in this formulation is the premise that while the communities of Globalized Space may not be rooted in territoriality, they are nonetheless founded on a
broad set of binding ties. The resources of a people may lead to common interests
that form the basis of, say, "natural economic territories" (NETs) – and, indeed,

NETs "are springing to life throughout the [Asia-Pacific] region"[9] – but these entities are not in themselves communities as the concept is used here. They have the material bases for being communities, but they presently lack the imagined ties in the sense that these must evolve out of cultural, social, and political foundations as well as economic complementarities. Out of the latter more encompassing ties may evolve, but not until signs of their evolution become manifest can it be said that a community is undergoing formation.

To be sure, since "some . . . sub-regions of nation-states are developing economic links with neighbors that may be more vital than links with the political centers of power that govern them," it is reasonable to ponder "the question of whether there is an emerging disjuncture between economic relations generated 'from below' and political authority administered 'from above' "[10] and then to conclude that in the long run NETs may prove to be powerful incentives for expanding into more encompassing communities. Possibly, that is, the integration of regions and subregions will be propelled through firms, families, and NGOs, with governments merely serving to implement the legal ramifications of the integrative processes. Conceivably, too, future communities that develop in Globalized Space will be configured in ways that are very different than the modern nation-state. Whatever the configuration of their economic, political, social, and cultural foundations, however, it is not until these are imagined to mesh together into a coherent whole that the bases for community development will be established.

In short, the processes of community formation are delicate and complex. Some nascent communities never make it. The people involved are unable to transform their imagined unity into agreed upon core values, or the material support necessary to widening the area of agreement is insufficient, or the material bases are ample but not conducive to imagining a more encompassing unity, or one or more of the groups within a nascent community break away and form communities of their own.

Nor are established communities free of disruptive tendencies. They may not be as vulnerable to collapse as are nascent communities, but there is no guarantee that their imagined coherence will withstand all challenges. A wide variety of dynamics can lead to a recognition that the ties that bind may be fraying and that other imagined communities may be more worthy of support and membership. All communities, in short, are always on the verge of change – if not of collapse, then of transition into a new set of imagined and material ties.[11]

Whether nascent communities make it – and whether established ones thrive – is increasingly problematic under the transformative conditions that mark present-day turbulence. The increasing access to new information technologies, the regionalization and globalization of economies, the spread of a consumerist culture, the worldwide shift to market economics and democratic politics, the heightened sensitivity to environmental threats, the growing salience of human rights issues, and the proliferation of ethnic strife and racial tensions are but a few of the dynamics that have dislodged, or at least have shaken up, the long-standing loyalties and identities through which people have reinforced their communities. And all of this is occurring in the context of the skill revolution, the deepening authority crises of collectivities, and the mounting competition between the multi- and state-centric worlds, the first two of which have further agitated the readiness of people and organizations to rethink and realign their commitments to their neighbors, towns, provinces, and countries, and the last of which has spawned alternative entities that can serve as foci of identity and loyalty.

Viewed in terms of a multiplicity of causal sequences such as these, it is hardly surprising that indigenous peoples have begun to coalesce into a worldwide movement, that ethnic groups hastened the break-up of Yugoslavia and Czechoslovakia, that Asians have begun to write with increasing vigor about shared cultural characteristics that differentiate them from the West,[12] that Australia has begun to perceive its future in Asian rather than European terms, that militia groups in the US have become more vocal in their effort to break out of the ties that bind their country, that separatists in Canada, Ireland, Sri Lanka, Chechnya, Palestine, and Scotland have become increasingly vociferous in their demands for autonomy, that European countries continue to cede authority to the European Union, that cyberspace has increasingly enabled people in far-flung locales to come together in issue, professional, and security networks they imagine as potentially new communities to which they can link, and that myriad other community-forming or community-dissolving episodes of this kind have become commonplace features of the global scene. Indeed, a serious and rich new literature – not to mention conferences like the one for which this paper was written – on the importance of identity, loyalty, place, and space has accompanied these developments, a literature that is so vast as to indicate such concerns are far more than a passing fad.[13] Equally striking, it appears to be a literature marked more by convergent formulations than divisive argumentations.[14] Whatever corner of the world they focus on, analysts appear to agree that identities and communities are undergoing restructuring. Globalized Space is not only a bee hive of activity; it is also a major intellectual preoccupation.

More and less encompassing communities

Whether they are real or imagined, not all communities are persisting through Globalized Space in the same direction. The dynamics of fragmegration lead some to draw the ties that bind tighter and others to redraw them so as to be more inclusive. The former, consisting mainly of groups that, for a wide variety of reasons, splinter off of larger aggregations in the hope of forming their own communities, are part and parcel of the worldwide tendencies toward localization, toward imagining and building material communities that serve particular concerns felt to be threatened or undermined by the more encompassing communities from which they break away. For want of a better term, we shall refer to these localizing entities as "Splinter Communities" in order to highlight that their origins stem from disaggregative rather than aggregative dynamics. In order to disaggregate, Splinter Communities normally associate their identity with particular territorial space that is seen as needing to be recognized and defended as theirs. Chechnya is a dramatic example of a Splinter Community in the sense that the cultural and historical ties imagined to bind Cheshnyans together in a specified geographic locale is deemed to be so strong and so exclusive that Cheshnyans have waged a bitter war to transform themselves into an independent material community. But Cheshnya is also an extreme example. The initial conditions of most Splinter Communities do not impel them to resort to force in order to achieve their localizing goals. Most either negotiate their autonomy or engage in practices that draw the ties that bind them together without offending, challenging, or otherwise provoking the more encompassing communities of which they are nominally a part.

However they gain momentum and come into being, and whatever success they may enjoy in transforming their imagined ties into material realities, Splinter Communities move quickly into Globalized Space. For them Globalized Space is a haven outside the nation-state system where they can seek support for their goals, cement their ties, find like-minded allies, recruit new adherents, advance their case for autonomy and exclusivity, and perhaps even eventually apply for admission back into the state-centric world. By being active in these ways in Globalized Space, moreover, Splinter Communities are no longer simply local entities; such activities are profoundly transnational even though they are rooted in aspirations to exclusivity. Diaspora are illustrative in this regard. Take the Armenian community in Los Angeles: it continuously reinforces its transnational ties to the Armenian Diaspora around the world even as it maintains its autonomy in Los Angeles.

In contrast to Splinter Communities are those with initial conditions that lead to the enlargement of their ranks, scope, horizons, or otherwise more encompassing coherence in Globalized Space through inclusivity. Driven by the diverse technological, economic, and cultural tendencies that foster globalization, these Inclusive Communities, as we shall call them, tend to have difficulty reinforcing their imagined ties with material foundations. Drawing as they do on ties that are not territorially based and must often span continents, Inclusive Communities need to make up in the clarity and creativity of their imagined links for what are chronic shortages in material expressions of their shared values, interests, and understandings. For instance, the history of regions such as Asia, Africa, Latin America, and the Middle East can be read as continuous processes of seeking to render concrete and material what some leaders and publics in the various countries of the regions imagine as commonalities that could serve as the ties of a regional community. Viewed in this way, it is hardly surprising that a proliferating of stress on Asian values is marked by efforts to link common cultural characteristics to the prospects for regional economic institutions.[15]

In evaluating these regional patterns, however, a distinction needs to be drawn between the notions of regionalization and regionalism. The former consists of projects promoted by states designed to serve their mutual interests rather than establish the foundation of communities, whereas the latter involves broader dynamics that transpire in Globalized Space and may eventuate in the evolution of communities through a combination of "historical and emergent structures – a complex articulation of established institutions and rules and distinctive new patterns of social interaction between non-state actors."[16] Thus it is that regionalization has led to formal state organizations such as the ASEAN, OAU, OAS, and Arab League, albeit normally the periodic meetings of their country's representatives fail to translate their imagined commonalities and aspirations into material support for concrete measures designed to strengthen regional ties. The recent decision of East African states to impose trade sanctions on land-locked Burundi as a means of preventing genocide and promoting a return to democratic rule is an exception to long-standing patterns in most regions of shying away from the hard steps large territorial regions must take to supplement their imagined unity with coordinated actions.[17] And so, of course, is the European Union an exception in this regard, one that involved the surmounting of numerous obstacles to the establishment of meaningful and coherent foundations.

But even as regionalization may falter in synthesizing the imagined and material bases of Inclusive Communities, regionalism maintains a steady pace in certain parts of the world, perhaps especially in the Asia-Pacific region. As one observer puts it, noting a "pattern of interaction emerging within the tripartite Asia Pacific regional policy communities – consisting of the key elite actors from within the corporate, governmental/bureaucratic and research communities" – the experience in the region "provides enough evidence to support a view that the development of a regional 'identity' . . . is developing along side, or even prior to, the consolidation of the economic indicators of region and indeed, even in the absence of some geographical and historical indicators of expected 'regionness.' "[18] Thus, for example, Globalized Space in that part of the world is increasingly populated by "NGOs, transnational networks, and international development agencies [that] have strengthened civil society and reshaped the discourse about sustainable development and democracy in Southeast Asia."[19]

Inclusive Communities with much narrower political agenda than regions encounter less formidable obstacles as they seek to give tangible expression to their perceived commonalities. Many professional associations, social movements, and nongovernmental issue organizations exemplify transnational entities that have lately managed to become increasingly coherent and effective as they move around in Globalized Space. On the other hand, the processes of community formation in cyberspace are presently so ad hoc, so lacking in leaders with the trappings of authority, that it is questionable whether common values discovered on the Internet can ever be transformed into material communities. The bulletin boards and home pages of cyberspace facilitate convergence around common concerns irrespective of locale and distance, but in the absence of any institutional structures, it seems unlikely that links established through wired connections can be sustained beyond the immediate issues that fashioned them. Put differently, Global Space is pervaded with criss-crossing networks that are rendering it ever more dense, complex, and nonlinear, but horizontal networks lack the nodes of authority that are minimally necessary to the formation of vertical communities.

Needless to say, Splinter and Inclusive Communities are as likely to conflict as to cooperate. Globalized Space is not a tranquil domain. Its imagined and material communities, along with the innumerable other actors who have no interest in becoming communities, compete for moral support and material resources under conditions where both are in short supply. As previously noted, moreover, not only are the localizing and globalizing processes of Globalized Space interactive, but they are also causally linked as Splinter Communities perceive their Inclusive counterparts as eager to expand and thus to undermine their coherence.[20]

If this is so, the question arises as to whether the cascading of these tensions through the networked complexity of Globalized Space will inhibit its potential emergence as a civil society in which diverse organizational activities are encouraged and tolerated. Also the focus of a growing literature,[21] the prospects for a global civil society are much too complex to probe at length here. The foregoing analysis does suggest, however, that the very existence of Globalized Space may create some of the initial conditions for such a society to evolve. Perhaps most important, it allows for the emergence of a global consciousness – a sense of globality as distinguished from one of nationality or locality – that is an obvious prerequisite to the development of societal structures. More accurately, to the extent that vibrant transnational actors and communities are increasingly recognized to function and flourish outside the international system – and the thrust of the foregoing reasoning is that a spreading recognition of Globalized Space constitutes a major hallmark of our fragmegrative epoch – then to that extent the bases for a global consciousness are laid. There is now, in other words, an increasingly level playing ground in which the organizational activities necessary to sustain a global civil society can take root.

Among the many initial conditions for a civil society to emerge and solidify, its members must evolve a nonzero-sum conception of identity. That is, they must come to accept the idea that people can have multiple identities and engage in diverse organizational activities that need not be mutually exclusive. This core value enables a community to become more integrative without foregoing diversity. As one analyst put it, "Multiple identities allow for broader relations and a larger empowerment . . . Thus, a Frenchman can also [identify] as a European, and in addition as (for example) a Catholic, a Parisian, a Frenchspeaker, a businessman in electronics, and so on, and can think and act along each of these parameters; when such a thought or action is inconsistent with the dictates of a competing identity, a choice is made without destroying either identification."[22] This foundation of a global community can already be discerned with respect to human rights issues. To be sure, agreement and practices in this regard are still far from universal, but in appreciating that people are entitled to certain rights even though their identities may be different, the basis for nonzero-sum approaches to identity is laid. Moreover, while agreement and practices around human rights issues fall short of universality, the fact that many states now join with NGOs and Inclusive Communities in demanding conformity to these values indicates that at least this dimension of a global civil society is likely to become increasingly pervasive.

In a curious, circuitous way, the vibrancy of numerous Splinter Communities in Globalized Space may also serve as a basic prerequisite for the emergence of a global civil society. Their active and intense presence, even their insistence on drawing ever tighter the binds that tie them together, offers protection from the homogenization that globalizing dynamics may generate. The test is the ability of those who comprise a society to tolerate the diverse ways and values of other members and, clearly, this test cannot be met when homogeneous conditions prevail. On the other hand, while Splinter Communities can be crucial to the emergence of a global civil society, they can also inhibit its evolution if they cling to a zero-sum conception of identity and thus refuse to accept the principle that the circumstances which allow them to persist intact involve a tolerance of their ways that obligates them to tolerate the practices of other actors in Globalized Space. Such a tolerance may not be easily developed by many Splinter Communities, fearing as they do that the rest of the world is intent upon undermining and altering the ties that bind them together. Indeed, since there are few signs that shared rules of engagement are coming to be accepted in the clash between Splinter and Inclusive Communities, it seems unlikely that the cosmopolitan perspectives necessary to a global civil society will evolve in the foreseeable future. Globalized Space provides the groundwork for such a society, but co-evolving the institutions that can transform it into a society will doubtless remain elusive for a long time to come.

7   Many globalizations, one international relations[1]

The advent of this journal is both a unique event and part of an explosive surge in the literature on globalization. It is unique in that most of the exploding literature consists of books and articles,[2] while journals remain narrowly disciplinary in their scope. Few are those journals that dare to focus on globalization in a broad interdisciplinary context – in this case so much so that an "s" is added to the end of its title in order to capture the vast scope of the subject.

It remains to be seen, however, if the journal can attract submissions that enable future issues to justify its plural title and commitment to treating globalization as a concern of numerous disciplines. More specifically, will its submissions compel it to become yet another journal of international relations (IR) authored and read mostly by scholars trained in political science? Unfortunately equating globalization with IR may well become a recurring theme because disciplinary habits are so strong that many analysts – natural as well as social scientists – are unable to think and probe beyond the boundaries of their fields. Such a theme would be extremely unfortunate because the study of globalization is *not* comparable to the study of IR. Rather globalization encompasses phenomena that can span all the social sciences and not a few of the natural sciences. Indeed, the literature on the subject is exploding precisely because every discipline and most of their sub-disciplines have occasion to focus on boundary-spanning activities that are not confined to structures and processes that occur within national or societal contexts.

Conceivably, in short, the onset of globalization could lead to drastic alterations in the disciplinary boundaries that have long prevailed in the teaching and research through which academic institutions have been organized. In a shrinking world where time and distance are increasingly irrelevant, all human activities, including those sustained through interaction with the natural environment, can no longer be readily examined through either the spatial or horizontal subdivisions that differentiate local, national, and international phenomena or the vertical subdivisions through which phenomena are differentiated by disciplines. The dynamics of globalization are such that narrow specializations will have to make way for broader inquiries. The pace at which this imperative will be realized, however, is likely to be slow and its extent is likely to be limited. The habits of specialization, and particularly the tendency to treat globalization as an aspect of

IR, are deep and long-standing, with all the professional (such as reputation, promotion, etc.) and intellectual (see below) incentives stacked against the need for broadened horizons.

The global and the international as separate foci

Before elaborating on the incentives that inhibit globalization perspectives, it is useful to note the several ways in which the study of globalization and IR are separate enterprises. The differences between the two are not immaterial. On the contrary, they are central to the lenses through which we assess the world, and they are stark differences, rooted in premises that can unknowingly take us down analytic paths we have no intention of traversing.

A prime difference concerns the state. It is located at the center of IR inquiries, whereas it may or may not be central to globalization studies. The very term "international" conjures up state-to-state relations or the interactions between states and publics. To be sure, the "nation" to which international also refers may not be a sovereign entity. Not only are there nonstate nations that do not aspire to statehood (though many do have such aspirations), but people and organizations in those nations that are also states can undertake actions abroad – such as tourism or corporate restructuring – that are independent of the states they regard as their home base. Nevertheless, as the term "international" has come to be used, it conventionally connotes the presence and relevance of states. Few, if any, are the international inquiries that explicitly indicate states are excluded from the analysis. Almost invariably states lurk implicitly in the background of international inquiries, and far more often than not they are explicitly in the foreground. The term globalization, on the other hand, encompasses a host of phenomena – such as the spread of ideas, disease, or technology – in which the state is either absent or peripheral. Globalization studies do not dismiss, discount, or otherwise ignore the state, but neither do they locate them at the center of their analyses. In short, it makes sense to conclude, at the risk of resorting to poor grammar, that while it is reasonable to speak of many globalizations, there is essentially only one international relations.

This distinction between international and globalization studies underlies the reason why political scientists predominate in the former field. With the line between "international" and "interstate" blurred, with states viewed as the prime actors on which political science must focus, and with war and governance major issues high on the global agenda, IR has long been predominately the province of scholars trained in political science. Ever since its founding, for example, the International Studies Association has aspired to attracting sociologists, psychologists, economists, geographers, anthropologists, natural scientists, and scholars from other disciplines into its membership; but its record in this regard is dismal. Most of its members are, or were, trained as political scientists, and apparently the prospects for enlarging the mix are very dim indeed. IR is conceived to be the province of political scientists and, contrariwise, there are remarkably few in other disciplines who address problems in which international political processes are considered core phenomena. To be sure, one can cite exceptions in this regard. Some economists, particularly those who trace the movement of goods and money across national boundaries, undertake IR inquiries, but they are few in number and can readily be regarded as exceptions that prove the rule. The same can be said of sociologists who probe world systems theory.

Given IR's personnel and its preoccupation with war and governance, it is hardly surprising that research and writing in the field has not broken the habit of locating the state as central to analyses undertaken by its practitioners. Indeed, the habit is so deep-seated that those who call attention to it and urge a broadening of the field's scope tend to be viewed as mavericks, as eccentrics whose work is marginal, if not irrelevant. Put differently, IR has long been marked by an orthodoxy that gets passed on to new generations of scholars who then start down a path wherein they are ensconced in paradigms that tend not to allow for change and that address a narrow range of issues. Problems associated with technological innovation, cultural values, and generational differences, for example, are rarely foci of inquiry, as if questions of war and peace are too urgent to permit exploration of such peripheral and unrelated subjects.

By its very broad and varied nature, on the other hand, globalization encourages inquiries into every facet of the human condition that extends beyond conventional boundaries, from the plight of individuals to the networks of groups to the strains of societies, from concerns about health, language, and consumption to those evoked by crime, sports, and music. Globalization spans such a huge array of phenomena that it has become a preoccupation in all the disciplines, thus leading increasingly to the practice of referring to diverse globalizations. Students of the several globalizations are not unmindful of the state and its interstate system, but neither are they inclined to treat them as central and ponder their relevance to all the subjects they undertake to probe. Indeed, in many instances the state is peripheral to the issues explored, with the habit of IR scholars to make it the centerpiece of their inquiries replaced by a concern for the nature of boundary-spanning processes and structures. Accordingly, many students of globalization do not even refer to international relations, preferring instead to speak of world affairs or world politics when their attention turns to the panoply of interactions that transcend national boundaries and involves states as well as other types of collectivities.

It can even be argued that increasingly IR scholars are coming to recognize that the broader scope of globalization is superseding what now appears to be the narrower scope of IR. In the words of one distinguished and long-time IR scholar, the terrorist attacks of September 11 revealed underlying changes in the structures of world affairs that render "most problematic . . . the assumptions in international relations theory about the roles played by states. There has been too much 'international relations,' and too little 'world politics,' not only in work on security but also in much work on international institutions," thus suggesting that "it would be salutary for us to change the name of our field from 'international relations' to 'world politics,' "[3] (a conclusion that reinforced his realization that the long-standing terminology of IR has been "simply overtaken by 'globalization' as the fashionable language to describe increases in economic openness and integration"[4]).

The vast difference between the scope of globalization and IR phenomena highlights another difference between the two enterprises. Because it is unified around the role and activities of states IR lends itself much more readily to coherent theory than does globalization. Indeed, given the number and breadth of the issues, processes, and structures that sustain globalization, it does not lend itself to a single, unified theory. Those who focus on the economic dimension of globalization have developed viable theories, but these are hardly of any use when attention turns to, say, the cultural or technological dimensions. Thus it is unreasonable to expect that a single, unified theory of globalization will ever be developed and, indeed, to date none has come even close in this respect. And even if one were to approach such a formulation, it would likely amount to an over-arching theory too general to be of any value. To seek to account for all the diverse dimensions of globalization is to take the theoretical task to a rarified level of abstraction that would be inapplicable to any specific set of concerns. Perhaps the most that can be hoped for is a series of theories addressed to the prime dimensions of globalizing dynamics – economic, political, cultural, technological, social, environmental – that overlap sufficiently to allow for the framing of inte-grated hypotheses about specific phenomena. One can imagine a globalization curriculum that is comprised of seminars on its various dimensions with an intro-ductory course that brings them together for the purpose of demonstrating the variability of the subject; but it is difficult to foresee a theory seminar that treats the subject as a unified whole integrated by the notion that each of its components involves expansion beyond national boundaries. The requirements of theory, in other words, once again necessitate a conception of many globalizations, of diverse, tangentially linked theories that share a focus on boundary-spanning phenomena.

It follows that to posit many globalizations is not imply that the subject is an academic discipline. Clearly, that is not the case. All the globalizations may share a focus on boundary-spanning phenomena, but this commonality is not sufficient to regard the diverse phenomena that comprise the field as having disciplinary char-acteristics in the sense of present-day social and natural science disciplines. Just as the field does not lend itself to coherent, unified theory, so does it fall short of the coherence an academic discipline normally requires. Given their wide scope and diverse foci, the many globalizations lend themselves to courses and curricula, but these are bound to be loosely linked around the notion of boundary-spanning concerns.[5]

Much the same can be said about IR. Even though it is predominantly organ-ized around states and their international systems as the central actors, IR also lacks the coherence to be treated as a discipline. It too is a hybrid field and, as such, can theoretically serve as the organizing basis for scholars from different fields to come together, collaborate, and exchange perspectives.

The problem of incentives

As previously noted, the accelerating preoccupation with globalization across numerous disciplines has the potential for offsetting tendencies toward narrow specialization. The obstacles to the realization of this potential are of two kinds, one professional and the other intellectual.

Professional obstacles

There are practitioners in most disciplines who apply their training to those problems of globalization they view as covered by their disciplines. Thus geographers write about how globalizing dynamics are affected by spatial dynamics, just as sociologists probe how the dynamics affect family and group cohesion, and just as economists examine the ways in which investment and trade flows are shaped by global considerations. In effect, therefore, such studies tend to remain within prescribed disciplinary boundaries and do not stray beyond them in order to account for relevant phenomena that are the domain of other disciplines. Why? Why do most globalization studies tend to be so narrowly conceived when reaching beyond the confines of their discipline could enrich them? The professional answer to this question is an old story: for a geographer, sociologist, or economist to collaborate with colleagues in other disciplines, or for them to reach out to other disciplines on their own, is to run the risk of isolation and not advancing professionally. The rewards in each discipline go to those who do not stray, who publish in the right journals, who do not collaborate outside their discipline such that the results fall outside the discipline's mainstream. It is the same old problem that has hindered interdisciplinary inquiries for decades, but it is an even more severe problem because of the broad scope of globalizing processes.

To be sure, there are individual scholars who manage to circumvent the problem by virtue of their broad-ranging concerns and their already having distinguished themselves in their disciplines. The trilogy by Manuel Castells[6] and works by Appadurai, Bauman, Giddens, and Held exemplify inquiries not inhibited by disciplinary boundaries,[7] but these are individuals whose careers were established, allowing them not to worry about adhering to orthodox approaches. Younger professionals tend to avoid breaks with orthodoxy and by the time they become senior and acquire tenure their disciplinary habits have become so deep-seated that many of them cannot break out of their orthodoxy. If this is an accurate assessment of the professional disincentives to avoid developing or participating in genuinely interdisciplinary globalization programs and curricula, then disciplinary specialization will not readily give way to more general, cross-disciplinary orientations. Only as time and space continue to shrink and render the distant ever more proximate and the global ever more local will the obsolescence of prevailing habits begin to become powerfully self-evident and slowly yield to an inclination to see the world through globalization lenses.[8]

Intellectual obstacles

No less difficult to overcome is at least one substantive barrier to globalizing perspectives – namely, the way in which at least three of the social sciences conceptualize the terminal entity that serves as the foundation of their discipline. For political science that entity is the state, for sociology it is the society, and for economics it is the international economy. In none of them is it a global community that serves as the site for globalization. But why do these disciplines cling to their long-standing terminal entities in the face of evidence suggesting they need to make them more encompassing? In addition to the professional incentives already noted, I think the answer lies in the large extent to which deeply rooted analytic habits have cumulated around the prevailing terminal entities.

Many political scientists in the IR field, for example, are so excessively oriented toward the nation state and the international system that they overlook a vast array of issues and problems in which the role states play is matched by, if not secondary to, those of other actors and systems. Likewise, just as political scientists are trained to treat the state as the terminal entity that stands above and supersedes all other political actors in its claim on the loyalties of people, so are sociologists taught early that society is the terminal entity with respect to which organizations, groups, and individuals conduct their affairs. Yes, the boundaries that separate states and societies have become increasingly porous in an age of globalization. And yes, loyalties and identities have proliferated to the point of undermining commitments to states and societies. And yes, the Internet and other microelectronic technologies have considerably lessened the relevance of time and distance, thereby further weakening the ties that bind states and societies. And yes, the vast movement of people of all kinds around the world has led to multicultural and sub-cultural bonds that weaken the competence of states and societies. And yes, the huge proliferation of transnational advocacy groups, corporations, and professional societies has served to highlight a vast array of interactions that circumvent the authority of states and societies. But, no, with the exception of an occasional sociologist[9] and members of the American Sociological Association's section on the Political Economy of the World System, such developments are not sufficient to alter the notion that the state and the society are the terminal entities on which analyses should be founded.

And what underlies the prevailing resistance to reconceptualizing terminal entities in the face of such dynamic transformations? Why are able scholars in these disciplines still mired in long-standing and conventional perspectives? Partly habit, both on the part of analysts and the orientations of citizens, who are seen as so locked into historical and habitual ways that their ultimate identities and loyalties are never treated as problematic. Partly, too, notions of power in which both the society and the state are seen as so fully ensconced on the high moral ground and so fully endowed with the physical instruments of coercion that their attenuation as a terminal entity is viewed as highly improbable, if not impossible.

No matter that in many parts of the world private security forces outnumber those of their state. No matter that increasingly noticeable numbers of young men avoid military service in different parts of the world or that, in Israel, a substantial group refused to remain on duty in Palestine. No matter that multi-cultural communities have replaced either the dominant ethnic or the melting-pot society. Such developments are seen as aberrations rather than possible signs of emergent central tendencies. As aberrations they preserve the state and society as terminal entities.

Nonetheless, strong and powerful as the state and society premises may be, I am inclined to anticipate that sooner or later such conceptual orientations will ultim-ately give way to new formulations of terminal entities, probably to diverse schemes in which a multiplicity of entities are conceived to be terminal. As the age of globalization continues to shrink time and distance, and as reactions against globalization continue to stress the local community and its values, so eventually are all the social science disciplines likely to relax their long-standing boundaries and allow for transnational and sub-national perspectives that are not cast in the shadow of the national society and the nation-state.

To be sure, getting out from under those shadows will not be easy. Social scientists, like the people they study, are prone to habitual modes of behavior, and thus are more likely to cast their inquiries into habitual frameworks that are taken for granted than to treat their organizing premises as problematic. In the case of political scientists the habitual framework is reinforced by a restless preoccupation with comprehending war, which is viewed as being initiated, sustained, and ter-minated by states. For sociologists the continuing strength of analytic habits derives from an overriding concern with systems and subsystems, which are seen as marked by endless interactions and frictions that unfold in the context of societies as the ultimate arbiter. Yet, and to repeat, such habits are presently under assault by the dynamics of globalization and are likely to give way eventually to new and different organizing premises. Already, for example, many political scientists posit intrastate wars as much more of a central tendency than interstate wars, a shift that is freeing them up to recognize and assess the degree to which sovereignty is undergoing transformation and the limits within which states can exercise their power. Likewise, I have the impression that sociologists are increas-ingly focusing on ethnic tensions, a shift that enables them to by-pass the society as the adjudicator of system–subsystem tensions. Perhaps historians, who are accustomed to subdividing their discipline into periods marked by centuries, wars, dynasties, and other major developments, will be the quickest to acknowledge the advent of the age of globalization and adjust their conceptual perspectives accordingly.

Methodological challenges

Given the nonlinear, complex, and messy nature of the various globalizations, analysts clearly face severe methodological problems in trying to generate and analyze empirical data that reveal and clarify the underpinning of the diverse globalizing processes. At the very least, they will have to relax the strict criteria of parsimony that IR researchers employ to probe international phenomena. Unlike the ability of the latter to posit states as prime actors and then to treat their actions as rooted in rationality, students of globalization must confront a welter of unalike actors whose goals, procedures, and interactions are too complex to lend themselves readily to rational-choice methodologies. In effect, they must treat feedback loops as no less central to their analyses than linear sequences. Such a conclusion obtains not only because there are many globalizations and probing their overlaps deepens the complexity of the empirical circumstances, but it is also the case within any of the globalizations, all of which are marked by a multiplicity of diverse actors whose behavior does not conform to linear analysis. As one observer put it,

> [G]lobalization is never complete. It is disordered, full of paradox and the unexpected. Racing across the world are complex mobile connections that are more or less intense, more or less social, more or less "networked" and more or less occurring "at a distance." There is a complex world, unpredictable yet irreversible, fearful and violent, disorderly but not simply anarchic. Small events in such systems are not forgotten but can reappear at different and highly unsuspected points in time and space.[10]

One possible means of addressing these methodological challenges is to borrow from complexity theory and use computer simulations and agent-based modeling to trace the complex, interactive dynamics that unfold on the different global stages. Such methods can identify feedback loops. They move analysis well beyond the conventional methods of specifying independent variables and discerning how their variation give rise to varying patterns on the part of dependent variables. The latter orthodoxy just does not serve to clarify the dynamism of any or all the globalizations. To be sure, computer simulations and agent-based modeling also have their limits as methodologies, thus emphasizing the need to ponder the methodological as well as the substantive problems posed by many globalizations. Perhaps some of these problems can be offset by case histories, but even these in combination with simulations and agent-based modeling are far from sufficient to meet the methodological challenges posed by the complexity of globalizing dynamics. Hopefully the pages of this journal will attract, and be open to, essays that address the methodological as well as the substantive problems inherent in the various globalizations.

Conclusion

Even more hopefully, the journal will become increasingly central and, as the complexity theorists put it, undergo a pulsating and dynamic emergence. Indeed, it has the potential of becoming the house organ for a broad association of scholars from many disciplines who share its concerns even as they employ different methodologies and rely on different theoretical commitments.

In sum, while globalization studies ought not and likely will not supersede international inquiries, the foregoing differences between the two are not trivial. The emergence of globalization foci will probably lead to more interdisciplinary work and the exchange of alternative perspectives, outcomes very much to be desired in a complex, messy world that is marked by a shortage of pervasive and sufficient understandings of the contemporary human condition.

8 The globalization of globalization[1]

As one whose professional life exceeds that of ISA, I have mixed feelings about the invitation to reflect critically on the accomplishments, failures, debates, standards, approaches, and future agendas of international relations (IR) and its subfields. On the one hand, I have no doubt that our shared past is marked by enormous growth and progress. The conceptual and methodological equipment with which IR is probed today is far more elaborate, incisive, and diverse than was the case at the outset – back in the 1950s when a few isolated, non-Ivy-League scholars first came together around common interests to form a professional association, replete with a journal (called *Background* before being changed to the *International Studies Quarterly*) and with a membership so small that it convened annually on campuses because it was unable to reach the minimum registration required for reduced rates at hotels.

On the other hand, for all the progress that has marked IR's evolution, I am plagued with doubts about the field's capacity for adapting to the transformations at work in the world today. And my doubts extend to questioning the wisdom of engaging in introspective assessments of inter- and intra-paradigmatic debates. Perhaps out of fatigue generated by a history of vigorous involvement in such debates and perhaps because I have progressively moved away from the IR mainstream, but more likely out of a conviction that change has left us so far in arrears that we need to focus our energies on assessing substantive dynamics rather than evaluating our colleagues, their theories and their standards. Several years ago I gave up wondering, worrying, and writing about the fit between my thinking and that of Realists and Liberals. To articulate such concerns struck me as needless ritual that diverted valuable time and space from focusing on what was transpiring outside academe in what students call "the real world." The problem was me and my understanding, which required an agenda framed by my own reasoning and not one devised by others. Put differently, exercises like the present one can be a substitute for thinking about the nature of the world and how it should be studied, and I think that too often we resort to this substitute when the course of events seem too complex and obscure to comprehend.

So the ensuing paragraphs stray beyond the assigned topics. They are rooted in a sense of déjà vu all over again, to quote an insightful philosopher. In 1968 I wrote that all the signs were pointing in the same direction, that a spate of articles, textbooks, conferences, and curricula signified the emergence of a subfield (comparative foreign policy),[2] and now an even greater variety and number of indicators are heralding the arrival of another new preoccupation, one that is so pervasive that it has not only spread quickly through our ivory towers, but it has also galvanized action in the world's streets, markets, foreign offices, boardrooms, legislative chambers, city halls, cyberspaces, and every other site where people converge. And its pervasiveness in academe is such that it may emerge as our field and not just as a subfield. On Tuesday, January 19, 2000, while preparing a syllabus for a new course on globalization, three insightful newspaper stories, two soon-to-be-published manuscripts, a large book of readings, invitations to two conferences (one in Washington and one in Israel), and the lead article in the December issue of *Foreign Affairs* came my way – all of them concentrating on one or another aspect of globalization. That was just one day's take. Previously the flow of such indicators was no less continuous or voluminous, with word of new courses, conferences, dissertations, books, and papers on the subject amounting to a flow of tidal proportions. In effect, the preoccupation with the dynamics of globalization, both good and bad, has undergone globalization.

But there is a difference between the 1968 article and the recent déjà vu experience. The former involved a flow located entirely in the IR academic community, whereas the second is predominantly inundating other communities both outside and within the academy. The outside flow is evident in the huge extent to which globalization encompasses a cluster of issues at the top of the agenda of communities at every level of aggregation. The inside preoccupation with such issues is sustained by scholars in anthropology, sociology, economics, geography, and social psychology, with political science and IR trailing way behind. More accurately, within the American IR community, globalization is not a primary focus of most inquiries. The articles, books, and conference proposals I received on January 19 were the work either of colleagues abroad or of journalists, defense officials, and economists. It is almost as if our political science and IR communities are shying away from the forces of globalization because their complexity does not fit readily within the extant frameworks. These forces are so pervaded by nonlinear feedback mechanisms, by confounding nuances, that confronting them runs the risk of finding that one's hard-won intellectual perspectives are inadequate to the explanatory tasks and may have to be abandoned, or at least greatly modified.

If that seems like sour grapes and a violation of my commitment not to worry or write about the approach of others, let me articulate my out-of-the-mainstream perspectives not in terms of others having gone astray, but in terms of four major dimensions of globalization that strike me as urgently needing to be addressed. There are, of course, a number of other dimensions that should command focused attention, but these four can be seen as prerequisites to focusing on the others.

Change

If one assumes, as I do, that the world, its societies and its people, are undergoing transformations so profound as not to be fully appreciated, then a major conceptual challenge needs to be faced: how do we know change when we see it? How do we differentiate between evolutionary and breakpoint change? At what levels of aggregation are deep and enduring changes most likely? Do changes at, say, micro levels necessitate comparable changes at macro levels, and vice versa? Are some forms of change illusory, amounting to no more than brief disruptions of under-lying patterns? With few exceptions, such questions have not been the focus of conceptual inquiries by IR scholars.[3] Most of us tend to take for granted that salient changes in the actors and structures of world affairs will be manifest as they unfold. Sure, when a regime collapses or an alliance breaks up, when markets decline precipitously, or when situations deteriorate abruptly, we have little dif-ficulty discerning the end of one historical sequence and the onset of another. Ascribing change to such developments is easy, but assessing the durability of the changes, or discerning the early indicators of regime, alliance, situational, or market collapses, is where our conceptual equipment is rudimentary, if not altogether lacking. This is why all too often we are surprised by the turn of events.

There are, of course, no magic formulas for understanding and anticipating different forms of change. Still, there are ways of maximizing our ability to assess when transformations may ensue. One is to assume that systems are always on the edge of collapse, an assumption which compels us to be sensitive to, even in awe of, the capacity of systems to get from one moment, week, year, or decade in time to the next. To proceed from the opposite assumption – that systems are likely to persist – is to limit our readiness to recognize the formation and early stages of change dynamics. Another way of coping with the challenge of change is to allow our variables to vary – that is, to mentally imagine a wide range of possible shifts in the values of all the variables relevant to our concerns. Most of us, for example, did not allow for the possibility that the Cold War and the Soviet Union would come to abrupt ends. In retrospect, such failures border on the inexcusable. Or at least if we had been more sensitive to the susceptibility of systemic collapse and thus been alert to variations in the two structures expressive of such tendencies, it may have been less surprising.

Fragmegration

Of the numerous change dynamics presently shaping world affairs, two clusters stand out as paramount – those that foster globalization, centralization, and inte-gration on the one hand and those that promote localization, decentralization, and fragmentation on the other. While these polarities move the course of events in opposite directions, they are continuously, simultaneously, and often causally interactive, giving rise to the prime tensions with which individuals and their collectivities must contend. As indicated in prior chapters, in order to capture the inextricable and pervasive character of these interactions, I use the concept of "fragmegration," which is admittedly grating but at the same time reminds us that the processes of globalization and localization tend to be one and the same. Indeed, it can readily be argued that the emergent epoch is one of fragmegration and not simply one of globalization. The so-called "battle of Seattle" in late

November, 1999, offers a quintessential illustration of fragmegrative dynamics: as the representatives of states gathered for the integrative purpose of negotiating new trade agreements, so did various NGOs and individuals take to the streets in order to demonstrate their opposition and to highlight the fragmenting nature of such agreements.

While anthropologists, sociologists, journalists, and business executives have recognized the importance of fragmegrative processes,[1] these crucial dynamics have not been accorded centrality by the IR community. To the extent that globalizing or localizing forces are examined, they tend to be explored and traced separately, with only passing attention being paid to the ways in which each set of forces impacts on the other. One reason for this conceptual gap probably concerns the simultaneity of fragmegrative dynamics. The processes whereby the several polarities are linked to each other are comprised largely of feedback mechanisms, of nonlinear sequences that present enormous methodological dilemmas (see below). Most of us are accustomed to linear analysis, to discerning how dependent variables vary in response to the operation of various independent variables. The idea that each dependent variable becomes instantaneously an independent variable tends to be too mind-boggling to acknowledge, much less serving as the basis for inquiry. So fragmegrative studies languish for want of an effective methodology.

Equally important, the conceptual gap is by-passed because of the number and variety of sources that contribute to and sustain the processes of fragmegration. One of these sources consists of what I have earlier labeled "the skill revolution" wherein people everywhere are increasingly able to construct scenarios that trace the course of distant events back into their homes and pocketbooks. A second source involves the large degree to which collectivities around the world are undergoing authority crises, by which is meant the paralysis and stalemates that prevent them from framing and moving toward their goals. A third focuses on the bifurcation of global structures whereby the long-standing state-centric world now has a rival in an emergent multi-centric world of diverse actors such as ethnic minorities, NGOs, professional societies, transnational corporations, and the many other types of private collectivities that now crowd the global stage. A fourth is what I call the "organizational explosion" that has witnessed a huge proliferation of associations and networks at every level of community. A fifth I call the "mobility upheaval," by which is meant the vast and ever-growing movement of people around the world, a movement that includes everyone from the tourist to the terrorist and from the jet-setter to the immigrant. A sixth consists of the many microelectronic and transportational technologies that have collapsed time and space. A seventh involves the complex processes through which territoriality, states, and sovereignty have weakened to the point where it can be reasonably asserted that landscapes have been supplemented – and in some cases replaced – by mediascapes, financescapes, technoscapes, ethnoscapes, and ideoscapes.[5] An eighth concerns the large degree to which national economies have been globalized. How these eight major sources (and doubtless others could be identified) interactively generate and sustain the dynamics of fragmegration is an enormous analytic challenge, but even prior to assessing their interaction is the need to probe each of them for their fragmegrative content and consequences (see Table 8.1 below).

Micro–macro links

Still another critical aspect of fragmegrative dynamics involves the links between individuals at the micro level and collectivities at the macro level. Like change and fragmegration, these links have not been the focus of extensive conceptualization and investigation. While few analysts would deny that the flow between the two levels is central to how collectivities come into being and sustain themselves through time, how their macro–macro relationships are configured, and how people are shaped by the collectivities to which they belong, the interaction across these levels has been largely taken for granted or, in one well-known case, assessed to be beyond systematic comprehension.[6] We simply do not have any viable theory that anticipates how individuals will vary in response to varying macro inputs or how the structures and policies of macro collectivities might be undermined, redirected, sustained, or otherwise affected by new patterns at the micro level. Again, this is a preoccupation in some of the social sciences,[7] but IR scholars have essentially ignored the puzzles posed by the links among the levels of aggregation. Indeed, a major paradigm in the field, realism, proceeds from the premise that the only relevant action is that of states at the macro level, that individuals at the micro level can be assumed to follow the lead of their states.

The reasons for this seeming obliviousness to micro–macro links are not difficult to identify. Tracing such links is extremely difficult theoretically and thus even more challenging empirically. Those of us who do not subscribe to realist formulations intuitively know that the links are endlessly operative, that what collectivities and individuals do on the global stage are in part reactions to each other; but faced with the task of tracing their interactions, we tend to find it easier to take them for granted than to wrestle with the puzzles they pose. I do not claim to have made any progress in solving the puzzles, but I do contend that comprehension of world affairs increasingly requires us to address the challenge and frame models that offer a chance to fit some of the pieces of the puzzles together. As the skill revolution, authority crises, structural bifurcation, the organization explosion, the mobility upheaval, microelectronic technologies, the weakening of territoriality, states, and sovereignty, and the globalization of national economies accelerate and extend their impact on fragmegrative dynamics, so does it become all the more urgent that we collectively work to confront the causal interactions thereby established. Table 8.1 is an effort to highlight the vast domain across which such theorizing must roam. The entries in its cells are no more than impressionistic hypotheses as to how the sources of fragmegration may play out at the micro, macro, macro-macro, and micro-macro levels, but hopefully they are suggestive of some of the paths inquiry into such relationships should follow.

Table 8.1 Some possible sources of fragmegration at four levels of aggregation

Source of Fragmegration	Level of Aggregation			
	MICRO	MACRO	MACRO-MACRO	MICRO-MACRO
Skill Revolution	expands peoples' horizons on a global scale; sensitizes them to the relevance of distant events; facilitates a reversion to local concerns	enlarges the capacity of government agencies to think "out of the box," seize opportunities, and analyze challenges	multiplies quantity and enhances quality of links among states; solidifies their alliances and enmities	constrains policy making through increased capacity of individuals to know when, where and how to engage in collective action
Authority Crises	redirect loyalties; encourage individuals to replace traditional criteria of legitimacy with performance criteria	weaken ability of both governments and other organizations to frame and implement policies	enlarge the competence of some IGOs and NGOs; encourage diplomatic wariness in negotiations	facilitate the capacity of publics to press and/or paralyze their governments, the WTO, and other organizations
Bifurcation of Global Structures	adds to role conflicts, divides loyalties, and foments tensions among individuals; orients people toward local spheres of authority	facilitates formation new spheres of authority and consolidation of existing spheres in the multi-centric world	generates institutional arrangements for cooperation on major global issues such as trade, human rights, the environment, etc.	empowers transnational advocacy groups and special interests to pursue influence through diverse channels
Organizational Explosion	facilitates multiple identities, subgroupism, and affiliation with transnational networks	increases capacity of opposition groups to form and press for altered policies; divides publics from their elites	renders the global stage ever more transnational and dense with non-government actors	contributes to the pluralism and dispersion of authority; heightens the probability of authority crises

Continued

Table 8.1 continued

Source of Fragmegration	Level of Aggregation			
	MICRO	MACRO	MACRO-MACRO	MICRO-MACRO
Mobility Upheaval	stimulates imaginations and provides more extensive contacts with foreign cultures; heightens salience of the outsider	enlarges the size and relevance of subcultures, diasporas, and ethnic conflicts as people seek new opportunities abroad	heightens need for international cooperation to control the flow of drugs, money, immigrants, and terrorists	increases movement across borders that lessens capacity of governments to control national boundaries
Microelectronic Technologies	enable like-minded people to be in touch with each other anywhere in the world	empower governments to mobilize support; renders their secrets vulnerable to spying	accelerate diplomatic processes; facilitates electronic surveillance and intelligence work	constrain governments by enabling opposition groups to mobilize more effectively
Weakening of Territoriality, States, and Sovereignty	undermines national loyalties and increases distrust of governments and other institutions	adds to the porosity of national boundaries and the difficulty of framing national policies	increases need for interstate cooperation on global issues; lessens control over cascading events	lessens confidence in governments; renders nationwide consensus difficult to achieve and maintain
Globalization of National Economies	swells ranks of consumers; promotes uniform tastes; heightens concerns for jobs	complicates tasks of state governments vis-à-vis markets; promotes business alliances	intensifies trade and investment conflicts; generates incentives for building global financial institutions	increases efforts to protect local cultures and industries; facilitates vigor of protest movements

Methodology

The conceptual challenges posed by the dynamics of change, fragmegration and micro–macro interactions share a methodological dilemma. Each is pervaded with feedback processes and thus they pose the difficult question of how to explore them systematically. In other words, each is rooted in events that unfold virtually simultaneously, making it fruitless to cast analyses in terms of the interaction of independent and dependent variables. More accurately, analyses cast in a conventional linear framework seem bound to fall short in terms of capturing the interactive, high-speed nature of the phenomena of interest. How, then, to proceed? What methodologies might be available for probing nonlinear sequences of interaction? Are we bound to rely exclusively on case studies that, hopefully, somehow reveal the underlying tendencies that drive the transformative impacts of fragmegration and micro–macro links? Can nonlinear methodologies drawn from mathematics and statistics be adapted to the needs of the IR student? If we are not ourselves adept at such methods, how do we make an effective case for students employing them?

Never having been very sophisticated as a methodologist, I do not have very precise answers to these questions. I know they are important and I presume there are colleagues who can answer them with some authority. Still, ignorance is no excuse. If the mysteries of a fragmegrative world are to be fathomed, we cannot shy away from the methodological questions on the grounds of inexperience. Herewith, then, a partial, somewhat informed response to the methodological challenge: while case studies can surely be of value, there are also nonlinear procedures that have become more feasible as a result of advances in computer technologies. As I understand it, there is now the prospect of computer chips that will be 10 billion (yes, 10 billion) times faster than those in use today.[8] This heightens the potential of using computer simulations based on complexity theory, of building nonlinear feedback mechanisms into models that simulate the dynamics of change, fragmegration, and micro–macro interactions. To recur to points made earlier, conceptualizations of these three sets of dynamics are in short supply and obviously need to be refined before computer models can be applied. If it is assumed that such refinements will eventually be developed, however, then computer simulations may prove to be a useful methodology in unraveling the mysteries of a fragmegrative world.

As for the problem of motivating and equipping students to take advantage of the technological advances that lie ahead, let me report on a teaching aid that I have found highly effective semester after semester for the last several years. It is a book entitled *Complexity: The Emerging Science at the Edge of Order and Chaos*, by M. Mitchell Waldrop.[9] In more than fifty years of teaching I have never given an assignment that has had such pervasive consequences. Each semester the first week's assignment is to read the entire book and write a five-page evaluation of it. The reactions are consistently impressive. Even though the book refers only occasionally and peripherally to the relevance of complexity theory for world affairs, and even though much of the book is about matters far removed from the concerns of social science – it is the story of the Santa Fe Institute in New Mexico – the students find the outlines of complexity theory eye-opening and virtually every week of the semester one or another student mentions the book and voices an idea they picked up from it. No book I have ever assigned lingers so persistently in the memory banks of students. In the last few years several students have rethought their study plans in the direction of tooling up in computer science.

In sum, I find myself persuaded that the future of our field, its capacity to confront the huge conceptual and methodological challenges that have eluded our generation, lies in the training of those who will enter the field in the future. We need to acknowledge our own limitations and alert those we train to the necessity of their breaking with past paradigmatic assumptions and finding new ways of understanding and probing the enormous challenges posed by the dynamics of change, fragmegration, and micro–macro interactions. If we can orient our students along these lines, the globalization of globalization will have moved on to a higher and more secure analytic plane.

Part III
Globalization

9 The complexities and contradictions of globalization[1]

A mall in an Asian airport has a food court with fifteen companies, all but one of which offers menus to cater to local tastes, while the fifteenth, McDonald's, is the only one crowded with customers. In New York city real estate developers are increasingly prone to consult experts in *feng shui*, an ancient Chinese craft aimed at harmonizing the placement of man-made structures in nature, in order to attract a growing influx of Asian buyers who would not be interested in purchasing buildings unless their structures were properly harmonized.

Most people confronted with these examples would probably not be surprised by them. They might even view them as commonplace, as comparable examples of day-to-day life late in the twentieth century in which local practices spread to new and distant sites. In the first case the spread is from West to East and in the second it is from East to West, but both share a process in which practices spread and become established in profoundly different cultures. And what immediately comes to mind when contemplating this process of spread? The answer can be summed up in one word: globalization, a label that is presently in vogue to account for peoples, activities, norms, ideas, goods, services, and currencies that are decreasingly confined to a particular geographic space and its local and established practices.

Indeed, some might contend that "globalization" is the latest buzz word to which observers resort when things seem different and they cannot otherwise readily account for them. That is why, it is reasoned, a wide variety of activities are labeled as globalization, with the result that no widely accepted formulation of the concept has evolved. Different observers use it to describe or assess different phenomena and often there is little overlap among the various usages. Even worse, the elusiveness of the concept of globalization is seen as underlying the use of a variety of other similar terms – world society, interdependence, centralizing tendencies, world system, globalism, universalism, internationalization, globality – that come into play when efforts are made to grasp why public affairs today seem significantly different from the past.

Such reasoning is misleading. The proliferation of diverse and loose definitions of globalization as well as the readiness to use a variety of seemingly comparable labels are not so much a reflection of evasive confusion as they are an early stage in a profound ontological shift, a restless search for new ways of understanding unfamiliar phenomena. The very lack of precise formulations may suggest the presence of buzz words for the inexplicable, but a more convincing interpretation is that such words are voiced in so many different contexts because of a shared sense that the human condition is presently undergoing deep, enduring, and profound transformations in all of its aspects.

What is globalization?

Let us first make clear where globalization fits among the many buzz words that share a concern for something new in world affairs which is moving the loci and foci of activities and concerns beyond the national seats of power that have long served as the foundations of economic, political, and social life. While all the buzz words seem to cluster around the same dimension of the present human condition, useful distinctions can be drawn among them. Most notably, if it is presumed that the prime characteristic of this common dimension is that of change, of practices and norms that are undergoing transformation, then the term "globalization" seems appropriate to denote the "something" that is changing humankind's preoccupation with territoriality and the traditional arrangements of the interstate system. It is a term that directly implies change – something is being globalized – and thus differentiates it as a process rather than as a prevailing condition or a desirable end state of affairs.

Conceived as an underlying process, in other words, globalization is not the same as "globalism," which points to aspirations for an end state of affairs wherein values are shared by or pertinent to all the world's five billion people, their environment, and their role as citizens, consumers, or producers with an interest in collective action designed to solve common problems. And it can also be distinguished from "universalism," which refers to those values that embrace all of humanity (such as the values that science or religion draw upon), at any time or place, hypothetically or actually. Nor is it co-terminous with complex interdependence, which signifies structures that link people and communities in various parts of the world.

Although related to these other concepts, the notion of globalization developed here is narrower in scope and more specific in content. It refers neither to values nor to structures, but to sequences that unfold either in the mind or in behavior, to interaction processes that evolve as people and organizations go about their daily tasks and seek to realize their particular goals. What distinguishes globalizing processes is that they are not hindered or prevented by territorial or jurisdictional barriers. As indicated by the two examples presented at the outset, such processes can readily spread in diverse directions across national boundaries and are capable of reaching into any community everywhere in the world. They consist of all those forces that impel individuals, groups, societies, governments, institutions, and transnational organizations toward engaging in similar forms of behavior or participating in more encompassing and coherent processes, organizations, or systems. Contrariwise, localization derives from all those pressures that lead people, groups, societies, governments, and transnational organizations to narrow their horizons, participate in dissimilar forms of behavior, and withdraw to less encompassing processes, organizations, or systems. In other words, any technological, psychological, social, economic, or political developments that foster the expansion of interests and practices beyond established boundaries are both sources and expressions of the processes of globalization, just as any developments in these realms that limit or reduce interests are both sources and expressions of localizing processes.

Note that the processes of globalization are conceived as only *capable* of being worldwide in scale. In fact, the activities of no group, government, society, or company have ever been planetary in magnitude, and few cascading sequences actually encircle and encompass the entire globe. Televised events such as civil wars and famines in Africa or successful protests against governments in eastern Europe may sustain a spread that is worldwide in scope. But such a scope is not viewed as a prerequisite of globalizing dynamics. As long as it has the potential of an unlimited spread that can readily transgress national jurisdictions, any interaction sequence is considered to reflect the operation of globalization. Obviously, the differences between globalizing and localizing forces also give rise to contrary conceptions of territoriality. Globalization is rendering boundaries and identity with the land less salient while localization, being driven by pressures to narrow and withdraw, is highlighting borders and intensifying the deep attachments to land that can dominate emotion and reasoning.

In short, globalization is boundary-broadening and localization is boundary-heightening. The former allows people, goods, information, norms, practices, and institutions to move about oblivious to or despite boundaries. The boundary-heightening processes of localization are designed to inhibit or prevent the movement of people, goods, information, norms, practices, and institutions. Efforts along this line, however, can be only partially successful. Community or state boundaries can be heightened to a considerable extent, but they cannot be rendered impervious. Authoritarian societies try to make them sealproof, but such policies are bound to be undermined in a shrinking world with increasingly interdependent economies and communications technologies that cannot be easily monitored. Thus it is hardly surprising that some of the world's most durable tensions flow from the fact that no geographic borders can be made so airtight as to prevent the infiltration of ideas and goods. Stated more emphatically, some globalizing dynamics are bound, at least in the long run, to prevail.

The boundary-expanding dynamics of globalization have become highly salient precisely because recent decades have witnessed, for a variety of reasons, a mushrooming of the facilities, interests, and markets through which a potential for worldwide spread can be realized. Likewise, the boundary-contracting dynamics of localization have also become increasingly significant, not the least because some people and cultures feel threatened by the incursions of globalization. Their jobs, their icons, their belief systems, and the lives of their communities seem at risk as the boundaries that have sealed them off from the outside world in the past no longer assure protection. And there is, of course, a basis of truth in these fears. Globalization does intrude; its processes do shift jobs elsewhere; its norms do undermine traditional mores. The responses to these threats can vary considerably. At one extreme are adaptations which accept the boundary-broadening processes and make the best of them by integrating them into local customs and practices. At the other extreme are responses intended to ward off the globalizing processes by resort to ideological purities, closed borders, and economic isolation, to mention only the main ways in which boundaries are heightened.

The dynamics of fragmegration

It follows that the core of world affairs today consists of tensions between the dynamics of globalization and localization, that the two sets of dynamics are causally linked, almost as if every increment of globalization gives rise to an increment of localization, and vice versa. As noted in several of the previous chapters, I have long used the term "fragmegration" to account for these tensions, an awkward and perhaps even grating label that has the virture of capturing the pervasive interactions between the fragmenting forces of localization and the integrative forces of globalization.[2] One can readily observe the unfolding of fragmegrative dynamics in the struggles of the European Union to cope with proposals for monetary unification or in the electoral campaigns and successes of Jean-Marie Le Pen in France, Patrick Buchanan in the United States, and Pauline Hansen in Australia – to mention only two of myriad examples that could be cited.

It is important to keep in mind that fragmegration is not a single dynamic. Both globalization and localization are clusters of forces which, as they interact in different ways and through different channels, contribute to more encompassing processes in the case of globalization and to less encompassing processes in the case of the localizing cluster. These various dynamics, moreover, are conceived to operate in all realms of human activity, from the cultural and social through the economic and political. In the political realm globalizing dynamics underlie any developments that facilitate the expansion of authority, policies, and interests beyond the existing socially constructed, territorial boundaries, whereas the polit-ics of localization involve any trends in which the scope of authority and policies undergoes contraction and reverts to concerns, issues, groups and/or institutions that are less extensive than the prevailing socially constructed, territorial boundar-ies. In the economic realm globalization encompasses the expansion of produc-tion, trade, and investments beyond their prior locales, while localizing dynamics are at work when the activities of producers and consumers are constricted to narrower boundaries. In the social and cultural realms globalization operates to extend ideas, norms, and practices beyond the settings in which they originated, and localization is operative whenever the original settings are high-lighted or compressed and the inroad of new ideas, norms, and practices thereby inhibited.

It must be stressed that the dynamics unfolding in all these realms are long-term processes. They express fundamental human needs and thus span all of human history. The expansion processes of globalizing dynamics derive from people's need to enlarge the scope of their self-created order so as to increase the goods, services, and ideas available for their well-being. The agricultural revolution, followed by the industrial and post-industrial transformations, are among the major sources that have sustained globalization. Even as these expansion-driven forces have been operating, however, so have contrary tendencies toward contraction been continuously at work. Localizing dynamics derive from people's need for the psychic comforts of close-at-hand, reliable support – for the family and neighborhood, for local cultural practices, for a sense of "us" that is distinguished from "them." Put differently, globalizing dynamics have long fostered large-scale order, whereas the history of localizing dynamics as sources of pressure for small-scale order has been no less lengthy. Fragmegration, in short, has always been an integral part of the human condition.

The eventual predominance of globalization

Notwithstanding the complexities inherent in the emergent structures of world affairs, observers have not hesitated to anticipate what lies beyond fragmegration as global history unfolds. All agree that while the contest between globalizing and localizing dynamics is bound to be marked by fluctuating surges in both directions, the underlying tendency is for the former to prevail over the latter. Eventually, that is, the dynamics of globalization are viewed as likely to serve as the bases around which the course of events are organized. Consensuses along these lines break down, however, when estimates are made as to whether the predominance of globalization is likely to have desirable or noxious consequences. Those who welcome globalizing processes stress the power of economic variables relative to social and political institutions and patterns. The globalization of national economies through the diffusion of technology, consumer products, the rapid transfer of financial resources, and the efforts of transnational companies to extend their market shares is seen as so forceful and durable as to withstand and eventually surmount any and all pressures toward fragmentation. Sure, this line of theory acknowledges, the diffusion that sustains the processes of globalization is a centuries-old dynamic, but the difference is that the present era has achieved a level of economic development in which it is possible for innovations occurring in any country or any sector of their economies to be instantaneously transferred to and adapted in any other country or sector:

> When this process of diffusion collides with cultural or political protectionism, it is culture and protectionism that wind up in the shop for repairs. Innovation accelerates. Productivity increases. Standards of living improve. There are setbacks, of course – the newspaper headlines are full of them. But we believe that the time required to override these setbacks has shortened dramatically in the developed world. Indeed, recent experience suggests that, in most cases, economic factors prevail in less than a generation, probably within one or two political cycles (five to ten years).

Thus understood, globalization – the spread of economic innovations around the world and the political and cultural adjustments that accompany this diffusion – cannot be stopped. . . . As history teaches, the political organizations and ideologies that yield superior economic performance survive, flourish, and replace those that are less productive.[3]

While it is surely the case that robust economic incentives sustain and quicken the processes of globalization, this line of theorizing nevertheless suffers from not allowing for its own negation. As summarized, the theory offers no alternative interpretations as to how the interaction of economic, political, and social dynamics will play out. One cannot demonstrate the falsity – if falsity it is – of the theory because any contrary evidence is seen merely as "setbacks," as expectable deviations from the predicted course that are presumed to be temporary. The day may come, of course, when events so perfectly conform to the predicted patterns of globalization that one is inclined to conclude that the theory has been affirmed. But in the absence of alternative scenarios, the theory offers little guidance as to how to interpret intervening events, especially those that highlight the tendencies toward fragmentation. Viewed in this way, it is less a theory and more an article of faith to which one can cling without concern about the relevance of patterns evidential of localizing tendencies.

Other observers are much less sanguine about the future development of fragmegration. They highlight a "litany" of noxious consequences that are seen as following from the eventual predominance of globalization: ". . . its economism; its economic reductionism; its technological determinism; its political cynicism, defeatism, and immobilism; its de-socialization of the subject and re-socialization of risk; its teleological subtext of inexorable global 'logic' driven exclusively by capital accumulation and the market; and its ritual exclusion of factors, causes or goals other than capital accumulation and the market from the priority of values to be pursued by social action."[4]

Still another approach allowing for either desirable or noxious outcomes has been developed by Michael Zurn. He identifies a mismatch between the rapid extension of boundary-crossing transnational activities and the scope of effective governance. Consequently, states are undergoing what is labeled "uneven denationalization," a primary process "where . . . the rise of international governance is still remarkable, but not accompanied by mechanisms for their democratic control, people, in addition, become alienated from the remote political process. . . . The democratic state in the Western world is confronted with a situation in which it is undermined by the process of globalization and overarched by the rise of international institutions.[5]

While readily acknowledging the difficulties of anticipating where the process of uneven denationalization is driving the world, Zurn is able to derive two possible scenarios that may unfold: "Whereas the pessimistic scenario points to instances of fragmentation and emphasize the disruption caused by the transition, the optimistic scenario predicts, at least in the long run, the triumph of centralization."[6] The latter scenario rests on the presumption that the increased interdependence of societies will propel them to develop ever more effective democratic controls over the very complex arrangements on which international institutions must be founded.

Uneven fragmegration

My own approach to theorizing about the fragmegrative process builds upon these other perspectives and a key presumption of my own – that there is no inherent contradiction between localizing and globalizing tendencies – to develop an overall hypothesis that anticipates fragmegrative outcomes and that allows for its own negation: *the more pervasive globalizing tendencies become, the less resistant localizing reactions will be to further globalization.* In other words, globalization and localization are anticipated to co-exist, but the former sets the context for the latter. Since the degree of co-existence will vary from situation to situation, depending on the salience of the global economy and the extent to which ethnic and other noneconomic factors actively conduce to localization, I refer, borrowing from Zurn, to the processes depicted by the hypothesis as *uneven fragmegration*. The hypothesis allows for continuing pockets of antagonism between globalizing and localizing tendencies even as increasingly (but unevenly) the two accommodate to each other. It does not deny the pessimistic scenario wherein fragmentation disrupts globalizing tendencies; rather the reasoning underlying the hypothesis treats the process inherent in the pessimistic scenario as more and more confined to particular situations that may eventually be led by the opportunities and requirements of greater interdependence to conform to the optimistic scenario.

For globalizing and localizing tendencies to accommodate to each other, individuals have to come to appreciate that they can achieve psychic comfort in collectivities through multiple memberships and multiple loyalties, that they can advance both local and global values without either detracting from the other. The hypothesis anticipates a growing appreciation along these lines because the contrary premise that psychic comfort can only be realized by having a highest loyalty is becoming increasingly antiquated. To be sure, people have long been accustomed to presuming that, in order to derive the psychic comfort they need through collective identities, they had to have a hierarchy of loyalties and that, consequently, they had to have a highest loyalty that could only be attached to a single collectivity. Such reasoning, however, is a legacy of the state system, of having encountered for centuries crises when one felt compelled to place nation-state loyalties above all others. It is a logic that long served to reinforce the predominance of the state as the "natural" unit of political organization and that probably reached new heights during the intense years of the Cold War. But if it is the case, as the foregoing analysis stresses, that conceptions of territoriality are in flux and that the failure of states to solve pressing problems has led to a decline in their capabilities and a loss of their performance legitimacy, it follows that the notion that people must have a "highest loyalty" will also decline and give way to the development of multiple loyalties and an understanding that local, national, and transnational affiliations need not be mutually exclusive. For the reality is that human affairs are organized at all these levels for good reasons, that people have needs that can only be filled by close-at-hand organizations and other needs that are best served by distant entities at the national or transnational levels.

In addition, not only is an appreciation of the reality that allows for multiple loyalties and memberships likely to grow as the effectiveness of states and the salience of national loyalties diminish, but it also seems likely to widen as the benefits of the global economy expand and people become increasingly aware of the extent to which their well-being is dependent on events and trends elsewhere in the world. At the same time, the distant economic processes serving their needs are impersonal and hardly capable of advancing the need to share with others in a collective affiliation. This need was long served by the nation-state, but with fragmegrative dynamics having undermined the national level as a source of psychic comfort and with transnational entities seeming too distant to provide the psychic benefits of affiliation, the virtues of the satisfactions to be gained through more close-at-hand affiliations are likely to seem ever more compelling.

Complexities and contradictions

Even as it seems clear that the age of fragmegration has become an enduring feature of global life, so is it also evident that globalization is not a buzz word, that it encompasses pervasive complexities and contradictions that have the potential of both enlarging and degrading our humanity. In order to ensure that the enlargement is more prevalent than the degradation, it is important that people and their institutions become accustomed to the multiple dimensions and nuances wherein our world is undergoing profound and enduring transformations. To deny the complexities and contradictions in order to cling to a singular conception of what globalization involves is to risk the many dangers that accompany oversimplification.

10 Toward a viable theory of globalization[1]

Notwithstanding the proliferation of inquiries into globalization and a continuing clarification of its various dimensions, synthesizing theories that combine different globalizing dynamics which, in turn, foster varied outcomes remain elusive. Students of international trade and their counterparts who analyze financial flows do proceed from a sound theoretical base, to be sure, but their studies are narrow in scope and limited to the economic dimension. Efforts to develop broad-gauged theory that explains the social, political, and cultural dimensions and how they interact with economic dynamics are conspicuously lacking. It is almost as if globalization defies the theoretical enterprise, being too amorphous and complex to allow for the framing and testing of incisive and empirical hypotheses. How, then, to begin to develop a viable theory of globalization that accounts for its underlying dynamics? How to free ourselves from conventional procedures and thereby possibly break through the barriers that make the task so difficult?

I am far from sure I can negotiate a breakthrough that facilitates surmounting the barriers and allows for a break from the conceptual and methodological jails that inhibit our analytic imaginations, but here I want to outline two possible and related paths to viable theory. One may seem outrageous at first glance, but it serves to facilitate movement down the second path.

The first path amounts to reversing the conventional links between theory and method. Ordinarily we employ methodology to affirm or reject theoretical propositions, but can this sequencing be altered, even reversed? Is it possible to employ a method that opens up previously unrecognized theoretical vistas? The section that follows offers at least a partial attempt to develop a positive response to these questions.

From method to theory

If it is assumed (as I do) that all the dimensions of globalization are sustained by individuals at the micro level as well as by diverse organizations at the macro level, one is faced by the enormous theoretical task of grasping how actors at the two levels shape each other's orientations and behavior. The task is enormous because a preponderance of the inquiries into globalization focuses almost exclusively on macro phenomena. Many of them include individual leaders and officials as central to globalizing processes, but they are included as heads of macro organizations while the role of individuals who are not leaders – those innumerable people who contribute to the collective actions of publics – are ignored, or at least not regarded as theoretically relevant. In effect, therefore, attention to micro–macro interactions has yet to make its way into the globalization literature. Note may be taken of protest marches and counter rallies during times of turmoil and mass unrest, but even these micro manifestations are not built into theoretical formulations in the form of propositions that link them to the macro actions or reactions of states and other organizations.

In short, it is arguable that there can be no viable theory without a micro–macro component. If it is assumed that people count – that all globalizing actions originate with individuals who may then form aggregate entities that engage in salient behavior – then it clearly follows that an adequate theory of globalization must perforce allow for micro–macro interactions.[2] Put differently, the quick spread of the Internet and the advent of suicide bombers highlight the large degree to which world affairs have undergone transformations that accord ordinary people the capacity to meaningfully affect the course of events.

Of what is this an instance?

In order to generate theoretical insights that insure the inclusion of micro phenomena, I have long argued there is a powerful, six-word question that stimulates, even forces, us to proceed theoretically from the micro level.[3] The question is, of what is this an instance? The key word here is "this," as it refers to anything we observe, whether it be in personal, professional, political, or global life and irrespective of whether it occurs in our immediate environment, is read in print, or is seen on television. The question is powerful because it compels us to climb the ladder of abstraction to find a more encompassing phenomenon of which the observed "this" is an instance. Once we ask the question, in short, we have no choice but to engage in generalization and thus to undertake the first steps toward theory. The steps may be crude and ambiguous, but they nonetheless get us up to the rungs on the ladder where of necessity theory is constructed if by "theory" we mean explanations of why clusters of phenomena cluster and behave as they do. Yet, to cling precariously to the higher rungs on the ladder is not enough. There is no automatic connection between asking the of-what-is-this-an-instance question and the generation of micro–macro theoretical propositions. And it is here, in the link between the question and meaningful theoretical formulations, that a methodological procedure may be helpful.

A journalistic method

Strange as it may seem coming from a social scientist, the method I have in mind has its roots in journalism. Every newspaper in developed societies begins most of its stories with a paragraph or two descriptive of a micro incident – an individual in trouble, a family divided, a community aroused – that is then used as an example of a more general situation, process, or institution. One can readily imagine a hardened newspaper editor saying to new, cub reporters, "Be sure and start out your story with an account of particular circumstances that is illustrative of what you want to write about." Put in my terms, the editor is saying, "Make sure you go from the micro to the macro!" Such phrasing suggests methodology as a means of theorizing.

It is not, of course, an elaborate methodology and there is a lot about it that may not be reliable. It offers no means of checking on whether the move from the micro to the macro is accurate or whether the micro situation is typical of the macro pattern it is claimed to exemplify. Nevertheless, it is a point of departure, a method that has the great virtue of getting students of globalization to cast their analyses in micro–macro terms before they move on to other concerns.

For analysts who are inclined to take micro phenomena for granted and are thus disinclined to employ the method, starting with a journalistic technique will not be easy. One has to build up the habit of relying on the of-what-is-this-an-instance methodology for it to become a meaningful analytic tool. More accurately, one has to assume that individuals are illustrative of more encompassing processes and structures, not an assumption that can readily be developed into a habit by observers who have long assumed that states, international organizations, and other macro collectivities are the entities that sustain and structure world affairs. On the other hand, it is a habit that quickly becomes engrained once one begins to pose the question and finds how clarifying it can be. For the question has no single answer when asked about any situation, nor any answer that is erroneous. There can be as many answers as one's knowledge and imagination can generate. If one's mind is alive, a micro event or action can be illustrative of a host of diverse macro situations, thus enabling the analyst to differentiate between fruitful and fruitless theoretical lines of inquiry. Put more strongly, if one cannot come up with any responses to what a micro event is an instance of, then his or her conceptual jail is deeply incarcerating.

A simple example highlights the utility of this journalistic method. Suppose analysts have developed the of-what-is-this-an-instance habit and want to incorporate the cultural dimension into a comprehensive theory of globalization when they come upon the following brief newspaper story:

> After six months of tough negotiations with a group of Taiwanese investors, Barry Lewen, a real-estate broker, thought he was just two days from completing the $14-million sale of a building at 366 Madison Avenue when he was unexpectedly told there was one last detail.
>
> The investors insisted that before anything more was done, a Chinese mystic had to be flown from Taiwan to determine if the building's qi, or life force, was acceptable. "I thought they were joking," said Mr. Lewen . . .
>
> A few days later, however, he anxiously watched as a practitioner of the

ancient Chinese craft of feng shui paced the site for 30 minutes before giving his approval.

"I wasn't sure if he was a witch doctor or what," Mr. Lewen said. "I can tell you there were a lot of sweaty palms."

Long a tradition in the Far East, the millennia-old craft of feng shui (pronounced FUNG-shway) has begun to exert a subtle influence on the hard-edged world of real estate in America. Feng shui, which means "wind" and "water" in Chinese, is a blend of astrology, design and Eastern philosophy aimed at harmonizing the placement of man-made structures in nature.

Driven by the influx of investors from Hong Kong, Singapore, Taiwan and China, the use of feng shui has surfaced in the design and marketing of projects from mini-malls in Los Angeles to skyscrapers in Manhattan.[4]

A mind that is alive might view this micro account as an instance of the macro preeminence of commercial orientations. Or it might conclude this is an illustration of the complexity of commercial transactions. But such interpretations do not facilitate theorizing about the cultural dimension of globalization. However, if the instance is seen as indicating that cultural flows can move from west to east as well as east to west, globalization theorists can avoid the trap of assuming that globalization consists of the spread of American values and are thus in a better position to integrate the cultural dimension into their theoretical framework.

There is, of course, no magic in this journalistic method. It provides no guidance as to how the insight about cultural flows is best integrated into a theoretical framework. For this purpose a more encompassing micro–macro perspective is needed, one that combines the fruits of the of-what-is-this-an-instance question with a scheme that identifies the sources of globalization and generates hypotheses as to how they might operate in a micro–macro context. The next section is designed to be suggestive as a possible step in this direction.

A second step: eight sources of globalization

I conceive of globalization to consist of all those processes whereby flows expand across national borders – flows of goods, ideas, people, pollution, drugs, crime, disease, technology, and a host of other phenomena that are part and parcel of daily and national life. Given this perspective, the question becomes what are the prime sources that sustain the various flows? Again, there is no standard response to this question. Analysts have to develop their own answer depending upon how they understand the dynamics of globalization. I have found it useful to specify eight sources, all of which have been set forth previously in Table 8.1. The entries in the cells of the 4 × 8 matrix are crude and untested hypotheses designed to illustrate the kinds of outcomes to which the various sources can give rise at the several levels of aggregation. They are intended to be suggestive and anything but definitive. Indeed, presumably a number of hypotheses can be developed for each of the thirty-two cells.

Is this to imply that the most we can hope for in developing a viable framework for theorizing about globalization is a thirty-two cell matrix, some cells of which may not be meaningfully linked to others? Not at all. The task is to evolve a scheme that specifies how each of the hypothesized outcomes in one of the rows contributes to the outcomes in the other cells in the row and then, eventually, how the outcomes in all the cells (including hypotheses not included) link to the postulated reactions listed in all the other cells. A formidable task, but one has to start somewhere. No one claims that a viable framework for the analysis of globalization will be parsimonious or simple to develop.

Elsewhere I have spelled out the phenomena encompassed by each of the eight sources of globalization,[5] so that here it is sufficient to illustrate how the micro foundations of three of the sources might be probed through the method outlined above. Of the sources listed, one, the skill revolution, derives entirely from micro roots. It refers to a worldwide trend whereby analytically, emotionally, and imaginatively people are increasingly able to connect distant events to proximate circumstances. The reasons for these growing capacities are numerous, and they include some of the other sources listed in Table 8.1 such as the organizational explosion, the mobility upheaval, and authority crises. The operation of expanded skills can be initially probed by employing the journalistic method in such a way as to trace the ways in which specific individuals perceive and participate in collective actions (the fourth cell of the first row in Table 8.1).

The organizational explosion highlights a worldwide trend whereby new formal and informal organizations are being formed at every level of community and in every part of the world. The journalistic method can be used to trace this process by following how particular individuals are recruited to bring a specific organization into being which then mobilizes them to engage in protests against a specific community policy that, along with the protests of other like-minded organizations, undermines the viability of the community (any of the cells in the fourth row of Table 8.1) and amounts to an authority crisis for that community (any of the cells in the second row).

Conclusion

In sum, to develop viable theories of globalization is to face a formidable challenge. Some might argue that a better strategy is to eschew a comprehensive theory that encompasses all the dimensions of the subject and to opt instead for framing a theory for each of the prime dimensions. Such a strategy assumes that a theoretical linking of the dimensions is either not possible or too taxing. Such may be the case, but that can only be determined if an effort is first made to construct an overarching theory. The foregoing may demonstrate for some analysts that it is absurd to undertake such an effort. A conclusion along this line strikes me as premature. Or at least I am inclined to believe that a broad, all-encompassing theory is doable if one or, better, a team is dedicated to investing the time, energy, and creativity to pull it off.

11 Democracy and globalization[1]

To schedule a roundtable on "democracy and globalization" at a conference on new challenges to democracy is to run the risk of succumbing to what I call the "domestic analogy." This analogy involves the assumption that democracy flourishes best – or perhaps only in the context of a national state that has procedures for reflecting the will of its people and protecting their rights. Some might argue that the domestic analogy is a measuring stick, a framework for judging practices whereby communities govern themselves, but here I want to elaborate on the conclusion that it is a highly misleading analogy, that it is deceptive as a measuring stick and is best avoided if the dynamics of globalization are as powerful and pervasive as they seem to be at this moment in history. Put more strongly, the domestic analogy inhibits our imaginations and subverts our inquiries if globalizing processes serve as our analytic framework. It blinds us, undermines our creativity, and confounds our dialogues by preventing us from seeing virtues in political mechanisms and processes that do not conform to the domestic procedures of democratic governments. In short, democracy in a globalizing world is sharply different from democracy in a national or local world, and it is a mistake to assess the former from the perspective of the latter.

The processes of globalization undermine the domestic analogy and the prospect of centralized authority emerging to reflect the will of diverse peoples on a global scale in a number of ways. First and foremost perhaps, not only is there a lack of centralized authority at the global level, but the obverse has become prevalent: the central tendency of globalizing processes involves the disaggregation of authority as states have weakened and their boundaries have become increasingly porous, as nongovernmental organizations (NGOs) have proliferated, as people have become ever more mobile and their skills ever more refined, as issues have become more and more transnational, as public spaces have become increasingly privatized through global consumerism, as multinational corporations have acquired significant power to shape human identity and networks, as local groups have increasingly contested the encroachment of globalizing forces, and, not least, as the global stage becomes ever more crowded and enmeshes myriad collectivities in a dense network of complex relationships – to mention only some of the sources and consequences of the relentless disaggregation of authority. Stated more succinctly, there are innumerable spheres of authority (SOAs) that render the domestic analogy ever more irrelevant.

It follows, as I have argued elsewhere, that the actions, practices, and structures with which democracy at the global level must contend occurs on the frontier between domestic and foreign affairs,[2] a broad political space in which the central dynamics are the clash between globalizing and localizing forces, what I call "fragmegration" in order to capture in a single concept the endless interactions between fragmentation and integration at every level of community. And fragmegrative dynamics are accelerating at an increasingly swift pace as techno-logical developments, in transportation as well as electronics, have rendered the world ever smaller and interdependent. What is distant is now also proximate, and vice versa, and these distant proximities intrude so fully upon every aspect of life that the dynamics of local–global interactions have become central to the daily routines of peoples and crowded out national phenomena as the key to understanding why the course of events unfolds as it does.[3]

Under these circumstances, the likelihood of developing transnational institu-tions on a global scale that promote democratic practices – by maintaining instruments of governance that insure habitual compliance with law and adminis-trative regulations, that sustain fair representation of diverse orientations, and that effectively protect rights and minorities – is, to say the least, virtually nil. The disaggregation of authority is too great and the perquisites of states are too deep-seated to permit the evolution of transnational institutions founded on democratic premises and procedures. How, then, does the notion of democracy have to be reconceptualized to be relevant to a shrinking world dominated by distant proximities that transgress the domestic–foreign frontier in crazy-quilt ways? If the foregoing brief outline of global life today is accurate and moves the domestic analogy toward irrelevance, what kinds of practices and institutions can be developed to achieve at least a modicum of democracy?

Before responding to these questions, it useful to note that while the probability of authoritative democratic procedures evolving on a global scale is extremely low, there are some institutions at the transnational level that offer a modicum of democracy and accountability. Among these, for example, are an international court that has effective jurisdiction over certain issues; a central European Com-mission that can set rules for members of the EU; more than a few international regimes that operate effectively in certain issue areas;[4] and the United Nations and its Security Council which undertakes to resolve intense conflicts and intrude peace-keepers into volatile situations. While such mechanisms are not trivial, at the same time they are not sufficient to ensure democracy throughout much of globalized space; much of humankind does not have access to these transnational institutions, which, in any event, are creatures of the state system and are not as democratic as the institutions evolved by domestic systems.

To be sure, there is no lack of proposals for subjecting the processes of global-ization to the requirements of a democratic order. Perhaps most notably, more than a few concerned observers have called for the addition of a Peoples' Assembly as a new, second chamber of the United Nations, that "would inject into UN debates a more realistic appreciation of the insecurity experienced by a large fraction of humanity, and a greater degree of independence vis-à-vis the major centers of power and wealth."[5] As a body of elected officials who would represent constituencies other than states, the "Peoples' Assembly would, much like the European Parliament, function as a house of review, carefully monitoring the decisions and deliberations of the [established UN] departments and agencies. . . . Members of the Peoples' Assembly would be directly elected (perhaps every five years) by their constituencies on the basis of universal suffrage, a secret ballot and the principle of one vote one value (with each constituency having an approximate population of six million, that is an electorate of between three and four million). The boundaries of each constituency would be proposed by an Electoral Commission located within the UN Secretariat and jointly approved by the General Assembly and Peoples' Assembly."[6] A host of benefits are anticipated to flow from such an institution: elections would promote "widespread public debate"; they "would be organized by the relevant national government but closely monitored by an international inspection team . . . accountable to the Peoples' Assembly"; the UN membership of each state "would be conditional on compliance with these requirements"; such procedures "would exert significant pressures on authoritarian governments to apply over time the same democratic procedures, or some version of them, to their own national political system;" and they "would also encourage local populations to devote more attention to international affairs, offering them another vehicle for applying pressure on their respective governments, and slowly but steadily fostering the articulation of world public opinion."[7]

In addition, since "global insecurity is as much economic as military in its origins," and since "a great many actors other than states" thus shape the course of events, "[i]t is only prudent . . . that these non-state actors be brought into the decision-making process and made more accountable for their actions." How? By establishing a "third chamber, to be known as the Consultative Assembly, [that] would have a membership of approximately 1,000. Three main types of organizations would be represented: transnational firms (industrial, commercial and financial) through the intermediary of their respective international (or regional) umbrella associations; trade unions and professional associations (again through the intermediary of international or regional associations), and a range of educational, scientific, cultural, religious, and public-interest organizations active around issues central to the UN's agenda (for example, peace, environment, development, human rights, social welfare, education)."[8] The proposal further states that different UN organs would be involved in selecting the organizations that would be given consultative status, "but the ultimate decision would remain solely that of the General Assembly."[9] As for the question of including powerful corporations in the deliberations,

> . . . the answer is essentially twofold. The most powerful players in the market place must over time become more transparent and more accountable for their decisions. This will be one of the few arenas in which their views,

priorities and actions can be subjected to international public scrutiny, where they will need to interact and negotiate on a continuing basis with other parties wedded to very different objectives and perspectives. . . . [Second,] the membership dues which these organizations would be expected to pay in accordance with an agreed assessment formula would make a welcome contribution to the UN budgetary needs.[10]

The difficulty with proposals such as these is that their legitimacy derives from and their procedures are rooted in the domestic analogy – in the state system – a flaw that, given the self-interested orientations of states, seems bound to prevent their adoption. In effect, such proposals are more in the nature of wishful thinking than realistic ideas susceptible to implementation. They fly in the face of what the state-centric system will permit. To be sure, the sovereignty of states has undergone some attrition in recent years with respect to human rights and genocide, but it is hard to imagine them yielding to pressures that might limit their authority over the many issues on their agendas that are inextricably caught up in the world's pervasive interdependence. This is why I suggest above that the probabilities of authoritative democratic procedures evolving on a global scale range from low to nil. Re-conceptualizing democracy in a globalizing world requires putting aside conventional notions of representation and accountability. If this can be done, the probabilities of achieving compatibility between democracy and globalization rise well above low.

Needless to say, to give up the domestic analogy is not to abandon the aspiration to infuse democratic practices into the processes of globalization. Rather it is to give up the requirement that democratic processes must have roots in formal and legal documents. As I see it, there is more than a little potential for success in promoting a variety of informal mechanisms that mirror democratic practices at the domestic level and that, in so doing, become institutionalized without any legal foundations comparable to those operative on the domestic scene. Just as, say, the British constitution has been no less effective for not having been written out and formally adopted, so can informal democratic processes evolve and be maintained in a transnational and globalized world. Adherence to such processes may take awhile to develop, and they will doubtless undergo setbacks on occasion, but the power of globalizing dynamics – and the challenge to human security they pose – is such that the habits necessary to sustain the processes in the absence of formal constitutional prescriptions will surely and steadily evolve. Put differently, as informal standards of accountability become increasingly accepted, so will they become embedded in transnational norms that enlarge the realm of democratic practices sustained through globalization. Indeed, the more the world shrinks and becomes inextricably interdependent, the greater will be the recognition that self-interest requires adherence to the emergent practices expressive of democratic norms.

Five dynamics appear especially likely to foster the emergence of democratic practices equivalent to some of those that mark the domestic scene within countries. One involves the large extent to which globalization has generated an organizational explosion and a skill revolution, developments that have resulted in the global stage being ever more crowded with diverse collectivities comprised of ever more skillful leaders and followers.[11] These, in turn, have formed a multitude of SOAs that are able to exercise effective authority over the people and issues that form the basis of their coherence. More than that, the skill revolution has enlarged the mobilizing capacity of leaders because people are increasingly skilled at knowing when, where, and how to engage in collective action. Thus the global stage is not only crowded, but it is also an endlessly busy place, marked by restless, pressing, and competing actors striving to reach their particularistic goals even as they check on the activities of their competitors. The result is, so to speak, increasing degrees of transparency, of informal mechanisms whereby the various organizations monitor each other. Stated differently, democracy at the global level is enhanced by safety in numbers, by overlapping or parallel jurisdictions that increasingly subject all the diverse organizations – from the corporation to the professional society, from the humanitarian agency to the advocacy group, from the NGO to the labor union – to constraints that may approach the equivalent of democratic controls in the sense that it becomes progressively difficult for any single collectivity or cluster of them to exercise undue dominance.

A second and closely related informal mechanism is linked to a technology, the Internet, which has recently made such substantial advances as to facilitate transnational democratic processes. Its wide usage around the world enlarges the capacity of organizations to mobilize support and to render actions and aims on the global stage more transparent. The Internet now enables activists to form "citizen networks" that, in turn, contribute to the shaping of public policy. A compelling example is the coalescence of citizen networks that successfully lobbied to defeat the proposed Multilateral Agreement on Investment (MAI) in 1998.[12] Indeed, "linked through the Internet across state borders, the tentacles of these citizen networks have begun to infiltrate nearly every major international political issue-area, from security to human rights to the governance of the global economy. . . . [T]hey are seen as largely positive expressions of genuine democratic participation in world arenas that for far too long have been monopolized by states and planet-roaming corporations."[13] To be sure, interaction among activists with respect to transnational policies did not begin with the Internet. The fax machine, telephone, letters, and conferences have long provided means to sustain interaction, but by the time the proposed MAI entered the political arena the Internet had become available and added "a dense layer of daily interaction to these links, intensifying the bonds between disparate members and fomenting a sense of international commonality"[14] as well as providing "a tool to put direct pressure on politicians and policy makers in member states."[15] Furthermore, while the anti-MAI network was created with a specific goal in mind, it "shows definite signs of being sustained into the future," so much so in fact that today it is difficult to imagine the boards of international financial institutions meeting without precipitating organized opposition to their agendas.

There are, of course, reasons to be skeptical about the extent to which citizen networks sustained by the Internet have contributed a measure of democracy to globalizing processes. Some fear, for example, that the organizational explosion and the Internet are leading to a "logistical nightmare of thousands upon thousands of niche interest groups buzzing around every conceivable international forum where nothing is achieved but endless gridlock."[16] Others are concerned that instead of modifying their agendas and policies, states and corporations have co-opted the citizen networks rather than taking their contentions seriously. Still others argue that NGOs themselves may not be democratic, that often they are not accountable to the people they represent. Despite the skepticism, however, "in the wake of the MAI, standard operating procedures for dealing with citizen networks are undergoing significant transformations. A much greater emphasis has been placed on transparency. There is more of a forthcoming attitude about the release of documents and background papers. Invitations for feedback from the public and civil society groups on official position papers have been prominent. Consultations with interested citizen groups have been held."[17] Despite the potential for co-optation, in other words,

> One should not underestimate the extent to which such a transformation in standard operating procedures, however minimal, can raise expectations, create path-dependencies, and open doors that cannot be shut again. Ultimately however, such a transformation suggests that at the very least states and international organizations have *perceived* in the wake of the MAI an important change in the power citizen networks which needs to be addressed. Undertaking a "business-as-usual" position in regard to citizen networks has clearly been viewed as not a viable option – a shift that suggests that the citizen networks did indeed matter.[18]

Another technology that contributes to the global democratization involves an array of instruments that I call the politics of proof. New techniques of electronic surveillance and aerial photography, for example, enable private groups as well as governments to generate evidence that exposes wrong-doing and thus have the potential of contributing to a greater degree of transnational transparency and accountability – or at least such is the case within systems that share the same values on what constitutes evidence. To be sure, the same technologies of observation can be used to deceive, to doctor photographs and voice records, but nonetheless it is now possible to exercise democratic constraints by generating proofs that were not previously obtainable.

The fourth dynamic that contributes to democracy in a globalized world is the actions that the new technologies facilitate. In particular, strengthened by the Internet, the organizational explosion, and the skill revolution, people everywhere are ready to convene and march in street protests when the boards of international financial institutions gather. These protests have become a regular feature of the global scene and while they are hardly the equivalent of legislative votes that constrain policy makers, they do appear to have arrested the attention of public officials, the mass media, and otherwise uninvolved citizens. It is hard to imagine that transnational leaders who favor key globalization goals remain oblivious to the protesters and make their decisions without an eye to avoid further provocations of them. On the contrary, there is some evidence that the World Bank, the IMF, the World Economic Forum, and other international institutions have heard the protesters' messages and sought, at least minimally, to accommodate them. Such responses may not be as clear-cut as was the case with the MAI, but nor have they been trivial. To be sure, the protests attract diverse groups with diverse goals, thus diluting the clarity of the messages delivered, but the dilution has yet to appear so great as to prevent the delivery of the main messages. It is not far-fetched, therefore, to assert that protest marches on behalf of greater transparency in corporate and governmental policy-making will become the global equivalent of domestic forms of representation like elections, legislative bargaining, and judicial review.

Finally, a key dynamic involves the nature of compliance, that readiness on the part of publics which enables authorities to generate desired responses to their directives and thereby govern effectively. In the domestic analogy the generation of compliance is backed up by the force of law, by resort to police powers if noncompliance persists. In a globalizing world, on the other hand, compliance in transnational SOAs has to occur informally on the basis of shared values. In some issue areas and in some parts of the world the degree of consensus around shared values is not sufficient for voluntary compliance to be generated, but at the same time this key dimension of democracy is manifest in some SOAs. In the human rights area, for example, norms of voluntary compliance protecting the rights of minorities have emerged in various corners of the world – not as much nor in as many corners as one would wish, to be sure, but an emergence is detectable.[19] As the world becomes ever more complex and as publics become increasingly sensitive to the high degree of complexity, presumably the readiness to comply voluntarily with transnational directives will also intensify and spread. Put differently, as mechanisms for facilitating transparency in SOAs evolve, so will constraints on the exercise of arbitrary authority, and such mechanisms may be the prime instruments through which globalization undergoes transformation in a democratic direction.

There is, of course, no unseen hand that will bring about developments along this line. The self-corrective mechanisms of the market-place are not sufficient to foster political changes. Nor can the mass media be relied upon as corrective mechanisms. Sometimes referred to as mediademocracy, mediaism, mediapolitik, mediacracy, and teledemocracy, collectively the world's media tend to be reluctant to be critical and/or to give voice to the perspectives of their national or local governments rather than to shared global values. Thus the task boils down to requiring the seen hand of persistent efforts to render SOAs more and more responsive to the worlds over which they preside.

Admittedly none of the five mechanisms I have identified are as effective or desirable as those embedded in the domestic analogy, but they partially offset the limits imposed by globalization and we have to accept them until such time as more formal democratic institutions become pervasive on the global stage. And if these informal mechanisms also seem like wishful thinking and so out of phase with the state system as to be absurd, it bears repeating that globalizing dynamics compel us to think about democracy in different ways and relax some of our main assumptions about the nature of democracy. Furthermore, the very same dynamics that have curtailed the role of states virtually require creative thought about what the emergent global order permits with respect to democratic practices.

12 Think globally, pray locally

In the wake of John Paul II's death and the election of his successor, speculation about the future of the Catholic church focused on whether the papacy would revert back to an Italian pope, where it had been for 455 years prior to John Paul II. In this context, Cardinal Fiorenzo Angelini was quoted as observing, "Our perception of the church has broadened, to the point of reaching really global dimensions. You can't reason any more with a national mentality, and not even a Continental one."[1] Put differently, religious thinking, like reflections from many other perspectives, has become global in scope as new technologies have reduced time and distance among locales and peoples. We live and think in globalized space even as we may pray in localized space, a contradiction that has urgently posed the question of what kind of order does and should prevail in the world.

In other words, the concern with world order has not superseded preoccupations with local concerns, be they family, jobs, communities, or deities. Indeed, pervasive tensions between local and global forces have become a central feature of our time, and they seem likely to endure for as long as one can see into the future. To be sure, the proximate and the distant have always been uneasily linked, but in recent decades the "distant" has become global in scope, thus intensifying absorption with the prospects for world order and the dangers of world disorder. It is an absorption that has heightened religiosity everywhere, with many individuals and peoples feeling a need to find a more encompassing meaning in a world that has become ever more complex, both more proximate and more distant. This need has fostered a revival and spread of fundamentalism – of thought that leaves no room for doubt and answers all questions – in virtually every religion. In so doing, it has intensified tensions both within and among the several religions.

Irrespective of whether they prevail in religions or other aspects of life, these tensions between the local and the global, the proximate and the distant, have led to two contrary tendencies, one integration and the other fragmentation. John Paul II wanted to reach out to people of other faiths even as he and other Catholic leaders sought to return to strict doctrinal perspectives. The same contradictory tensions also prevail among Muslims, Jews, and other religions.

Viewed holistically, these contrary tendencies are instances of the worldwide clash of the integration and fragmentation processes that are unfolding simultaneously and endlessly interacting in all walks of life. I have labeled these interactive dynamics as "fragmegration,"[2] an awkward and grating designation but one that fills a gaping hole in our vocabulary.[3] Numerous analysts depict the present world order as marked by globalization, but this designation does not capture the two prime processes at work at every level of community. It does not allow for the propensity wherein organizations, communities, societies and international systems splinter and fragment into several parts as a means of resolving their tensions. We live in a messy, fragmegrative world sustained by forces that move in crazy-quilt and contradictory directions. The dynamics of fragmegration are sustaining a world order marked by high degrees of disorder. That is, while some of the prevailing structures and processes conduce to integration among and within groups, others foster disintegrative tendencies. The European Union is a conspicuous example of these fragmegrative dynamics: even as efforts to write a constitution further unifying the EU countries unfold, so are they accompanied by factions intent upon derailing the momentum in this direction. More to the point of this symposium, just as some Episcopalian churches ordain gay priests, so do others reject the practice and speak out against it.

Troubled by the uncertainties on which the pervasiveness of fragmegration rests, and often unable to comprehend its implications for themselves, numerous people in all parts of the world and in all walks of life are inclined to look for answers in spiritual outlooks that depict one or another form of world order. Of course, such inclinations are hardly new. Concerns about "final events," the "end of time," the "coming of Christ," the "return of the Buddha," the "new Jerusalem," the establishment of the Kingdom of God on earth, other worldliness, apocalyptic events, and Armageddon have a long history. What is new about such concerns is the intensity with which they are held and their spread on a global scale. Indeed, it can reasonably be observed that no other line of thought is as concerned about world order as those founded on spiritual sources and the fears induced by fragmegrative dynamics. If the clash between the global and the local cannot be readily resolved, if the disorder that follows from the intrusion of the distant upon the proximate cannot be easily managed, many people are inclined to search for meaning in the order that spiritual formulations provide.

Fundamentalism as a source of fragmegration

It follows that the spread of religious fundamentalism both mirrors and intensifies fragmegrative dynamics. Whatever may be their religious commitments, fundamentalists adhere to rigid values in their search for certainty, and they do so rigidly, leaving little or no room for compromise with fellow religionists whose views are more open and tolerant. In more than a few cases their fundamentalism reaches an extreme that results in violence and mayhem. In the case of a few Muslims, for example, the certainties born of uncertainties and hatred have led them to become suicide bombers. And even short of this extreme, their rigidity and intolerance tend to wreak havoc within societies where their numbers are sufficient to roil neighborhoods and communities. It can fairly be said that

fundamentalists of any religious stripe have a view of world order that so reso-
lutely rejects alternative perspectives as to generate enduring fragmegrative
conflicts. Illustrative in this regard are those who subscribe to Salafism, a funda-
mentalist school of Islam, and who constitute a radical fringe that advocates war
against non-Muslims.[4]

Disclaimers notwithstanding (such as religions of "any stripe"), it is highly
misleading to cite Muslims as the only example of fundamentalists. They and
their suicide bombers are very much in the news at the present time, but they are
hardly the only believers whose perspectives are rigid and intolerant and whose
violent actions can dominate the headlines. In the United States those known as
the "religious right" are no less conspicuous and no less strident. Their interpretation of Christianity that condemns abortion and gay marriage has come to
pervade much of the political scene, thereby lending credence to disorderly tendencies even as they promote the need for order. In some rare instances devotees
interpret world order as permitting the murder of doctors who perform abortions.
Likewise, in Israel some fanatic Orthodox Jews have resorted to acts of violence or
otherwise sought to block policies that would greatly alleviate tensions between
Israel is and Palestinians: in 1994, for example, Baruch Goldstein, a well-known
leader of the Jewish extremist Kach group, entered Al-Ibrahimi Mosque in the
West Bank town of Al-Khalil and emptied two clips of a machine-gun into Muslim
worshippers during the dawn prayer, killing at least 50 people and injuring 200
others. Extremism on behalf of a religious world order has also marred recent
history in Japan. Some 500 Japanese, for example, have subscribed to the religious
fanaticism of Asahara Shoko, who named his group Aum Shinrikyo. Aum is
Sanskrit for the "powers of destruction and creation in the universe," and Shinrikyo is the "teaching of the supreme truth," a perspective which, among other
violent acts, led to placing a deadly sarin gas in several Tokyo subway stations that
killed twelve people and incapacitated thousands.[5]

This is not to imply that religious fundamentalism necessarily culminates in
violence. As other essayists have plainly demonstrated, the eschatological foundations of diverse religions outline notions of world order without advocating resort
to brutality. To be sure, conceptions, even paintings, of hell as a form of world
order can be pervaded with savage barbarity that depicts extreme disorder.[6]
Nonetheless, for every account of a barbarous world one can point to more than a
few eschatological formulations that stress an orderly world in which peace and
nonviolence prevail. Such formulations are also marked by rigid certainties as to
how the world is or ought to be ordered, but they nevertheless stop short of urging
the use of violent methods to put the world on a proper path.

World order as disaggregated complexity

It is surely not surprising that the onset and dynamics of an ever more fragmegrated world have intensified religious fundamentalism and fostered concerns for a
more orderly world. Faced with disarray that seems threatening and irresolvable,
many people look for simple answers, or at least for clear-cut forms of world order

that allow them to presume better circumstances lie ahead. While constructing models of world order is relatively easy, all of them seem destined to be inappropriate in the sense of falling far short of the tendencies presently at work in the world. For not only are societies and their international systems increasingly complex, but the complexity appears to be rooted in processes whereby authority is increasingly disaggregated. New electronic technologies, increasingly skillful people everywhere, proliferating organizations that are crowding the global stage, the mounting movement of people around the world, the greater onset of authority crises in many societies and communities, the bifurcation of global structures that have led to the state-centric world having to cope with a multi-centric world comprised of nongovernmental organizations (NGOs), corporations, professional societies, and many other collective actors that have clambered onto the global stage – all these dynamics are fostering decentralization and new nodes of authority.[7]

More than that, the various dynamics are interactive and thus further deepen the complexities with which people and their collectivities have to cope. Unless one falls back on the clarity of religious convictions, the emergent epoch is thus marked as much by disorder as order, and it is difficult to imagine these dynamics coming to a halt or turning in aggregative directions. Some religious precepts may insist that progress is inevitable, but movement toward a world marked by order and decency is far from certain.

Still, as people increasingly develop the skills to manage the complexities they face in their large urban communities, the disorder of their worlds may seem increasingly manageable. The skill revolution is global in scope and it may not always foster more responsible citizens, but for the most part the expanded competence of individuals in all parts of the world seems likely to foster pockets of order within communities and societies.[8] Or at least such a likelihood seems greater as long as tendencies toward religious fundamentalism do not accelerate and overwhelm those fundamentalisms that preach love, tolerance, forgiveness, and other positive orientations. If devotees pray locally even as they think globally, the chances of disorder overwhelming the pockets of order will probably not increase and they may even lessen.

Part IV
Governance

13 Toward an ontology for global governance[1]

In an era marked by shifting boundaries, relocated authorities, weakened states, and proliferating nongovernmental organizations (NGOs) at local, provincial, national, transnational, international, and global levels of community, the time has come to confront the insufficiency of our ways of thinking, talking, and writing about government. And this imperative is all the greater because the dynamics of change, the shrinking of social, economic, and political distances, and the focus on the inherent weaknesses of the United Nations – to mention only the more conspicuous sources – have led to a surge of concern for a still amorphous entity called "global governance." Welcome as this new focus is, however, it suffers from a reliance on artifacts of the very past beyond which it seeks to move. While myriad books, journals, and study commissions have debated what such an entity involves and whether there are any prospects for its realization,[2] such inquiries are plagued by a lack of conceptual tools appropriate to the task of sorting out the underpinnings of political processes sustained by altered borders, redirected legitimacy sentiments, impaired or paralyzed governments, and new identities.

A depleted toolshed suggests that understanding is no longer served by clinging to the notion that states and national governments are the essential underpinnings of the world's organization. We have become so accustomed to treating these entities as the foundations of politics that we fall back on them when contemplating the prospects for governance on a global scale, thereby relegating the shifting boundaries, relocated authorities, and proliferating NGOs to the status of new but secondary dimensions of the processes through which communities allocate values and frame policies. To be sure, these dimensions are regarded as important and few observers would dismiss their impact as peripheral. Nonetheless, the predominant tendency is to cling to old ways of thought that accord primacy to states and national governments. Even an otherwise praiseworthy attempt to clarify and define the nature of global governance proved unable to break free of the conventional conception which posits states and governments as the organizng focus of analysis: while acknowledging the enormous changes at work in the world, the transformation of boundaries, the erosion of state authority, and the proliferation of NGOs, in the end this definitional undertaking falls back on old ways of thought and specifies that global governance involves "doing internationally what governments do at home."[3] Such a formulation amply demonstrates the large extent to which we remain imprisoned by the idea that the line dividing domestic and foreign affairs still serves as the cutting edge of analysis.

How, then, to update our perspectives so that they can more fully and accurately account for a world in which the dynamics of governance are undergoing profound and enduring transformations? How to render political inquiry more incisive, more able to treat seemingly anomalous developments as part and parcel of modern-day governance? How to equip ourselves so that we are not surprised by a Soviet Union that peacefully collapses overnight, by a Canada that borders on fragmentation, by a Yugoslavia that seeks membership in the European Union even as it comes apart, by a currency crisis that surfaces simultaneously around the world, by a South Africa that manages to bridge a long-standing and huge racial divide, by the splintering of a long-unified Israel, or by international institutions that intrude deeply into the domestic affairs of states (to mention only a few of the surprising developments of recent years)?

The answer to these questions lies, I believe, in the need to develop a new ontology for understanding the deepest foundations of governance. Such an ontology – and the paradigms that flow from it – should recast the relevance of territoriality, treat the temporal dimensions of governance as no less significant than the spatial dimensions, posit as normal shifts of authority to subnational, transnational, and nongovernmental levels, and highlight the porosity of boundaries at all levels of governance. Awesome as this task surely is, what follows offers some initial thoughts on what the outlines of a new ontology should encompass. The goal is not to specify in detail the key ontological premises (the details can be developed only as the ontology is used in empirical inquiries); rather it is that of briefly indicating the substantive shifts that people are likely to undergo as they think about the purposes, processes, structures, and loci of governance. By focusing on these prospective shifts, hopefully we can accelerate the pace at which they unfold.

Ontologies and paradigms

Let us start by drawing some conceptual distinctions. The concept of an ontology originates in the field of philosophy. It refers to the broad assumptions that people make about the nature of reality. Here the concept is adapted to the field of world politics and is conceived to involve the broad assumptions people make about the realities of global affairs. A paradigm, on the other hand, is conceived here as an empirical specification of what follows from the assumptions encompassed by an ontology. Stated differently, ontologies are foundational in that they highlight what basic elements are regarded as comprising the existing order, whereas paradigms are seen as referring to the range within which the elements are interactively organized and order thus imposed upon them. Put in still another way, ontologies are static in that they identify the essential components of the whole they comprise, but paradigms allow for movement on the part of the components and thus focus on the changes as well as the stabilities that comprise the whole. It follows that while one's ontology identifies *what* actors engage in *what* forms of behavior to sustain a particular form of global governance, one's paradigm focuses on *how* and *when* the actors are likely to maintain or vary their behavior.[4] Viewed from the more encompassing perspective in which people perceive and talk about reality, of course, ontologies and paradigms cannot be clearly delineated from each other. We separate them only for analytical purposes (combined together they constitute what is often referred to as the "social construction of reality").

The need for ontologies and paradigms derives from the fact that people can never grasp reality in its entirety and are thus forced to select some features of the ongoing scene as important and dismiss the rest as trivial. So as to tease a modicum of order out of the welter of phenomena they select as important, people need to link the various phenomena to each other coherently; that is, they need to render the world orderly so that they can understand and adapt to it. The way in which the important features are arranged in relation to each other form the bases of the ontologies and paradigms through which the course of events is interpreted and order imposed upon them. The end result for either individuals or collectivities is an intersubjective – and not an objective – understanding. As Cox puts it, "Reality is made by the collective responses of people to the conditions of their existence. Intersubjectively shared experience reproduces reality in the form of continuing institutions and practices."[5] In short, "Ontologies tell us what is significant in the particular world we delve into – what are the basic entities and key relationships. Ontologies are not arbitrary constructions; they are the specification of the common sense of an epoch."[6]

This is not to imply that either ontologies or paradigms are necessarily complex and pervaded with multiple layers. On the contrary, normally only a few features – such as the identity of major actors and the essential attributes of their activities – are selected out as crucial structures of governance that serve to explain how and why polities move in one direction rather than another. The prevailing ontology prior to World War II, for example, focused on the "balance of power" as the common sense of that epoch; in the subsequent period the "Cold War" with its superpower rivalry served to organize thinking about the world; and today neither of these perspectives pertain to the order that has emerged since the beginning of the 1990s. In other words, ontologies are so thoroughgoing and paradigms so all-encompassing in their empirical scope, so capable of accounting for all the developments that are perceived to be relevant to the maintenance or alteration of the political world, that people can summarize their understanding of complex phenomena by reference to a few organizing principles. They do not need to go back and forth between paradigms with the rationale that "it all depends on the issue." For ontologies and paradigms are cast at a level of understanding where the sources of behavior in world affairs are presumed to derive from roots more fundamental than those associated with issue differences.

How, then, do ontologies and paradigms, those specifications of the common sense of an epoch, undergo change? In either of two ways: either the prevailing conditions are so profoundly transformed that people are led by the cumulation and normalization of anomalies to alter the way they intersubjectively experience them, or their awareness of their existing conditions shifts in response to new technologies that enable them to perceive their prevailing circumstances in a new context. In the present era both sources of ontological transformation seem likely to operate and reinforce each other. The globalization of national economies, the emergence of a worldwide consumerist culture, the advent of global norms pertaining to human rights and the environment, the challenges of AIDS, the fragmentation of some societies and the integration of others, the drug trade, international crime syndicates, currency crises, and the ozone gap are only the more obvious changes that have become central features of the prevailing circumstances of world affairs today. At the same time the continuing spread of global television and many other features of the unending microelectronic revolution have greatly facilitated an intensified awareness of these new conditions with which people must cope.

Yet, however the altered conditions and the awareness of them may combine to foster new intersubjective experiences, a more appropriate ontology and its concomitant paradigms will be slow to evolve and difficult to frame. As previously implied, ontologies are so deep-seated, so rooted in as the bases of analytic habits, that they do not readily yield to evidence of obsolesence. The concept of regimes is a good case in point. Conceived originally as an issue-area in which the relevant actors share the rules, norms, principles, and procedures through which decisions are made and implemented, the preponderance of the literature that has since mushroomed lays emphasis upon states as comprising the members of regimes.[7] Little attention is paid to other than governmental actors despite considerable evidence that in many regimes (e.g. oil), firms, NGOs, and other types of actors play crucial roles. If it is the case that regimes are a major institutional form through which global governance is carried forward, then it is virtually impossible to assess their contribution to governing processes if their ranks are conceived to consist exclusively of national governments. Nonetheless, analysts using the regime approach have yet to update their inquiries by allowing for NGOs and other types of actors to play major roles in the conduct of regimes.[8]

Stated more generally, faced with the case for an ontological shift, many people may acknowledge that changes are occurring in the territorial, temporal, and organizational underpinnings of governance, but in the same breath they are likely to insist that nevertheless states and national governments continue to retain the primary authority and power they have possessed for several centuries.[9] Yes, they would agree, the Cold War is over, but it is still an anarchical world of states where national governments and their power balances predominate. Understandable as it may be to presume that history has resumed from where it left off in 1939, such a reaction can only perpetuate and heighten the limits of our grasp of governance in a turbulent and transformative age. At the same time, the necessity of an ontological shift may seem less ominous and more palatable if it is appreciated that the ensuing formulation does not dismiss states and governments as secondary and peripheral; rather it posits them as central to and consequential for the course of events along with a host of other actors. In other words, a fine line needs to be drawn between treating states as the only players on the global stage and as diminished and aged players that have long since passed their prime. Given the necessity of not devoting exclusive attention to states and acknowledging that a wide range of nongovernmental actors increasingly need to serve as foci of intensive analysis, it follows that states and governments should be posited not as first among equals, but simply as significant actors in a world marked by an increasing diffusion of authority and a corresponding diminution of hierarchy. Yes, states retain their sovereign rights, but the realms within which these rights can be exercised have diminished as the world becomes ever more interdependent and as state boundaries become ever more porous. With the increasing diffusion of authority, states can no longer rely on their sovereignty as a basis for protecting their interests in the face of increasingly complex challenges.

As will immediately be seen, new ontologies require new labels to clearly differ-entiate the common sense of the new epoch from its predecessor and to facilitate the development of a widespread intersubjectivity as to the ways in which it breaks with the past. It must be stressed, however, that the label used here is offered tentatively, that it may prove too technical to generate broad usage, and that in all probability a less complex and more compelling terminology will evolve. Indeed, the label used here is not the first to be suggested: among others, for example, are "polyarchy,"[10] "panarchy,"[11] and "collibration,"[12] all three of which highlight the degree to which the world has undergone decentralization since the end of the Cold War. Whatever labels may eventually be adopted, in other words, they are likely to point incisively to the key arrangements that distinguish the epoch from its predecessors. It is not sufficient to designate the new epoch by the label of "post-Cold War," since this is a term that conveys no image of what the core dynamics of the new epoch involve. The Cold War label, like the "balance of power" epoch that preceded it, did point to substantive phenom-ena. It was a label that served to summarize the superpower rivalry and the structures thereby imposed on the rest of the world, whereas to speak now of the post-Cold War period is merely to highlight that the earlier period has ended. Awkward as the label used here may seem, it does capture the essential dynamic wherein the new epoch is marked by the simultaneity of continual tensions and interactions between the forces propelling the fragmentation of communities and those conducing to the integration of communities.

Globalization, localization, and fragmegration

It seems clear that powerful tendencies toward globalization not only underlie the shifting of boundaries, the relocation of authorities, the weakening of states, and the proliferation of NGOs, but they also provoke equally powerful tendencies toward localization that give rise to further consequences of this sort. If the interactions of sovereign states in an anarchical world lie at the heart of the old ontology, at the center of the new one are the interactions of globalizing and localizing forces, of tendencies toward integration and fragmentation that are so simultaneous and interactive as to collapse into an erratic but singular process here labeled "fragmegration."

It follows that we live in and study a fragmegrative world that cascades events through, over, and around the long established boundaries of states and, in so doing, relocates authority upwards to transnational and supranational organizations, sidewards to social movements and NGOs, and downwards to subnational groups. It is a world in which the logic of governance does not necessarily follow hierarchical lines, in which what is distant is also proximate, and in which the spatial and temporal dimensions of politics are so confounded by fragmegrative dynamics as to rid event sequences of any linearity they once may have had. Today's chains of causation follow crazy-quilt patterns that cannot be adequately discerned if one clings to an ontology that presumes the primacy of states and governments.

At the very least a more appropriate ontology will highlight the large extent to which the erosion of state authority and the proliferation of NGOs has resulted in a disaggregation of the loci of governance. Notwithstanding the overriding power of globalizing forces in the economic, communications, and cultural realms, and despite the signs of expanding integration to be found in Europe and other regions today, fragmegration has been accompanied by a dispersion of the sites out of which authority can be exercised and compliance generated. The weakening of states has not been followed by authority vacuums (although there may be situations where this is the case) so much as it has resulted in a vast growth in the number of spheres into which authority has moved. Fragmegration points to a redistribution of authority and not to its deterioration.

In short, if a map of the world based on the new ontology were drawn, it would depict global governance as highly disaggregated even as many of its spheres are overlapping. Global governance is not so much a label for a high degree of integration and order as it is a summary term for highly complex and widely disparate activities that may culminate in a modicum of worldwide coherence or that may collapse into pervasive disarray.[13] In the event of either outcome, it would still be global governance in the sense that the sum of efforts by widely disaggregated goal-seeking entities will have supplemented, perhaps even supplanted, states as the prime sources of governance on a global scale. And whichever outcome eventually predominates, both will surely be sufficiently cumbersome to prevent either from amounting to an effective arrangement for addressing the need for decisive and equitable policies that ameliorate the large problems comprising the global agenda.

Of course, the present era is not the only moment in history when disaggregation has marked the loci of governance. In earlier eras, for example, considerable authority was exercised by members of the Hanseatic League and the Medici and Rothschild families. Indeed, one can doubtless find numerous historical circumstances that parallel any examples that appear as central to the dynamics of boundary erosion and change today. Just as AIDS moves quickly through national boundaries today, so did the plague in the sixteenth century; just as the Internet, fax machine, and global television render boundaries ever more porous today, so did the advent of the printing press, the wireless, and the telephone spread ideas independently of national borders in earlier eras; and so on for all the channels whereby the processes of globalization and localization are presently expanding and contracting horizons. The difference in the current period is that the processes of aggregation and disaggregation are occurring and interacting so rapidly – more often than not instantaneously to the point of being literally simultaneous. That is, the pace of politics at all levels of community has accelerated to the extent that reactions to events occur roughly at the same time as the events themselves, leaving actors as always in a mode of seeking to catch up with the consequences of decisions to which they were also parties. It is for this reason that the emergent ontology will doubtless include a new understanding of the temporal dimension of politics.

Units of governance

It follows that the new ontology requires us to focus on those political actors, structures, processes, and institutions that initiate, sustain, or respond to globalizing forces as they propel boundary-spanning activities and foster boundary-contracting reactions. Approached in this way, states become only one of many sources of authority, only one of many organizations through which the dynamics of fragmegration shape the course of events. Stated differently, instead of initially positing a world dominated by states and national governments, the new ontology builds on the premise that the world is comprised of spheres of authority (SOA) that are not necessarily consistent with the division of territorial space and that are subject to considerable flux. Such spheres are, in effect, the analytic units of the new ontology. They are distinguished by the presence of actors who can evoke compliance when exercising authority as they engage in the activities that delineate the sphere. Authority, in other words, is conceived not as a possession of actors, nor as embedded in roles. Rather, authority is relational; its existence can only be observed when it is both exercised and complied with. A new occupant of a position may acquire formal authority upon taking up the duties of the position, but whether his or her authority is effective and enduring depends on the response of those toward whom the authority is directed. If they are responsive, then authority can be said to be operative; if they do not respond compliantly, then the formal prerequisites of the position are quite irrelevant.

It follows that SOAs can differ in form and structure, depending on the degree to which their relational foundations are hierarchically arrayed. They can vary from those founded on hierarchical arrangements that explicitly allow for unexplained orders backed up by the capacity to coerce or dismiss those who do not comply – command authority – as is the case in military organizations; to SOAs that involve an implicit capacity to force compliance if persuasion proves insufficient to achieve it – bureaucratic authority – as is the case when nonmilitary governmental or nongovernmental officials exercise authority; to SOAs in which authority derives from expertise – epistemic authority – as is the case when people comply because specialists concur in a recommendation.[14]

It also follows that a SOA may or may not be co-terminous with a bounded territory: those who comply may be spread around the world and have no legal relationship to each other, or they may be located in the same geographic space and have the same organizational affiliations. If the sphere involves the allocation of values through certifying and rating the reliability of bond issuers, for example, then its actors will include Moody's, Standard and Poor's, and a number of other credit rating agencies whose evaluations determine which firms, governments, and NGOs in various parts of the world get loans and which do not.[15] In contrast to these nonterritorial SOAs, on the other hand, are those in which the allocation of values remains linked to geographic space, thus enabling local, provincial, and national governments to achieve compliance when they exercise authority over taxes, parklands, police activities, and whatever other domains wherein they have not experienced a shift and contraction of their jurisdictions.

The advent of nonterritorial actors and relocated authorities helps to explain the recent tendency to focus on processes of governance rather than those of governments as the instruments through which authority is exercised. While governments are concrete actors accorded formal jurisdiction over specified territorial domains, governance is a broader concept that highlights SOAs that may not be territorial in scope and that may employ only informal authority to achieve compliance on the part of those within the sphere. Governance, in other words, refers to mechanisms for steering social systems toward their goals,[16] a conception which is far more amenable to understanding a world in which old boundaries are becoming obscure, in which new identities are becoming commonplace, and in which the scale of political thought has become global in scope. Indeed, it might well be that the shift to the emphasis on governance will prove to be the first major indicator that a new intersubjective ontology for understanding world affairs is already in the process of taking hold in the awareness of people.

Still another sign of the emergent ontology can be discerned in the variety of new terms that have evolved to designate units of governance which are not instruments of states and governments. At least ten such units have achieved acceptance in (and in some cases pervade) the literature on world politics: NGOs, nonstate actors, sovereignty-free actors, issue networks, policy networks, social movements, global civil society, transnational coalitions, transnational lobbies, and epistemic communities.[17] While an intersubjective consensus has yet to shake this terminology down into a shared vocabulary, clearly the proliferation of such terms expresses a restlessness with the prevailing ontological preoccupation with states and governments.

Hierarchy

In a disaggregated, decentralized world in which SOAs are relatively independent of each other, what might the new ontology specify as common sense with respect to the pervasiveness of hierarchy? Again it may be difficult to move on to new ways of thinking. Hierarchy involves power and the relative capability of actors, and we are so accustomed to positing pecking orders in these terms that it will not be easy to come to grips with a disaggregated array of actors whose power is limited to a particular expertise or set of issues, thus rendering them essentially autonomous and not dependent on where they stand in a pecking order. More specifically, the new ontology allows for within-sphere hierarchies since actors with similar goals in a SOA are likely to have different capabilities that differentiate their degree of influence, but there is no basis for presuming that a pecking order will develop among SOAs. Some credit rating agencies may be more influential than others, but there is no necessary basis for presuming either that the most high-status credit agency can achieve compliance from actors outside its sphere or that its compliance can be achieved by actors in other spheres. "Wait a minute," those wedded to the old ontology might exclaim, "what about the state's sovereignty? Surely that enables it to curb or override any credit agency operating within its borders!" Not at all, respond those who have adopted the new ontology, authority inheres in a sphere and if a state or national government succeeds in curbing or overruling the actions of a credit agency, such an outcome will be a consequence of the circumstances of the sphere in which the two actors compete rather than stemming from the state having sovereign authority which the credit agency lacks. Put differently, what enables an actor to obtain compliance from another actor in a disaggregated world is an interdependent convergence of needs and not a constitutional specification that assigns the highest authority exclusively to states and national governments. In addition, the hierarchy that derives from the military power over which states have a monopoly and through which they exercise their sovereignty in the last resort can no longer, given the disaggregation of SOAs, be translated into leverage over credit agencies.

What about bounded systems?

Given the widening porosity of conventional political boundaries, the shifting loci of authority, and the emergence of a nonterritorial, nonlinear politics, the question arises as to whether the foregoing analysis cannot also be applied to the governance of more circumscribed domains? If fragmegrative dynamics are as pervasive and significant as suggested here, are they not also operative within bounded societies? And if so, do they not also exert pressure for a new ontology to replace the one that has long served as the intersubjective basis for understanding "domestic" politics?

A positive answer to such questions can readily be asserted even if it may yet be premature to undertake specifying an ontology comparable to that organized around the notion of fragmegration. Certainly fragmegrative dynamics are no less relevant to societal systems than they are to the global system. Surely it is reasonable to think in terms of SOAs as units of governance within societies as it is between them. Doubtless the exercise of authority in societal processes is as likely as in global ones to cascade across space and time in an erratic fashion, flowing first in one direction, then in another, followed by still a third redirection, even a reversal to the point of origin, with the result that compliance cumulates, gets modified, or is terminated in nonlinear sequences. And given societies that are as disaggregated as the global system they comprise, they will in all likelihood be increasingly marked by an eroding between-SOA pecking order.

Indeed, given a conviction that "the governing capacity of political/administrative systems . . . either has crossed the threshold of the law of diminishing returns or is quite close to such a boundary,"[18] with the result that "*political governance in modern societies can no longer be conceived in terms of external governmental control of society but emerges from a plurality of governing actors*,"[19] signs of efforts to specify a new common sense of societal governance in the emergent epoch are already manifest. An entire symposium, for example, has been devoted to probing "new patterns of interaction between government and society" and thereby to "discovering other ways of coping with new problems or of creating new possibilities for governing."[20] It seems clear, in short, that the foregoing ruminations are part and parcel of a larger thrust to update our common sense understanding of politics in a turbulent world.

14 Governance in the twenty-first century[1]

To anticipate the prospects for global governance in the decades ahead is to discern powerful tensions, profound contradictions, and perplexing paradoxes. It is to search for order in disorder, for coherence in contradiction, and for continuity in change. It is to confront processes that mask both growth and decay. It is to look for authorities that are obscure, boundaries that are in flux, and systems of rule that are emergent. And it is to experience hope embedded in despair.

This is not to imply the task is impossible. Quite to the contrary, one can discern patterns of governance that are likely to proliferate, others that are likely to attenuate, and still others that are likely to endure as they always have. No, the task is not so much impossible as it is a challenge to one's appreciation of nuance and one's tolerance of ambiguity.

Conceptual nuances

In order to grasp the complexities that pervade world politics, we need to start by drawing a nuanced set of distinctions among the numerous processes and structures that fall within the purview of global governance. Perhaps most importantly, it is necessary to clarify that global governance refers not only to the formal institutions and organizations through which the management of international affairs is or is not sustained. The United Nations system and national governments are surely central to the conduct of global governance, but they are only part of the full picture. Or at least in the ensuing analysis global governance is conceived to include systems of rule at all levels of human activity – from the family to the international organization – in which the pursuit of goals through the exercise of control has transnational repercussions. The reason for this broad formulation is simple: in an ever more interdependent world where what happens in one corner or at one level may have consequences for what occurs at every other corner and level, it seems a mistake to adhere to a narrow definition in which only formal institutions at the national and international levels are considered relevant. In the words of the Council of Rome,

> We use the term governance to denote the *command* mechanism of a social system and its actions that endeavor to provide security, prosperity, coherence,

order and continuity to the system. . . . Taken broadly, the concept of
governance should not be restricted to the national and international systems
but should be used in relation to regional, provincial and local governments
as well as to other social systems such as education and the military, to private
enterprises and even to the microcosm of the family.[2]

Governance, in other words, encompasses the activities of governments, but it
also includes the many other channels through which "commands" flow in the
form of goals framed, directives issued, and policies pursued.

Command and control

But the concept of command can be misleading. It implies that hierarchy, perhaps
even authoritarian rule, characterizes governance systems. Such an implication
may be descriptive of many forms of governance, but hierarchy is certainly not a
necessary prerequisite to the framing of goals, the issuing of directives, and the
pursuit of policies. Indeed, a central theme of the ensuing analysis is that often
the practices and institutions of governance can and do evolve in such a way as to
be minimally dependent on hierarchical, command-based arrangements. Accordingly, while preserving the core of the Council of Rome formulation, here we
shall replace the notion of command mechanisms with the concept of *control* or
steering mechanisms, terms that highlight the purposeful nature of governance
without presuming the presence of hierarchy. They are terms, moreover,
informed by the etymological roots of "governance": the term "derives from the
Greek 'kybenan' and 'kybernetes' which means 'to steer' and 'pilot or helmsman'
respectively (the same Greek root from which 'cybernetics' is derived). The process of governance is the process whereby an organization or society steers itself,
and the dynamics of communication and control are central to that process."[3]

To grasp the concept of control one has to appreciate that it consists of
relational phenomena which, taken holistically, comprise systems of rule. Some
actors, the controllers, seek to modify the behavior and/or orientations of other
actors, the controllees, and the resulting patterns of interaction between the former and the latter can properly be viewed as a system of rule sustained by one or
another form of control. It does not matter whether the controllees resist or
comply with the efforts of controllers; in either event, attempts at control have
been undertaken. But it is not until the attempts become increasingly successful
and compliance with them increasingly patterned that a system of rule founded
on mechanisms of control can be said to have evolved. Rule systems and control
mechanisms, in other words, are founded on a modicum of regularity, a form
of recurrent behavior that systematically links the efforts of controllers to the
compliance of controllees through either formal or informal channels.[4]

It follows that systems of rule can be maintained and their controls successfully
and consistently exerted even in the absence of established legal or political
authority. The evolution of intersubjective consensuses based on shared fates and
common histories, the possession of information and knowledge, the pressure of

active or mobilizable publics, and/or the use of careful planning, good timing, clever manipulation, and hard bargaining can – either separately or in combination – foster control mechanisms that sustain governance without government.[5]

Interdependence and proliferation

Implicit in the broad conception of governance as control mechanisms is a premise that interdependence involves not only flows of control, consequence, and causation within systems, but that it also sustains flows across systems. These micro–macro processes – the dynamics whereby values and behaviors at one level get converted into outcomes at more encompassing levels, outcomes which in turn get converted into still other consequences at still more encompassing levels – suggest that global governance knows no boundaries, geographic, social, cultural, economic, or political. If major changes occur in the structure of families, if individual greed proliferates at the expense of social consciences, if people become more analytically skillful, if crime grips neighborhoods, if schools fail to provoke the curiosity of children, if racial or religious prejudices become pervasive, if the drug trade starts distributing its illicit goods through licit channels, if defiance comes to vie with compliance as characteristic responses to authority, if new trading partners are established, if labor and environmental groups in different countries form cross-border coalitions, if cities begin to conduct their own foreign commercial policies – to mention only some of the more conspicuous present-day dynamics – then the consequences of such developments will ripple across and fan out within provincial, regional, national, and international levels as well as across and within local communities. Such is the crazy-quilt nature of modern interdependence. And such is the staggering challenge of global governance.

And the challenge continues to intensify as control mechanisms proliferate at a breathtaking rate. For not only has the number of UN members risen from 51 in 1945 to 184 a half-century later, but the density of nongovernmental organizations (NGOs) has increased at a comparable pace. More accurately, it has increased at a rate comparable to the continuing growth of the world's population beyond 5 billion and a projected 8 billion in 2025. More and more people, that is, need to concert their actions to cope with the challenges and opportunities of daily life, thus giving rise to more and more organizations to satisfy their needs and wants. Indeed, since the needs and wants of people are most effectively expressed through organized action, the organizational explosion of our time is no less consequential than the population explosion. Hastened by dynamic technologies that have shrunk social, economic, political, and geographic distances and thereby rendered the world ever more interdependent, expanded by the advent of new global challenges such as those posed by a deteriorating environment, an AIDS epidemic, and drug trafficking, and further stimulated by widespread authority crises within existing governance mechanisms,[6] the proliferation of organizations is pervasive at and across all levels of human activity – from neighborhood organizations, community groups, regional networks, national states, and transnational regimes to international systems.[7]

Not only is global life marked by a density of populations, in other words; it is also dense with organized activities, thereby complicating and extending the processes of global governance. For while organizations provide decision points through which the steering mechanisms of governance can be carried forward, so may they operate as sources of opposition to any institutions and policies designed to facilitate governance. Put in still another way, if it is the case, as many (and this author) argue, that global life late in the twentieth century is more complex than ever before in history, it is because the world is host to ever greater numbers of organizations in all walks of life and in every corner of every continent. And it is this complexity, along with the competitive impulses which lead some organizations to defy steerage and resort to violence, that make the tasks of governance at once so difficult and so daunting.

Disaggregation and innovation

An obvious but major conceptual premise follows from the foregoing: namely, there is no single organizing principle on which global governance rests, no emergent order around which communities and nations are likely to converge. Global governance is the sum of myriad – literally millions – of control mechanisms driven by different histories, goals, structures, and processes. Perhaps every mechanism shares a history, culture, and structure with a few others, but there are no characteristics or attributes common to all mechanisms. This means that any attempt to assess the dynamics of global governance will perforce have multiple dimensions, that any effort to trace a hierarchical structure of authority which loosely links disparate sources of governance to each other is bound to fail. In terms of governance, the world is too disaggregated for grand logics that postulate a measure of global coherence.

Put differently, the continuing disaggregation that has followed the end of the Cold War suggests a further extension of the anarchic structures that have long pervaded world politics. If it was possible to presume that the absence of hierarchy and an ultimate authority signified the presence of anarchy during the era of hegemonic leadership and superpower competition, such a characterization of global governance is all the more pertinent today. Indeed, it might well be observed that a new form of anarchy has evolved in the current period – one that involves not only the absence of a highest authority, but that also encompasses such an extensive disaggregation of authority as to allow for much greater flexibility, innovation, and experimentation in the development and application of new control mechanisms.

In sum, while politicians and pundits may speak confidently or longingly about establishing a new world order, such a concept is only meaningful as it relates to the prevention or containment of large-scale violence and war. It is not a concept that can be used synonymously with global governance if by the latter is meant the vast numbers of rule systems that have been caught up in the proliferating networks of an ever more interdependent world.

Emergence and evolution

Underlying the growing complexity and continuing disaggregation of modern governance are the obvious but often ignored dynamics of change wherein control mechanisms emerge out of path-dependent conditions and then pass through lengthy processes of either evolution and maturation or decline and demise. In order to acquire the legitimacy and support they need to endure, successful mechanisms of governance are more likely to evolve out of bottom-up than top-down processes. As such, as mechanisms that manage to evoke the consent of the governed, they are self-organizing systems, steering arrangements that develop through the shared needs of groups and the presence of developments that conduce to the generation and acceptance of shared instruments of control.

But there is no magic in the dynamics of self-organization. Governance does not just suddenly happen. Circumstances have to be suitable, people have to be amenable to collective decisions being made, tendencies toward organization have to develop, habits of cooperation have to evolve, and a readiness not to impede the processes of emergence and evolution has to persist. The proliferation of organizations and their ever greater interdependence may stimulate felt needs for new forms of governance, but the transformation of these needs into established and institutionalized control mechanisms is never automatic and can be marked by a volatility that consumes long stretches of time. Yet, at each stage of the transformation, some form of governance can be said to exist, with a preponderance of the control mechanisms at any moment in time evolving somewhere in the middle of a continuum that runs from nascent to fully institutionalized mechanisms, from informal modes of framing goals, issuing directives, and pursuing policies to formal instruments of decision making, conflict resolution, and resource allocation.

No matter how institutionalized rule systems may be, in other words, governance is not a constant in these turbulent and disaggregated times. It is, rather, in a continuous process of evolution, a becoming that fluctuates between order and disorder as conditions change and emergent properties consolidate and solidify. To analyze governance by freezing it in time is to insure failure in comprehending its nature and vagaries.

The relocation of authority

Notwithstanding the evolutionary dynamics of control mechanisms and the absence of an overall structural order, it is possible to identify pockets of coherence operating at different levels and in different parts of the world that can serve as bases for assessing the contours of global governance in the future. It may be the case that "processes of governance at the global level are inherently more fragile, contingent, and unevenly experienced than is the case within most national political systems,"[8] but this is not to deny the presence of central tendencies. One such tendency involves an "upsurge in the collective capacity to govern": despite the rapid pace of ever greater complexity and decentralization – and to some extent because of their exponential dynamics – the world is undergoing "a remarkable expansion of collective power," an expansion that is highly disaggregated and unfolds unevenly but that nevertheless amounts to a development of rule systems "that have become (1) more intensive in their permeation of daily life, (2) more permanent over time, (3) more extensive over space, (4) larger in size, (5) wider in functional scope, (6) more constitutionally differentiated, and (7) more bureaucratic."[9] Global governance in the twenty-first century may not take the form of a single world order, but it will not be lacking in activities designed to bring a measure of coherence to the multitude of jurisdictions that are proliferating on the world stage.

Perhaps even more important, a pervasive tendency can be identified in which major shifts in the location of authority and the site of control mechanisms are underway on every continent and in every country, shifts that are as pronounced in economic and social systems as they are in political systems. Indeed, in some cases the shifts have transferred authority away from the political realm and into the economic and social realms even as in still other instances the shift occurs in the opposite direction.

Partly these shifts have been facilitated by the end of the Cold War and the lifting of the constraints inherent in its bipolar global structure of superpower competition. Partly they have been driven by a search for new, more effective forms of political organization better suited to the turbulent circumstances that have evolved with the shrinking of the world by dynamic technologies.[10] Partly they have been driven by the skill revolution that has enabled citizens to more clearly identify their needs and wants as well as to more thoroughly empower them to engage in collective action.[11] Partly they have been stimulated and sustained by subgroupism – the fragmenting and coalescing of groups into new organizational entities – that has created innumerable new sites from which authority can emerge and toward which it can gravitate.[12] Partly they have been driven by the continuing globalization of national and local economies that has undermined long-established ways of sustaining commercial and financial relations.[13] And, no less, the shifts have been accelerated by the advent of interdependence issues – such as environmental pollution, AIDS, monetary crises, and the drug trade – that have fostered new and intensified forms of transnational collaboration as well as new social movements that are serving as transnational voices for change.[14]

In short, the numerous shifts in the loci of governance stem from interactive tensions whereby processes of globalization and localization are simultaneously unfolding on a worldwide scale. In some situations the foregoing dynamics are fostering control mechanisms that extend beyond national boundaries and in others the need for the psychic comfort of neighborhood or ethnic attachments are leading to the diminution of national entities and the formation or extension of local mechanisms. The combined effect of the simultaneity of these contradictory trends is that of lessening the capacities for governance located at the level of sovereign states and national societies.[15] Much governance will doubtless continue to be sustained by states and their governments initiating and implementing policies in the context of their legal frameworks – and in some instances national governments are likely to work out arrangements for joint governance with rule systems at other levels – but the effectiveness of their policies is likely to be undermined by the proliferation of emergent control mechanisms both within and outside their jurisdictions.[16] In the words of one analyst, "the very high levels of interdependence and vulnerability stimulated by technological change now necessitate new forms of global political authority and even governance."[17]

Put more emphatically, perhaps the most significant pattern discernable in the criss-crossing flow of transformed authority involves processes of bifurcation whereby control mechanisms at national levels are, in varying degrees, yielding space to both more encompassing forms of governance and to narrower, less comprehensive forms. For analytic purposes, we shall refer to the former as transnational governance mechanisms and the latter as subnational governance mechanisms, terms that do not preclude institutionalized governmental mechanisms but that allow for the large degree to which our concern is with dynamic and evolving processes rather than with the routinized procedures of national governments.

While transnational and subnational mechanisms differ in the extent of their links across national boundaries – all the former are by definition boundary-spanning forms of control, while some of the latter may not extend beyond the jurisdiction of their states – both types must face the same challenges to governance. Both must deal with a rapidly changing, ever more complex world in which people, information, goods, and ideas are in continuous motion and, thus, endlessly reconfiguring social, economic, and political horizons. Both are confronted with the instabilities and disorder that derive from resource shortages, budgetary constraints, ethnic rivalries, unemployment, and incipient or real inflation. Both need to contend with the ever greater relevance of scientific findings and the epistemic communities that form around the findings. Both are subject to the continuous tensions that spring from the inroads of corrupt practices, organized crime, and restless publics that have little use for politics and politicians. Both must cope with pressures for further fragmentation of subgroups on the one hand and for more extensive transnational links on the other. Both types of mechanisms, in short, have severe adaptive problems and, given the fragility of their legal status and the lack of long-standing habits of support for them, many of both types may fail to maintain their essential structures intact.[18] Global governance, it seems reasonable to anticipate, is likely to consist of proliferating mechanisms that fluctuate between bare survival and increasing institutionalization, between considerable chaos and widening degrees of order.

Mechanisms of global governance

Steering mechanisms are spurred into existence through several channels: through the sponsorship of states, through the efforts of actors other than states at the transnational or subnational levels, or through states and other types of actors jointly sponsoring the formation of rule systems. They can also be differentiated by their location on the aforementioned continuum that ranges from full institutionalization on the one hand to nascent processes of rule-making and compliance on the other. Although extremes on a continuum, the institutionalized and nascent types of control mechanisms can be causally linked through evolutionary processes. It is possible to trace at least two generic routes that link the degree to which transnational governance mechanisms are institutionalized and the sources that sponsor these developments. One route is the direct, top-down process wherein states create new institutional structures and impose them on the course of events. A second is much more circuitous and involves an indirect, bottom-up process of evolutionary stages wherein nascent dynamics of rule-making are sponsored by publics or economies that experience a need for repeated interactions that foster habits and attitudes of cooperation which, in turn, generate organizational activities that eventually get transformed into institutionalized control mechanisms.[19] Stated more generally, whatever their sponsorship, the institutionalized mechanisms tend to be marked by explicit hierarchical structures, whereas those at the nascent end of the continuum develop more subtly as a consequence of emergent interaction patterns which, unintentionally and without prior planning, culminate in fledgling control mechanisms for newly formed or transformed systems.

Table 14.1 offers examples of the rule systems derivable from a combination of the several types of sponsors and the two extremes on the continuum, a matrix that suggests the considerable variety and complexity out of which the processes of global governance evolve. In the table, moreover, there are hints of the developmental processes whereby nascent mechanisms become institutionalized: as indicated by the dotted arrows, some of the control mechanisms located in the right-hand cells have their origins in the corresponding left-hand cell as

Table 14.1 The sponsorship and institutionalization of control mechanisms

	nascent	*institutionalized*
transnational	–nongovernmental organizations	–internet
	–social movements	–European Environmental Bureau
not state sponsored	–epistemic communities	–credit rating agencies
	–multinational corporations	–American Jewish Congress
subnational	–ethnic minorities	
	–micro regions	–the Greek lobby
	–cities	–crime syndicates
state sponsored	–macro regions	–United Nations System
	–European community	–European Union
	–GATT	–World Trade Organization
jointly sponsored	–cross-border coalitions	–election monitoring
	–issue regimes	–human rights regime

interdependence issues that generate pressures from the nongovernmental world for intergovernmental cooperation which, in turn, lead to the formation of issue-based transnational institutions. The history of more than a few control mechanisms charged with addressing environmental problems exemplify how this subtle evolutionary path can be traversed.

However they originate, and whatever pace at which they evolve, transnational governance mechanisms tend to be essentially forward-looking. They may be propelled by dissatisfactions over existing (national or subnational) arrangements, but their evolution is likely to be marked less by despair over the past and present and more by hope for the future, by expectations that an expansion beyond existing boundaries will draw upon cooperative impulses which may serve to meet challenges and fill lacunae that would otherwise be left unattended. To be sure, globalizing dynamics tend to create resistance and opposition, since any expansion of governance is bound to be detrimental to those who have a stake in the status quo. Whether they are explicitly and formally designed or subtly and informally constructed, however, on balance transnational systems of governance tend to evolve in a context of hope and progress, a sense of breakthrough, an appreciation that old problems can be circumvented and moved toward either the verge of resolution or the edge of obsolescence. Relatively speaking, on the other hand, subnational mechanisms are usually (though not always) energized by despair, by frustration with existing systems that seems best offset by contracting the scope of governance, by a sense that large-scale cooperation has not worked and that new subgroup arrangements are bound to be more satisfying. This distinction between transnational and subnational governance mechanisms can, of course, be overstated, but it does suggest that the delicacies of global governance at subnational levels may be greater than those at transnational levels.

In order to highlight the variety of forms transnational governance may take in the twenty-first century, the following discussion focuses on examples listed in Table 14.1. Due to space limitations, only some of the listed examples are subjected to analysis, and even the discussion of these is far from exhaustive. But hopefully both the table and its elaboration convey a sense of the degree to which global governance is likely to become increasingly pervasive and disaggregated in the years ahead.

Nongovernmental organizations

Irrespective of whether they are volunteer or profit-making organizations, and quite apart from whether their structures are confined to one country or span several, NGOs may serve as the basis for, or actually become, nascent forms of transnational governance. Why? Because in an ever more interdependent world the need for control mechanisms outstrips the capacity or readiness of national governments to provide them. There are a variety of types of situations where governments are unwelcome, or where they fear involvement will be counterproductive, or where they lack the will or ability to intrude their presence. (And as noted below, there are also numerous circumstances where governments find it expedient to participate in rule systems jointly with organizations from the private sector.)

Put more specifically, just as at the local level "community associations are taking over more of the functions of municipal governments,"[20] and just as in diplomatic situations distinguished individuals from the private sector are called upon when assessments are made which assert, in effect, that "I don't think any governments wanted to get involved in this,"[21] so are NGOs of all kinds to be found as the central actors in the deliberations of control mechanisms relevant to their spheres of activity. Whether the deliberations involve the generation and allocation of relief supplies in disaster situations around the world or the framing of norms of conduct for trade relationships – to mention only two of the more conspicuous spheres in which transnational governance occurs – volunteer associations or business corporations may make the crucial decisions. In the case of alliances fashioned within and among multinational corporations, for example, it has been found that

> transnational actors, unlike purely domestic ones, have the organizational and informational resources necessary to construct private alternatives to governmental accords, alternatives which may well correspond more closely to their interests. Intergovernmental accords may even encroach on spheres previously organized by means of private alliances, thereby threatening transnational interests. In this case, the presence of transnational alliances would make international agreements *less* likely.[22]

And even if only a small proportion of NGOs preside over steering mechanisms, their contribution to global governance looms as substantial when it is appreciated that over 17,000 international nongovernmental organizations in the nonprofit sector were active in the mid-1980s and that in excess of 35,000 transnational corporations with some 150,000 foreign subsidiaries were operating in 1990.[23]

Furthermore, the activities of both volunteer and profit-making organizations are not unmindful of their role in nascent control mechanisms. This can be discerned in the charters of the former and in the public pronouncements of the latter. An especially clear-cut expression along this line was made by the Chairman and CEO of the Coca-Cola Company,

> . . . four prevailing forces – the preeminence of democratic capitalism, the desire for self-determination, the shift in influence from regulation to investment, and the success of institutions which meet the needs of people – reinforced by today's worldwide communications and dramatic television images, . . . all point to a fundamental shift in global power. To be candid, I believe this shift will lead to a future in which the institutions with the most influence by-and-large will be businesses.[24]

Social movements

Much less structured but no less important, social movements have evolved as wellsprings of global governance in recent decades. Indeed, they are perhaps the quintessential case of nascent control mechanisms that have the potential of developing into institutionalized instruments of governance. Their nascency is conspicuous: they have no definite memberships or authority structures; they consist of as many people, as much territory, and as many issues as seems appropriate to the people involved; they have no central headquarters and are spread across numerous locales; and they are all-inclusive, excluding no one and embracing anyone who wishes to be part of the movement. More often than not, social movements are organized around a salient set of issues – like those that highlight the concerns of feminists, environmentalists, or peace activists – and as such they serve transnational needs that cannot be filled by either national governments, organized domestic groups, or private firms. Social movements are thus constituent parts of the globalizing process. They contribute importantly to the non-economic fabric of ties facilitated by the new communications and transportation technologies. They pick up the pieces, so to speak, that states and businesses leave in their wake by their boundary-crossing activities: just as the peace movement focuses on the consequences of state interactions, for example, so has the ecological movement become preoccupied with the developmental excesses of transnational corporations. Put even more strongly, "The point about these anti-systemic movements is that they often elude the traditional categories of nation, state, and class. They articulate new ways of experiencing life, a new attitude to time and space, a new sense of history and identity."[25]

Despite the lack of structural constraints which allow for their growth, however, social movements may not remain permanently inchoate and nascent. At those times when the issues of concern to their members climb high on the global agenda, they may begin to evolve at least temporary organizational arrangements through which to move toward their goals. The International Nestlé Boycott Committee is illustrative in this regard: it organized a seven-year international boycott of Nestlé products and then was dismantled when the Nestlé Company complied with its demands.[26] In some instances, moreover, the organizational expression of a movement's aspirations can develop enduring features. Fearful that the development of organizational structures might curb their spontaneity, some movement members might be aghast at the prospect of formalized procedures, explicit rules, and specific role assignments, but clearly the march toward goals requires organizational coherence at some point. Thus have transnational social movement organizations (TSMOs) begun to dot the global landscape.[27] Oxfam and Amnesty International are two examples among many that could be cited of movement spinoffs that have evolved toward the institutionalized extreme of the continuum. The European Environmental Bureau (EEB), which was founded in 1974, has moved less rapidly toward this extreme, but it now has a full-time staff quartered in a Brussels office and shows signs of becoming permanent as the environmental movement matures.[28]

Cities and micro regions

The concept of regions, both the macro and micro variety, has become increasingly relevant to the processes of global governance. Although originally connotative of territorial space, it is a concept that has evolved as a residual category encompassing those new patterns of interaction that span established political boundaries and at the same time remain within a delimited geographic space. If that space embraces two or more national economies, it can be called a macro region, whereas a space that spans two or more subnational economies constitutes a micro region.[29] As can be inferred from Table 14.1, both types of regions can emerge out of bottom-up processes and thus evolve out of economic foundations into political institutions. This evolutionary potential makes it "difficult to work with precise definitions. We cannot define regions because they define themselves by evolving from objective, but dormant, to subjective, active existence."[30]

Abstract and elusive as it may be, however, the notion of micro and macro regions as residual categories for control mechanisms that span conventional boundaries serves to highlight important features of transnational governance. In the case of micro regions, it calls attention to the emergent role of certain cities and "natural" economic zones as subtle and nascent forms of transnational rule systems that are not sponsored by states and that, instead, emerge out of the activities of other types of actors which at least initially may foster a relocation of authority from the political to the economic realm. To be sure, some micro regions may span conventional boundaries within a single state and thus be more logically treated as instances of subnational control mechanisms, but such a distinction is not drawn here because many such regions are, as noted in the ensuing paragraphs, transnational in scope. Indeed, since they "are interlinked processes,"[31] it is conceivable that the evolution of micro regions contributes to the emergence of macro regions, and vice versa.

An insightful example along these lines is provided by the developments that have flowed from the success of a cooperation pact signed in 1988 by Lyon, Milan, Stuttgart, and Barcelona, developments that have led one analyst to observe that "a resurrection of 'city states' and regions is quietly transforming Europe's political and economic landscape, diminishing the influence of national governments and redrawing the continental map of power for the 21st century."[32] All four cities and their surrounding regions have an infrastructure and location that is more suited to the changes at work in Europe.[33] They are attracting huge investment and enjoying a prosperity that has led to new demands for greater autonomy. Some argue that, as a result, the emerging urban centers and economies are fostering "a new historical dynamism that will ultimately transform the political structure of Europe by creating a new kind of 'Hanseatic League' that consists of thriving city-states."[34] One specialist forecasts that there will be nineteen cities with at least 20 million people in the greater metropolitan area by the year 2000, with the result that "Cities, not nations, will become the principal identity for most people in the world."[35] Another offers a similar interpretation based on the coastal rim of maritime Asia. Cities such as Tokyo, Hong Kong, Bangkok, Seoul, Singapore, Osaka, and Taipei are the hubs for most of Asia's air and sea transportation, its international entrepreneurship, its pattern of direct overseas investment . . . As a rough approximation, we can say that less than a dozen urban centers in Asia (representing perhaps 4% of the total population) are the locus of 90% of the international finance, of international transportation, of trade oriented manufacturing, and international information networks. To underscore the fact that capitalistic growth centers on a small selection of Asia's cities, is to highlight their contrast with the national societies that make up the bulk of Asia's geography and population. Certainly the intensity of international activities are tens to hundreds of times higher per capita in these cities than in the nation states that we typically focus on.[36]

Still another anticipates that "a desire to bring government closer to the people could make nationhood obsolete. By the middle of the next century, he believes there could be multinational security alliances while real government is carried out by what he calls 'the international metropolitans' ":

> In just a few decades, nation states such as the United States, Japan, Germany, Italy and France will no longer be so relevant. Instead, rich regions built around cities such as Osaka, San Francisco and the four motors of Europe will acquire effective power because they can work in tandem with the transnatonal companies who control the capital.[37]

Yet another observer stresses the obsolescence of traditional state boundaries even more forcefully:

> The nation state has become an unnatural, even dysfunctional, unit for organizing human activity and managing economic endeavor in a borderless world. It represents no genuine, shared community of economic interests; it defines no meaningful flows of economic activity. In fact, it overlooks the true linkages and synergies that exist among often disparate populations by combining important measures of human activity at the wrong level of analysis.[38]

And what unit is evolving in the place of the nation state as a natural unit for organizing activity within the economic realm? Again the data point to the emergence of control mechanisms that are regional in scope:

> . . . the lines that now matter are those defining what may be called "region states." The boundaries of the region state are not imposed by political fiat. They are drawn by the deft but invisible hand of the global market for goods and services. . . . Region states are natural economic zones. They may or may not fall within the geographic limits of a particular nation – whether they do is an accident of history.[39]

This is not to say, however, that region states are lacking in structure. On the contrary, since they make "effective points of entry into the global economy because the very characteristics that define them are shaped by the demands of that economy, [r]egion states tend to have between five million and 20 million people. The range is broad, but the extremes are clear: not half a million, not 50 or 100 million. A region state must be small enough for its citizens to share certain economic and consumer interests but of adequate size to justify the infrastructure – communication and transportation links and quality professional services – necessary to participate economically on a global scale. . . . It must, for example, have at least one international airport and, more than likely, one good harbor with international-class freight-handling facilities."[40]

Needless to say, since the borders of regional states are determined by the "naturalness" of their economic zones and thus rarely coincide with the boundaries of political units, the clash between the incentives induced by markets and the authority of governments is central to the emergence of transnational governance mechanisms. Indeed, it is arguable that a prime change at work in world politics today is a shift in the balance between these two forces, with political authorities finding it increasingly expedient to yield to economic realities. In some instances, moreover, political authorities do not even get to choose to yield:

> Regional economic interdependencies are now more important than political boundaries. In Seattle . . . Japan is seen as neighbor and valued trading partner, while New York and the East Coast are regarded as distant. Illustrating this point is the regional economic community that had developed across the US–Canadian border among five American states and two Canadian provinces without the approval of Washington, D.C., or Ottawa.[41]

Put differently, "The implications of region states are not welcome news to established seats of political power, be they politicians or lobbyists. Nation states by definition require a domestic political focus, while region states are ensconced in the global economy."[42]

This potential clash, however, need not necessarily turn adversarial. Much depends on whether the political authorities welcome and encourage foreign capital investment or whether they insist on protecting their noncompetitive local industries. If they are open to foreign inputs, their economies are more likely to prosper than if they insist on a rigorous maintenance of their political autonomy. But if they do insist on drawing tight lines around their authoritative realms, they are likely to lose out:

> Region states need not be the enemies of central government. Handled gently, region states can provide the opportunity for eventual prosperity for all areas within a nation's traditional political control. . . . Political leaders, however reluctantly, must adjust to the reality of economic regional entities if they are to nurture real economic flows. Resistant governments will be left to reign over traditional political territories as all meaningful

participation in the global economy migrates beyond their well-preserved frontiers.[43]

It seems clear, in short, that cities and micro regions are likely to be major control mechanisms in the world politics of the twenty-first century. Even if the various expectations that they replace states as centers of power prove to be exaggerated, they seem destined to emerge as either partners or adversaries of states as their crucial role becomes more widely recognized and they thereby move from an objective to an intersubjective existence.

Macro regions

Although largely nursed into being through the actions of states, macro regions may be no less nascent than cities and micro regions. And like their micro counterparts, the macro regions which span two or more states are deeply ensconced in a developmental process that may, in some instances, move steadily toward institutionalization while in others the evolutionary process may either move slowly or fall short of culminating in formal institutions. Movement toward institutionalization – or in Hettne's felicitous term, "regionness" – occurs the more a region is marked by "economic interdependence, communication, cultural homogeneity, coherence, capacity to act and, in particular, capacity to resolve conflicts."[44]

Whatever their pace or outcome, these processes have come to be known as the "new" regionalism which is conceived to be different from the "old" regionalism in several ways. While the latter was a product of Cold War bipolarity, the former has come into being in the context of present-day multipolarity. The old regionalism was, in effect, created on a top-down basis from the outside by the superpowers. The new regionalism, on the other hand, consists of more spontaneous processes from within that unfold largely on a bottom-up basis as the constituent states find common cause in a deepening interdependence. As one observer put it,

> The process of regionalization from within can be compared with the historical formation of nation states with the important difference that a coercive centre is lacking in processes of regionalization which presuppose a shared intention among the potential members. . . . The difference between regionalism and the infinite process of spontaneous integration is that there is a politically defined limit to the former process. The limitation, however, is a historical outcome of attempts to find a transnational level of governance which includes certain shared values and minimizes certain shared perceptions of danger. Like the formation of ethnic and national identities, the regional identity is dependent on historical context and shaped by conflicts. And like nations and ethnies, regional formations which have a subjective quality . . . [are] "imagined communities." . . . [D]espite enormous historical, structural, and contextual differences, there is an underlying logic behind contemporary processes of regionalization.[45]

Presently, of course, the various new regions of the world are at very different stages of development, with some already having evolved the rudiments of control mechanisms while others are still at earlier stages in the process. As noted below, Europe has advanced the most toward institutionalized steering mechanisms, but the decline of hegemons, the advent of democracies, and the demise of governmentally managed economies throughout the world has fostered the conditions under which the new regionalism can begin to flourish. Pronounced movements in this direction are discernible in the Nordic region, in the Caribbean, in the Andean Group, and in the Southern Cone of South America.[46] Lesser degrees of regionness are evident in the three Asia-Pacific regions – East Asia, Southeast Asia, and the European Pacific – and the former Soviet Union, while the regionalization process has yet to become readily recognizable in South Asia, the Middle East, and Africa.[47]

Whatever the degree to which the new regionalism has taken hold in various parts of the world, however, it seems clear that this macro phenomenon is increasingly a central feature of global governance. Indeed, the dynamics of macro regions can be closely linked to those of micro regions in the sense that as the former shift authority away from national states, so do they open up space for the latter to evolve their own autonomous control mechanisms. "This can be seen all over Europe today. . . ."[48] As stressed elsewhere, the dynamics of globalization and localization are intimately tied to each other.[49]

Issue regimes

Despite a mushrooming of literature around the concept of international regimes as the rules, norms, principles, and procedures that comprise the control mechanisms through which order and governance in particular issue-areas are sustained, there has been little convergence around a precise and shared notion of the essential attributes of regimes. Indeed, "scholars have fallen into using the term regime so disparately and with such little precision that it ranges from an umbrella for all international relations to little more than a synonym for international organizations."[50] Notwithstanding this conceptual disarray, however, the conception of governance used here as steering mechanisms that are located on a nascent-to-institutionalized continuum serves to highlight regimes as important sources of global governance. Most notably, since they allow for the evolution of a variety of arrangements whereby nongovernmental as well as governmental actors may frame goals and pursue policies in particular issue-areas, regimes meet the need for "a wider view" that includes not only states, international organizations, and international law, "but also the often implicit understandings between a whole range of actors, some of which [are] not states, which [serve] to structure their cooperation in the face of common problems."[51] In some instances the control mechanisms of issue-areas may be informal, disorganized, conflictful, and often ineffective in concentrating authority – that is, so rudimentary and nascent that governance is spasmodic and weak. In other cases the control mechanisms may be formalized, well organized, and capable of effectively exercising authority

– that is, so fully institutionalized that governance is consistent and strong. But in all regimes, regardless of their stage of development, "the interaction between the parties is not unconstrained or is not based on independent decision making."[52] All regimes, that is, have control mechanisms to which their participants feel obliged to accede even if they do not do so repeatedly and systematically.

It is important to stress that irrespective of whether they are nascent or institutionalized, the control mechanisms of all regimes are sustained by the joint efforts of governmental and nongovernmental actors. This shared responsibility is all too often overlooked in the regime literature. More accurately, although the early work on regimes allowed for the participation of nongovernmental organizations, subsequent inquiries slipped into treating regimes as if they consisted exclusively of states that were more or less responsive to advice and pressures from the nongovernmental sector. However, from a global governance perspective in which states are only the most formalized control mechanisms, the original conception of regime membership as open to all types of actors again becomes compelling. And viewed in this way, it immediately becomes clear that issue regimes evolve through the joint sponsorship of state and nonstate actors. To be sure, as regimes evolve from the nascent toward the institutionalized extreme of the continuum, the more will intergovernmental organizations acquire the formal authority to make decisions; but movement in this direction is likely to be accompanied by preservation of the joint sponsorship of state and nonstate actors through arrangements that accord formal advisory roles to the relevant nongovernmental organizations. No issue regime, it seems reasonable to assert, can prosper without control mechanisms that allow for some form of participation by all the interested parties. As one observer put it with respect to several specific issue regimes,

> Increasingly, this transnationalization of civic participation is redefining the terms of governance in North America, not only in the commercial arena but also on issues such as the environment, human rights, and immigration. Nongovernmental organizations, particularly grassroots groups, located throughout these societies are playing a growing role in setting the parameters of the North American agenda, limiting the ability of public officials to manage their relationship on a strict government-to-government basis, and setting the stage for a much more complex process of interaction.[53]

As indicated in Table 14.1, it follows that not all the steering mechanisms of issue regimes are located at the nascent end of the continuum. Some move persistently toward institutionalization – as was recently the case in the human rights regime when the UN created a High Commissioner for Human Rights – while others may be stalemated in an underdeveloped state for considerable periods of time. However, given the ever greater interdependence of global life, it seems doubtful whether any issue area that gains access to the global agenda can avoid evolving at least a rudimentary control mechanism. Once the problems encompassed by an issue area become widely recognized as requiring attention and amelioration, it can hardly remain long without entering at least the first stage of the evolutionary process toward governance. On the other hand, given the disaggregated nature of the global system, it also seems doubtful whether any regime can ever become so fully institutionalized that its rule system evolves a hierarchy through which its top leadership acquires binding legal authority over all its participants. Rather, once a regime acquires a sufficient degree of centralized authority to engage in a modicum of regulatory activities, it undergoes transformation into an international organization, as is suggested in Table 14.1 by the evolution of GATT into the World Trade Organization.

How many issue regimes are there? Endless numbers, if it is recalled that issue-areas are essentially a conglomeration of related smaller issues and that each of the latter evolves identifiable mechanisms for governance that are at some variance with other issues in the same area. The global agenda is conceived in terms of large issue-areas only because they are more easily grasped and debated, but it is on the smaller issues that particularistic activities requiring special governance arrangements focus.

Cross-border coalitions

Some issue regimes, moreover, are so disaggregated as to encompass what have been called "cross-border coalitions."[54] These can be usefully set aside for separate analysis as instances of jointly sponsored, nascent control mechanisms. The emphasis here is on the notion of coalitions, on networks of organizations. As previously noted, INGOs are by definition cross-border organizations, but their spanning of boundaries tends to occur largely through like-minded people from different countries who either share membership in the same transnational organization or who belong to national organizations that are brought together under umbrella organizations that are transnational in scope. Cross-border coalitions, on the other hand, consist of organizations that coalesce for common purposes but do not do so under the aegis of an umbrella organization. Some of these may form umbrella INGOs as they move on from the nascent stage of development, but at present most of the new coalitions are still in the earliest stage of formation. They are networks rather than organizations, networks that have been facilitated by the advent of information technologies such as e-mail and electronic conferencing and that thus place their members in continuous touch with each other even though they may only come together in face-to-face meetings on rare occasions. Put more dramatically, "[r]ather than be represented by a building that people enter, these actors may be located on electronic networks and exist as 'virtual communities' that have no precise physical address."[55]

It is noteworthy that some cross-border coalitions may involve local governments located near national boundaries that find it more expedient on a variety of issues to form coalitions with counterparts across the border than to work with their own provincial or national governments. Such coalitions may even be formed deliberately in order to avoid drawing "unnecessary or premature attention from central authorities to local solutions of some local problems by means of informal contacts and 'good neighborhood' networks. Often it [is] not a deliberate deception, just an avoidance of unnecessary complications."[56]

That cross-border coalitions are a nascent form of issue regimes is indicated by the fact that they usually form around problems high on the agendas of their communities. During the 1993 debate over the North American Free Trade Agreement (NAFTA), for example, a number of advocacy groups concerned with environmental, human rights, labor, and immigration issues linked up with their counterparts across the US–Mexican boundary and, in some instances, the networks spanned the sectoral issue areas as the implications of NAFTA were discovered to have common consequences for otherwise disparate groups. This is not to say that the advent of cross-border coalitions reduced the degree of conflict over the question of NAFTA's approval. As can be readily expected whenever a control mechanism is at stake, coalitions on one side of the issue generated opposing coalitions.

In short, "the new local and cross-border NGO movements are a potential wild card. They may be proactive or reactive in a variety of ways, sometimes working with, sometimes against, state and market actors who are not accustomed to regarding civil society as an independent actor."[57]

Credit rating agencies

Turning now to transnational control mechanisms that are located more toward the institutionalized extreme of the governance continuum, the dimension of the global capital markets in which risk is assessed and credit-worthiness legitimated offers examples of both discernible rule systems that came into being through the sponsorship of states and others that evolved historically out of the private sector.[58] The International Monetary Fund (IMF) and the World Bank are illustrative of the former type of mechanism, while Moody's Investors Service and Standard & Poor's Ratings Group (S&P) dominate the ratings market in the private sector. Although the differences between the two types are in some ways considerable – unlike the agencies in the private sector, the IMF and the World Bank derive much of their capacity for governance from the sponsorship and funding by the state system that founded them – they are in one important respect quite similar: in both cases their authority derives at least partially from the specialized knowledge on which their judgments are based and the respect they have earned for adhering to explicit and consistent standards for reaching their conclusions as to the credit-worthiness of enterprises, governments, and countries.[59] And in both cases the judgments they render are authoritative in the sense that the capital markets acquiesce to and conduct themselves on the basis of their ratings. To be sure, fierce debates do break out over the appropriateness of the standards employed to make the risk assessments of debt security, but the credibility of the private rating agencies has not been so effectively challenged as to diminish their status as control mechanisms.

That the private agencies are transnational in scope is indicated by the fact that both Moody's and S&P have branches in London, Paris, Frankfurt, Tokyo, and

Sydney. Most of the other agencies in this trillion-dollar market are domestically focused and confine their assessments to the credit-worthiness of borrowers in the countries where they are located, albeit there are signs that a Europe-wide agency is in the process of evolving.

In sum, the private ratings agencies are a means through which key parts of national and transnational economies are, relatively speaking, insulated from politics. By presiding over this insulation the agencies have become, in effect, control mechanisms. Put differently, "rating agencies seem to be contributing to a system of rule in which an intersubjective framework is created in which social forces will be self-regulating in accord with the limits of the system."[60]

Crime syndicates

It is a measure of the globalization of governance that crime syndicates have evolved institutional forms on a transnational scale, that they can properly be called "transnational criminal organizations" (TCOs). Their conduct, of course, violates all the norms that are considered to undergird the proper exercise of authority, but their centrality to the course of events is too conspicuous not to note briefly their role among the diverse control mechanisms that presently comprise global governance.[61] Indeed, upon reflection it seems clear that "with the globalization of trade and growing consumer demands for leisure products, it is only natural that criminal organizations should become increasingly transnational in character," that they have been "both contributors to, and beneficiaries of, . . . a great increase in transactions across national boundaries that are neither initiated nor controlled by states,"[62] and that

> Not only is transnational activity as open to criminal groups as it is to legitimate multinational corporations, but the character of criminal organizations also makes them particularly suited to exploit these new opportunities. Since criminal groups are used to operating outside the rules, norms and laws of domestic jurisdictions, they have few qualms about crossing national boundaries illegally. In many respects, therefore, TCOs are transnational organizations *par excellence*. They operate outside the existing structures of authority and power in world politics and have developed sophisticated strategies for circumventing law enforcement in individual states and in the global community of states.[63]

A good measure of how new opportunities have facilitated the explosiveness of TCOs in the present era is provided by the pattern of criminal activities that have evolved in the former Soviet Union since the collapse of the Soviet empire. "More than 4,000 criminal formations comprising an estimated 100,000 members now operate in Russia alone" and, of these, some "150 to 200 . . . have international ties."[64]

While TCOs operate outside the realm of established norms, and while they are marked by considerable diversity in their size, structures, goals, and memberships, they are nevertheless institutionalized in the sense they control their affairs in patterned ways that often involve strategic alliances between themselves and national and local criminal organizations, alliances that "permit them to cooperate with, rather than compete against, indigenously entrenched criminal organizations."[65] Yet, TCOs have not succumbed to excessive bureaucratization. On the contrary, "they are highly mobile and adaptable and able to operate across national borders with great ease . . . partly because of their emphasis on networks rather than formal organizations."[66] It is interesting and indicative of the dynamics of globalization that legitimate multinational corporations have recently come to resemble TCOs in two ways: first, by developing more fluid and flexible network structures that enable them to take advantage of local conditions and, second, by resorting to strategic alliances that facilitate development on a global scale.

United Nations system

The UN is an obvious case of a steering mechanism that was sponsored by states and that took an institutional form from the inception of its founding. To be sure, its processes of institutionalization have continued to evolve since 1945 to the point where it is now a complex system of numerous subagencies that, collectively, address all the issues on the global agenda and that amount to a vast bureaucracy. The institutional histories of the various agencies differ in a number of respects, but taken as a whole they have become a major center of global governance. They have been a main source of problem-identification, information, innovation, and constructive policies in the fields of health, environment, education, agriculture, labor, family, and a number of other issues that are global in scope.

This is not to say that the collective history of the UN depicts a straight-line trajectory toward ever greater effectiveness. Quite to the contrary, not only have its many agencies matured enough to be severely and properly criticized for excessive and often misguided bureaucratic practices, but also – and even more important – its primary executive and legislative agencies (the Secretary General, the General Assembly, and the Security Council) have compiled a checkered history with respect to the UN's primary functions of preventive diplomacy, peacekeeping, and peacemaking under Chapter VII of its Charter. For the first four decades its record in these regards was that of a peripheral player in the Cold War, an era in which it served as a debating arena for major conflicts, especially those that divided the two nuclear superpowers, but accomplished little by way of creating a new world order that provided states security through the aggregation of their collective strength. Then, at the end of the Cold War, the UN underwent both a qualitative and quantitative transformation, one that placed it at the very heart of global governance as states turned to the Security Council for action in a number of the major humanitarian and conflict situations that broke out with the end of superpower competition. The inclination to rely on the UN, to centralize in it the responsibility for global governance, reached a peak in 1991 with the successful multilateral effort under UN auspices to undo Iraq's conquest of Kuwait.

It is not difficult to demonstrate the quantitative dimensions of the UN's transformation at the end of the Cold War. In 1987 the UN had assigned some 10,000 peace-keepers – mostly troops in blue helmets who were supposed to resort to force only if attacked – to five operations around the world on an annual budget of about $233 million. Seven years later the number of troops had risen to 72,000 in eighteen different situations at an annual cost of more than $3 billion. Similarly, where the Security Council used to meet once a month, by 1994 its schedule involved meeting every day and often twice a day. Put differently, during the first forty-four years of its history the Security Council passed only six resolutions under Chapter VII in which "threats to the peace, breaches of the peace, acts of aggression" were determined to exist. Between 1990 and 1992, on the other hand, the Security Council adopted thirty-three such resolutions, on Iraq (21) the former Yugoslavia (8), Somalia (2), Liberia (1), and Libya (1).

Even more impressive are the qualitative changes that underlay the UN's transformation: as the Cold War wound down and ended, two remarkable developments became readily discernible. One was the advent of a new consensus among the five permanent members of the Security Council with respect to the desirability of the UN's involvement in peacekeeping activities and the other was the extension of this consensus to the non-permanent members, including virtually all of the non-aligned states elected to the Council. These changes are evident in the fact that the number of unanimously adopted Security Council resolutions jumped from 61 percent (72 of 119) in 1980–5 to 84 percent in 1986–1992 (184 of 219). In 1993 alone, the Security Council passed more than 181 resolutions and statements, all of which high-mindedly addressed peacekeeping issues (such as a demand for the end of ethnic cleansing in the former Yugoslavia).

Furthermore, these transformations rendered the UN into a control mechanism in the military sense of the term. The organization's operations in both Somalia and Bosnia found the Secretary General conducting himself as commanding general and making the final decisions having to do with the application of air power, the disposition of ground forces, and the dismissal of commanding officers.

Yet, despite these transformations in its role and orientations, the UN's performances have not lived up to the surge of high hopes for it that immediately followed the end of the Cold War. Rather than sustaining movement toward effective global governance, it foundered in Somalia, dawdled in Bosnia, and cumulatively suffered a decline in the esteem with which it is held by both governments and publics.[67] The reasons for this decline are numerous – ranging from a lack of money to a lack of will, from governments that delay paying their dues to publics that resist the commitment of troops to battle – but they add up to a clear-cut inability to carry out and enforce the resolutions of the Security Council. Consensus has evolved on the desirability of the UN intervening in humanitarian situations, but there is a long distance between agreement on goals and a shared perspective on the provision of the necessary means: the readiness to implement multilateral goals and thereby enhance the UN's authority so as to achieve effective governance is woefully lacking, leading one analyst to describe the organization's activities in the peacekeeping area as "faint-hearted multilateralism."[68]

But the checkered history of the UN's institutionalization suggests that its present limitations may undergo change yet again. The organization continues to occupy a valued and critical position in the complex array of global control mechanisms. The need for collective action in volatile situations is bound to continue, so that it is likely that the world will seek to fill this vacuum by again and again turning to the UN as the best available means of achieving a modicum of governance. And in the processes of doing so, conceivably circumstances will arise that swing faint-hearted commitments back in the direction of a more steadfast form of multilateralism.[69]

The European Union

Much more so than the UN, the history of the European Union (EU) is a record of the evolutionary route to institutionalization. Even a brief account of this history is beyond the scope of this analysis,[70] but suffice it to say that it is one macro region that has passed through various stages of growth to its present status as an elaborately institutionalized instrument of governance for the (increasing number of) countries within its jurisdiction. Sure, it was states that formalized the institutionalization, but they did so as a consequence of transformations that culminated in the member countries holding referenda wherein the establishment of the EU was approved by citizenries. In this sense the EU offers a paradigmatic example of the dynamics that propel evolutionary processes from nascent to institutionalized steering mechanisms. As one observer puts it, this transformation occurred through "the gradual blurring of the distinction made between the 'Community' and the 'nation-states' which agreed to form that community in the first place. . . . Although the two are by no means linked as tightly as are subnational units to the center in the traditional state, the Community-state entanglement is such that the Community is very far from being a traditional regional organization."[71] Indeed, such is the evolution of the EU that it

> is now better conceptualized as a union of states rather than as an organization. The international law doctrine that actors are either states or organizations has become unrealistic. . . . In [a 1992] decision the Court of Justice established that Community law within its sphere is equal in status to national law. Further, the court has successfully maintained that, because law should be uniform, Community law must take precedence over conflicting national law.[72]

In short, while the EU does not have "federal law because Community legislation suffers from the defect that its statutes are not legitimized by a democratic legislature,"[73] it does have a rule system in the combination of its executive and judicial institutions.

Election monitoring

A good illustration of how control mechanisms can evolve toward the institutionalized end of the governance continuum through the sponsorship of both states and NGOs is provided by the emergence of clear-cut patterns wherein it has become established practice for external actors to monitor the conduct of domestic elections in the developing world.[74] Indeed, the monitoring process has become quite elaborate and standardized, with lengthy instructional booklets now available for newcomers to follow when they enter the host country and shoulder their responsibilities as monitors.[75] And no less indicative of the degree of institutionalization is that some of the monitors, say the UN or the National Democratic Institute, send representatives to observe virtually all elections in which outside monitors are present.

But does external monitoring constitute a control mechanism? Most certainly. Whatever hesitations the host countries may have about the presence of outsiders who judge the fairness and propriety of their election procedures, and irrespective of their attempts to circumvent the monitors and load the electoral outcome, now they yield both to the pressure for external monitoring and to the judgments the outsiders make during and after election day. Elections have been postponed because of irregularities in voter lists detected by the external monitors, "dirty tricks" uncovered during the balloting have been terminated at the insistence of monitors, and the verdict of outsiders that the final tallies were fraudulent have resulted in the holding of new elections. To be sure, a few countries still adamantly refuse admission to outside monitors or do not allow them to be present on a scale sufficient to allow for legitimation of the electoral outcome, but the monitoring process has become so fully institutionalized that normally the host countries overcome their reluctance as they begin to recognize the problems they cause for themselves by refusing to acquiesce to the monitoring process. Put differently, the advent of established procedures for the external monitoring of elections demonstrates the large extent to which control mechanisms derive their effectiveness from information and reputation even if their actions are not backed up by constitutional authority. It might even be said that governance in an ever more complex and interdependent world depends less on the issuance of authoritative directives and more on the release of reliable information and the legitimacy inherent in its detail.

As for the presence of both state and NGO actors, the spreading norm that the establishment of democracy justifies the international community's involvement in domestic elections attracts both official and unofficial groups to train and send monitors. Whatever organizations may have led the negotiations that result in the acceptance of outside observers, a number of others (such as the Organization of American States, the Socialist International, and the Latin American Studies Association in the case of Paraguay's 1993 election) find reasons important to their membership to be present and there are few precedents for denying admission to some monitoring teams while accepting others. Although the monitoring process may not be free of friction and competition among the numerous teams, the more procedures have been institutionalized, the greater has been the collaboration among the teams. It is not stretching matters to conclude that not only does the international community turn out in force for domestic elections in distant countries, but it does so with representatives from many of its diverse segments. In the 1990 Nicaraguan election, for example, 2,578 accredited observers from 278 organizations were present on election day.[76]

Subnational governance mechanisms

Although space constraints do not permit a comparable analysis of the variety of control mechanisms that have emerged within states, it is useful to reiterate that as interdependence mounts what is local may also be global and what is subnational may also be transnational. A full picture of what are likely to be the contours of global governance in the decades ahead thus requires attention to the dynamics of localization and how they are in part responses to the dynamics of globalization, responses which give rise to what can be called "distant proximities" that may well become systems of rule with diverse types of control mechanisms.[77]

Although some localizing dynamics are initiated by national governments – as when France decided to decentralize its steering apparatus and reduce Paris's control over policy and administrative issues – perhaps the preponderance of them are generated at subnational levels, some with the help and approval of national agencies but many in opposition to national policies, which then extend their scope abroad. The tendencies toward strengthened ethnic subgroups that have surfaced since the end of the Cold War are a case in point. Even though these actors may not have direct ties to supporters in other countries, their activities on the local scene can foster repercussions abroad which thereby transform them into aspects of global governance.[78] The recent struggles in Bosnia, Somalia, and Rwanda are illustrative in this regard. Similarly, since so many of the world's resource, water, and air-quality problems originate in subnational communities, and since this level is marked by a proliferation of both governmental and non-governmental agencies that seek to control these problems within their jurisdiction and to do so through cooperative efforts with transnational counterparts, the environmental area offers another array of local issues that are central to the conduct of global governance.

Continuing forms of national governance

The emphasis here on transnational and subnational mechanisms is not, of course, to imply that national governments and states are no longer central loci of control in the processes of global governance. Needless to say, they are very central indeed. No account of the global system can ignore them or give them other than a prominent place in the scheme of things. Nevertheless, the preceding analysis should make clear that states have not only lost some of their earlier dominance of the governance system, but also that the lessening of their ability to evoke compliance and govern effectively is in part due to the growing relevance and potential of control mechanisms sustained by transnational and subnational systems of rule.

Governance in the twenty-first century

If the analysis were to end here, the reader, like the author, would likely feel let down, as if the final chapter of this story of a disaggregated and fragmenting global system of governance has yet to be written. It is an unfinished story, one's need for closure would assert. It needs a conclusion, a drawing together of the "big picture," a sweeping assessment which offers some hope that somehow the world can muddle through and evolve techniques of cooperation that will bridge its multitude of disaggregated parts and achieve a measure of coherence which enables future generations to live in peace, achieve sustainable development, and maintain a modicum of creative order. You need to assess the overall balance, one's training cries out, show how the various emergent centers of power form a multipolar system of states that will manage to cope with the challenges of war within and among its members. Yes, that's it, depict the overall system as polyarchical and indicate how such an arrangement can generate multilateral institutions of control that effectively address the huge issues which clutter the global agenda. Or, perhaps better, indicate how a hegemon will emerge out of the disaggregation and have enough clout to foster both progress and stability. At the very least, one's analytic impulses demand, you need to suggest how worldwide tendencies toward disaggregation and localization may be offset by no less powerful tendencies toward aggregation and globalization.

Compelling as these alternative interpretations may be, however, they do not quell a sense that it is only a short step from polyarchy to pollyanna and that one's commitment to responsible analysis must be served by not taking that step. The world is on a path dependent course, to be sure, and some of its present outlines can be discerned if, as noted at the outset, allowance is made for nuance and ambiguity. Still, in this time of continuing and profound transformations too much remains murky to project beyond the immediate present and anticipate long-term trajectories. All one can conclude with confidence is that in the twenty-first century the paths to governance will lead in many directions, some that will emerge into sunlit clearings and others that will descend into dense jungles.

15 Global governance as disaggregated complexity[1]

In focusing on the structures and processes of global governance (GG) one has to be wary of proceeding from an initial presumption that there is an empirical reality out there to be investigated. Since it suggests desirable and compelling values that ought to be promoted, GG invites wishful thinking, an unexamined premise that somehow our messy, tension-ridden world must be undergoing governance on a global scale marked by a modicum of coherence that can and should be analyzed.

My preoccupation with the dangers of wishful thinking in this regard derives from an understanding of how GG became central to the discourse on world affairs. Its emergence requires recognizing that widespread use of the word "governance" is essentially a recent phenomenon – indeed, it did not exist in some languages (e.g. German) – and that its increasing usage has paralleled the acceleration of globalization. With but few exceptions, in fact, governance tends to be employed only when it is modified by the adjective "global." Otherwise, for scales short of the global – whether local, provincial, or national – "government" is usually treated as the entity through which order is sought and goals framed and implemented. And why, then, have "global" and "governance" become inextricably linked in public discourse? The answer strikes me as stemming from three sources. One involves the need to refer to the exercise of authority beyond national borders and the implausibility of doing so by referring to global government inasmuch as such a structure neither exists nor hovers on the horizon. Second, the need to speak of transnational authority was intensified by the Apollo picture of the earth taken from outer space that depicted a lonely spheroid in a vast universe and thereby served to heighten a keen awareness of humankind as sharing a common fate.

Third, for a long time the world was described as increasingly interdependent, but not until the Cold War ended were people freed up to fully recognize that the dynamics of interdependence tended to have consequences that are global in scope. The problem of global warming, for example, knows no boundaries and reaches into every corner of the globe. Likewise, genocidal policies and practices in Rwanda and Kosovo have been experienced as challenges to all of humankind, as have financial crises and a growing gap between the rich and poor in developing countries. As such processes accelerated at a seemingly ever more rapid rate, and as new electronic technologies facilitated a collapse of time and distance, the notion quickly spread that interdependence is characteristic of the world as a whole. Accordingly, persuaded that many problems cannot be allowed to fester and endanger the well-being of people everywhere, and eager to bring a modicum of order and direction to the uncertainties and dislocations inherent in the vast degrees of interdependence, analysts have quite naturally begun to talk of the need for GG and the processes and structures that might foster and sustain it.

At first glance everything seems in place for a surge toward effective GG, however IT may be conceptualized. Both publics and their governments are keenly aware the world is a messy place – the "organized irresponsibility that rules the globe"[2] – and they all aspire to bringing some order and progress to it. A plethora of international and transnational organizations have come into being for this purpose, and there is no shortage of good minds and decent people working hard at framing ideas for improving existing institutions and founding new ones that may move the world along the path to more effective global governance. A huge and ever-growing literature, a seemingly endless spate of conferences, an outpouring of commitments by corporate boards and religious organizations, a flurry of activity by public officials in myriad issue-areas, and a turn toward new courses and programs in the academic world testify to the continuing expansion of the surging preoccupation with how IT might be realized.

Put differently, at first glance much of the world appears to have moved collectively from a fragmented NIMBY (not in my backyard) syndrome to a keen awareness of an integrated future symbolized by the aforementioned picture of the earth from outer space. Backyards remain marked by extensive local variation that cannot be ignored, but such differences are now somewhat more likely to be framed in a global context.

A post-international perspective

Despite the explosion of literature on the subject, none of the approaches to GG strike me as adequate. Too wedded to existing theories such as realism and liberalism, most formulations tend to underplay, even ignore in some cases, the messiness of the current world scene and the consequences of growing interdependence on a global scale that is at the same marked by undiminished local variations. Accordingly, I have developed my own theoretical perspective, one that stressed the changing nature of world affairs by treating the emergent structures and processes as post-international.[3] Such a perspective is rooted in the premise that the world is undergoing a profound transformation wherein three of its basic parameters have become variables rather than constants. One is at the micro level and involves the acquisition of new skills by people everywhere. A second is a macro parameter that posits a bifurcation of global structures such that the long-standing state-centric world now has to contend with a multi-centric world composed of diverse and numerous collectivities such as NGOs, corporations, professional societies, etc. The third is a micro–macro parameter that focuses on how the links between people at the micro level and collectivities at the macro level give rise to pervasive authority crises within most collectivities.

Structure

The major structural consequence of the transformations that mark post-international politics is the advent of an ever-greater number of spheres of authority (SOA) that, in effect, amount to a vast disaggregation of the mechanisms through which GG is exercised. In effect, therefore, the global stage has become increasingly dense and crowded, thereby lessening the probability that governance on a global scale can be effective. There are just too many centers of power and authority.

Yet, notwithstanding the huge extent to which the global stage has become crowded with diverse actors at every level of community who take positions and pursue policies that may have widespread repercussions beyond the scope of their authority, most discussions of GG start at the level of reforming international institutions and then note how the reforms have to be implemented by national and local governments. To be sure, the vulnerability of international institutions to the wishes of the member governments that created them is fully acknowledged and bottom-up solutions thereby hinted; but whether the solutions are top-down or bottom-up, they posit vertical flows of authority. The repeated calls for a World Environmental Organization similar to the World Trade Organization exemplifies the vertical perspective.[4] Such a perspective has led quite naturally to a widespread presumption that GG is founded on a coordinated structure, as if governance on a global scale involves a singular form of activity, or at least a set of activities that are in harmony with one another. No one quite says it that way, but the implication always seems to underlie GG formulations. More than that, GG is usually posited as a good thing, as consisting of desirable activities and outcomes. To be sure, simplistic approaches to GG are relatively scarce. Most analysts do acknowledge the complexity, but nonetheless they usually presume it is a manageable complexity, one that is potentially coherent and all-encompassing.

In short, efforts to develop viable solutions to GG problems are still cast in the context of traditional approaches to the nature of authority. They ignore the ways in which collectivities in both the public and private sectors sustain authority flows horizontally through networks as well as vertically through hierarchical structures, almost as if allowance for horizontal, network-like flows is just too complex to contemplate. Lip service is paid to the role of NGOs and publics and their modes of interaction, but in the end allowance for such dynamics is essentially limited. The state continues to be posited as the prime, if not the only, wielder of effective authority. Thus, still rooted in the notion that compliance involves those at the top persuading, instructing, or ordering that those down the chain of command conduct themselves in specified ways, no allowance is made for requests and suggestions that evoke compliance through nonhierarchical structures. In effect, the NIMBY syndrome has been elevated to the national level, thereby minimizing the extent to which we are sensitive to the variability that still prevails at local levels.

Put differently, our concern for the global problems posed by our recognition of the earth as a lonely spheroid in a vast universe serves to block our appreciation of the relevance of authority being exercised in local networks. The disaggregation of authority is thus a major reason why the challenges of GG are so daunting. In the words of one observer,

> So dominant in contemporary consciousness is the assumption that authority must be centralized that scholars are just beginning to grapple with how decentralized authority might be understood. . . . [T]he question of how to think about a world that is becoming "domesticated" but not centralized, about a world after "anarchy," is one of the most important questions today facing not only students of international relations but of political theory as well.[5]

If the world is conceived to be a disaggregated multiplicity of SOAs that collectively constitute a new global order, the key to understanding their various roles in GG lies not so much in focusing on their legal prerogatives, but rather in assessing the degree to which they are able to evoke the compliance of the people whom they seek to mobilize through the directives they issue. Achieving compliance is the key to leadership and politics, and it is not readily accomplished. The more complex societies and the world become, the more difficult it is to get people to respond to efforts to generate their compliance. States have an advantage in this regard because they have the legitimate right to employ force if their citizens fail to comply. But to stress this distinctive quality of states is to ignore the underpinnings of compliance. Most notable perhaps, it ignores the large degree to which compliance is rooted in habit, in an unthinking readiness to respond to directives issued by the authorities to which one has been socialized to be committed, responsive, and loyal, and the large degree to which such habits are no longer encompassed by the clear-cut province of states. With the proliferation of SOAs and the declining relevance of domestic–foreign boundaries, with the emergence of alternative authorities to which people can be responsive, analytic attention needs to focus on the ways in which compliance habits may be undergoing transformation.

It is not a simple matter to grasp global governance as congeries of diverse collectivities, only some of which are governments and states while most are NGOs, private groups, corporations, and a host of other boundary-spanning entities. Such a proliferation of transnational actors requires one to wrench free of the long-standing and unquestioned premise that the boundaries separating countries are firm and impassable without permission of the states that preside over them. This wrenching task is not easily accomplished. Our analytic capacities are rooted in methodological territorialism,[6] in a long-standing, virtually unconscious habit of probing problems in a broad, geographic or spatial context. This habit poses an acute problem because of the ever-growing porosity of domestic–foreign boundaries[7] that has rendered territoriality much less pervasive than it used to be even as all the social sciences construct their inquiries, develop their concepts, formulate their hypotheses, and frame their evidence-gathering procedures through spatial lenses. Nor are officials free to think in alternative contexts: as one analyst put it, "Trapped by the territoriality of their power, policy makers in traditional settings often have little choice but to address the symptoms rather than the causes of public problems."[8]

Yet, breaking out of the conceptual jail imposed by methodological territorialism is imperative because the processes of fragmegration so readily span foreign–domestic boundaries, thus making it difficult for states to exercise control over the flows of ideas, money, goods, pollution, crime, drugs, and terrorists; and they have only slightly greater control over the flow of people. Why? Because their capacities have been weakened by an ever-greater complexity embedded in some eight dynamics (outlined in Table 8.1) that have greatly increased transborder flows and rendered domestic–foreign boundaries ever more porous. With the collapse of time and distance, subnational organizations and governments that once operated within the confines of national boundaries are now so inextricably connected to far-off parts of the world that the legal and geographic jurisdictions in which they are located matter less and less. What matters, instead, are the spheres of authority to which their members are responsive.

Preferring a tidier, less complex conception of how global affairs are structured, some analysts reject the conception of GG as disaggregated centers of authority. They argue that positing the global stage as ever more crowded with SOAs amounts to such a broad conception as to make it "virtually meaningless both for theory construction and social action."[9] Here this argument is found wanting. Opting for a narrow conception may facilitate analysis, but doing so is also misleading in that it ignores the vast proliferation of SOAs that has emerged as a prime characteristic of the system of GG subsequent to the end of the Cold War.

The convergence of structure and process

Elsewhere I have suggested that the core of governance involves rule systems in which steering mechanisms are employed to frame and implement goals that enable organizations and communities to move in the directions they wish to go or that enable them to maintain the institutions and policies they wish to maintain.[10] Governance is not the same as government in that the rule systems of the latter are rooted in formal and legal procedures, while those of the former are also marked by informal rule systems.[11] It follows that the achievement of a modicum of governance on a global scale requires the development of steering mechanisms that evoke compliant actions, not just words, on the part of the innumerable individual and collective actors whose activities shape the course of events within and among communities throughout the world.

Three key challenges here are especially noteworthy. One concerns myriad local variations that resist overall global solutions. Some problems are global in scope, but the circumstances of different communities and issues can vary considerably, with the result that GG involves the exercise of authority in a host of diverse conditions. To aspire to transnational institutions that are relevant to situations everywhere is to drastically misread the governance problem. Needs at the local level must be met without encouraging or reinforcing the NIMBY syndrome.

The second challenge involves the fact that political entities are not the only ones that engage in governance. It is now commonplace to speak of market governance, of corporate governance, of environmental governance, of governance by NGOs, of media governance,[12] and so on across all the types of collectivities that may exercise authority on the global stage. It follows that an adequate conception of GG needs to incorporate all the various forms of extant governance. Not to do so would be to miss central features of the pervasive complexities that mark GG.[13]

The third challenge is posed by the nature of compliance, of getting relevant actors to put aside habitual responses and, instead, to yield to authorities who set new, more globally compatible standards for the systems of which they are a part. The challenge is huge not only because GG is a highly complex, disaggregated and minimally coordinated system of governance comprised of hundreds of thousands of formal and informal rule systems at all levels of the world's communities, but also because of an inclination not to confront the complexity it represents and, instead, to favor a more streamlined system that is hierarchically aggregated.

In short, since fragmegrative processes sustain authority flows that are not neatly structured and go every which way, emanating from a vast array of actors whose rule systems seek to evoke compliance through a variety of means, GG involves crazy-quilt arrangements wherein authority is exercised partly by hierarchical structures, partly by horizontal networks, and partly by oblique links among overlapping vertical and horizontal SOAs. Taken in its entirety, and as indicated in the previous chapter, the prevailing system of GG is comparable to a mobius strip or web. It is a system marked by patterns that unfold when the impetus to steer a course of events derives from networked and hierarchical interactions across levels of aggregation among transnational corporations (TNCs), international nongovernmental organizations (INGOs), NGOs, intergovernmental organizations (IGOs), states, elites, mass publics, and local or provincial communities, interactions that are elaborate and diverse enough to constitute a hybrid structure in which the dynamics of governance are so overlapping among the several levels as to form a singular, web-like process that is continuous and, like a mobius, neither begins nor culminates at any level or at any point in time. A mobius web is top-down, bottom-up and side-by-side governance all at once.[14]

Needless to say, the growing numbers of SOAs immensely complicate the challenges they face in evoking compliance. SOAs proliferate because increasingly people are capable of shouldering and managing multiple identities that lessen their allegiance to their states. As they get involved in more and more networks in the multi-centric world, so do their loyalties fractionate and become issue- and object-specific. To be sure, history in this era of fragmegration does record pockets of successful coordination among states in the state-centric world and among the diverse nongovernmental collectivities in the multi-centric world that are able to generate meaningful compliance. Even though SOAs vary widely in their ability to evoke compliance and thus in their contributions to the processes of global governance, some do manage to gain a measure of control over fragmegrative tensions. Rule systems developed through negotiation among national governments – such as the United Nations, the Kyoto Protocol on the Environment, the World Trade Organization, or the European Union – have the widest scope and, consequently, make perhaps the most substantial contribution to governance processes. Steering mechanisms maintained by SOAs in the multi-centric world – such as the calculations of credit-rating agencies that estimate the reliability of national economies,[15] the rulings of truth commissions designed to enable countries racked by civil strife to heal their wounds, or the practices of the insurance industry to offset climate changes[16] – exemplify effective instruments of governance with respect to specific issues.[17] To repeat, no less important are the many successful efforts at global governance that result from cooperation among collectivities in the state- and multi-centric worlds. In the words of one knowledgeable observer, "global regimes are increasingly the product of negotiations among state and nonstate actors."[18]

For every example of rule systems in world politics that achieve meaningful coordination and compliance, however, innumerable cases can be cited in which efforts to maintain effective steering mechanisms fail to generate the compliance necessary for governance. Indeed, such failures may well be more the rule than the exception in world affairs today. Our messy world is littered with paralyzed or stalemated governments and nongovernmental SOAs that fall far short of evoking the compliance appropriate to their goals and policies.

Universal science and indigenous knowledge[19]

Although there is no lack of appreciation that many governance problems originate in local communities, each of which has special circumstances that require responses tailored to their needs, it is useful to note that all too many officials and their expert advisers tend to assess the local variations under the rubric of science. The impulse to posit scientific findings as having universal relevance can thus serve as a conceptual block to grasping the dynamism of fragmegration. It has become so ingrained in the expertise of many economists, environmentalists, and other specialists that they tend to give little credence to the idea that there are occasions when indigenous knowledge is more accurate and relevant than the knowledge generated through scientific methods. After all, experts tend to assert, the local insights are idiosyncratic and may even prove false when subjected to the rigors of scientific testing. More than that, they invite their superiors and local counterparts to consider, say, global warming, a widening ozone layer, species diminution, polluted air carried by high winds, and other worldwide environmental problems as indicative of the limits of indigenous knowledge, stressing that it overlooks the big picture and is therefore less compelling than universal verities uncovered through science.

This is, of course, an oversimplified characterization. There are local experts whose knowledge is respected precisely because it stems from a familiarity with circumstances on the ground. What local specialists offer, however, may not be scientific findings, but rather the insights of experience gained through familiarity with local conditions. Still, for many experts the habit of positing scientific findings as more reliable than experiential understanding is a perspective not easily abandoned. For many experts forsaking the habit is viewed as a capitulation to local pressures. Expertise, in short, can be a basis for perpetuating rather than ameliorating fragmegrative tensions.

Sustainable development

For several decades the concept of sustainability has captured the imagination of those who worry about the long-term future of humankind. Originally conceived as referring to environmental challenges and the need to utilize nature's bounties without depriving future generations of the resources they will need, conceptual imprecision has subsequently developed as the core idea of sustainability has undergone a significant change of meaning. Now it has come to connote "sustainable development," with the emphasis on sustaining economies rather than nature, a semantic shift that has enabled a vast array of diverse actors to crowd under the umbrella of sustainability and to press their goals in the context of what they regard as unquestionable sets of values.[20] It is also a shift that has intensified controversies over whether the policies designed to achieve environmental sustainability should be undertaken by local jurisdictions or under the rubric of GG.

However activists and observers may use the concept, both environmental and economic sustainability have empirical and moral dimensions. On the one hand, it refers to those empirical processes whereby humankind preserves or exploits the resources of nature in such a way that subsequent generations do or do not have available access to comparable standards of living. Sustainability is thus readily understood as being about GG, about the future, about the long run, about the capacity of people to ponder the well-being of their unborn great grandchildren. But efforts to promote a desirable future for the unborn is loaded with values and it is here where sustainability is pervaded with moral dimensions, with questions of right and wrong, with loaded interpretations of scientific inquiries. Empirical data – the findings of science – on whether a particular practice promotes or deters sustainable development in the future can be interpreted in diverse ways, depending on the perspectives from which they are approached.

Accordingly, it is hardly surprising that the ongoing discourse about sustainable development is marked by florid affirmations and vivid denunciations. Whatever the solidity of the empirical findings that may be uncovered about the impact of economic development on species survival, pollution, resource utilization, and all the other foci that comprise the environmental issue-area, inevitably policies designed to achieve sustainability will be deeply ensconced in unending controversies and conflicts that make widespread compliance with the policies improbable. The chances of consensuses forming around the nature of environmental threats and the steering mechanisms appropriate to governing them thus pose severe obstacles to GG enhancing the prospects for the future. It is not difficult to imagine the great grandchildren of future generations living under even more dire conditions than prevail at present.

The governance of a fragmegrated world

Given a disaggregated and fragmegrative system of GG in which the global stage is dense with actors, large and small, formal and informal, economic and social, political and cultural, national and transnational, international and subnational, aggressive and peaceful, liberal and authoritarian, there is a serious question of whether it can be effectively governed and thereby facilitate movement to a more sane and orderly world. To be sure, the disparate collectivities in the state-centric and multi-centric worlds have in common that all of them sustain rule systems that range across the concerns of their members and that constitute the boundaries of their SOAs.[21] Clearly, however, this commonality may not be sufficient to allow for progress toward effective governance. The challenge is to insure that fragmegrative dynamics do not rupture evolving mobius forms of governance among two or more of the actors. The challenge is not easily met, as the tensions between integrative and fragmenting tendencies continually pose the possibility of rupture.

Put differently, there is no lack of either variety or number in the extant systems of governance. It is difficult to overestimate how crowded the global stage has become as the world undergoes a multiplication of all kinds of governance, from formal to multilevel governments, from formally sanctioned entities such as arbitration boards to informal SOAs, from emergent supranational entities such as the European Union to emergent issue regimes, from regional bodies to international governmental organizations (IGOs), from transnational corporations to neighborhood associations, from humanitarian groups to ad hoc coalitions, from certifying agencies to social movements, and so on across an ever-widening array of activities and concerns.

Of course, notwithstanding the increasing difficulty of generating compliance posed by the world's greater complexity, not every fragmegrative situation on the global agenda lacks governance. Some mobius webs are harmoniously structured and capable of resisting rupture. There are innumerable situations involving localizing responses to globalizing stimuli that are marked by a high, or at least an acceptable, quality of governance and that thus need not be of concern here. The vast proliferation of rule systems in recent decades includes a trend to devolve governance so that its steering mechanisms are closer to those who experience its policies. This trend is most conspicuously marked by the evolution of what has been called "multilevel" governance, a form of rule system in which authority is voluntarily and legally dispersed among the various levels of community where problems are located and local needs require attention. The European Union exemplifies multilevel governance, as does Scotland, Wales, the French provinces, US welfare programs, and many other federal systems in which previously centralized authority has been redistributed to provincial and municipal rule systems. Such systems are not lacking in tensions and conflicts, but relatively speaking the quality of governance is such that the tensions do not lead to violence, the loss of life, the deterioration of social cohesion, or the degradation of people. In short, in and of itself no fragmegrative process is inherently negative or destructive.

For all kinds of reasons, however, numerous fragmegrative situations are fragile, deleterious, violence-prone, and marked by publics who resent, reject, or otherwise resist the intrusion of global values, policies, actors, or institutions into their local affairs. It is these situations that pose the main problems for GG. To be sure, some of the global intrusions can be, depending on one's values, welcomed and applauded. The world's intrusion into the apartheid rule system, for example, was clearly worthwhile. But in a large number of cases – in those where fragmegrative situations involve local reactions to globalizing dynamics that result in internal fighting, external aggression, intensified crime, repressed minorities, exacerbated cleavages, sealed boundaries, glorified but exclusionary ideals, pervasive corruption, and many other patterns that run counter to human dignity and well-being – corrective steering mechanisms that upgrade the quality of governance seem urgently needed.

Part of the problem of achieving governance over deleterious fragmegrative situations, of course, is that often they require the use of external force against local authorities, a practice that has long been contrary to international law and only lately undergone revision, most notably with respect to Kosovo. But international military interventions into domestic arenas are only one part – and a small one at that – of the challenge of establishing rule systems for unwanted fragmegrative conditions. There are many situations in which organized violence is not the response to globalizing dynamics but which are nonetheless woefully lacking in appropriate steering mechanisms and thus in need of enlightened rule systems. The list of such circumstances is seemingly endless: they can involve situations in which boundaries are sealed, minorities silenced, crime tolerated, majorities deceived, societies ruptured, law flouted, tyrants enhanced, corruption ignored, oppositions jailed, people trafficked, pollution accepted, elections rigged, and thought controlled – to cite only the more conspicuous practices that are often protected by the conventions of sovereignty and that one would like to see subjected to a modicum of effective and humane mechanisms of GG. The thwarted aspirations of the Falun Gong, the people of Burma, the women of Afghanistan, and the recurring wars and pervasive poverty in Africa are only among the more conspicuous of many examples of continuing fragmegrative situations that elude efforts toward steerage in enlightened directions.

Nor are the protections of sovereignty the only hindrance to decent GG. Mobius governance on a global scale is also difficult because the globalizing and localizing interactions often occur across both cultures and issue-areas. For instance, while national governments can address – though not necessarily alleviate – the fears of their workers over the loss of jobs resulting from foreign trade with relative ease because they have some jurisdiction over both the well-being of their workers and the contents of trade regulation, the global scale of fragmegrative dynamics can also involve situations in which the parties to them are not located in the same jurisdiction, with the result that any attempt to steer them must be undertaken by diverse authorities that often have different interests and goals. Indeed, not infrequently a globalizing political or economic stimulus can provoke localizing cultural reactions far removed from the country, region, or issue-area in which the stimuli were generated; contrariwise, local events such as protest marches, coups d'état, or severe economic downturns, can have widespread consequences in distant places. The rapid spread of currency crises, for example, often seems ungovernable because authority for coping with the crises is so widely dispersed in this issue-area and because much of the action takes place beyond the reach of any extant governments, in cyberspace. Put more strongly, the processes of imitative, emulative, and isomorphic spread, as well as those that are direct and not circuitous, are so pervasive and powerful that developing steering mechanisms that prevent, or at least minimize their unwanted consequences, seems a staggering task under the best of circumstances.

Leadership

Some analysts contend that the dangers of rupture and disarray are not as great as they may seem, that tendencies in these directions are held in check – and in some cases reversed – by the leadership of the United States as the dominant actor in the post-Cold War arrangement of world politics. Frequently referred to as "hegemonic stability" a "unipolar structure," or an emergent empire the dominance of the United States and the democratic values it espouses is conceived to be a form of global governance. It is a conception that presumes the capabilities of the US are so unrivaled that it can generate the compliance necessary to preserve stability on a global scale even as it promotes human rights, democracy, and open markets. As I see it, such an approach is misguided. Not only does it ignore the reluctance of the American people to play an active role in the processes of global governance – a reluctance which takes the form of not paying in full its dues to the United Nations or otherwise not participating in numerous international rule systems to which most countries have agreed – but even more important it is a perspective that takes no account of the large degree to which authority is undergoing disaggregation. If the preceding analysis is correct that the global stage is ever more crowded with SOAs capable of independently pursuing their goals, then obviously hegemonic leadership can neither flourish nor endure. Much as many people in the US, ordinary citizens as well as leaders, might prefer to pursue unilateral policies, in most situations the country is forced to work within and through multilateral institutions and, in so doing, it often has to accept modification of its goals. And when it does not accept any modifications, when it proceeds unilaterally, its policies tend to flail aimlessly at best, or fail at worst. The world is simply too interdependent, and authority is too dispersed, for any one country to command the global scene as fully as empires once did.

Conclusions

To a large degree conclusions reached on the potential of GG depend on one's temperament – on whether one pessimistically stresses the disarray inherent in weakened states or optimistically focuses on humankind's capacities for innovation and adaptation. Although basically an optimist, I am inclined to offer some pessimistic inferences followed by a couple of upbeat observations that may offset at least some of the downbeat interpretations. My bleak assessment of the prospects for GG derives from the crazy-quilt nature of global structures and processes, along with the failure to conceptually allow for them. For processes founded on effective authority that inches the world toward sanity, a wide variety of numerous actors, both individuals and collectivities, have to be coordinated and their differences at least minimally subordinated to the interests of their great grandchildren. More than that, given the boundary-spanning nature of fragmegrative dynamics, all concerned have to recognize that people everywhere have an interest in your great grandchildren as well as their own.

The chances of such mobius webs being fashioned as effective rule systems seem very slim indeed. Too many actors can intrude ruptures in the webs. Whether they are corporate executives who sacrifice the well-being of future generations for the sake of immediate profits, states that pursue economic goals at the expense of sustainable environments, sovereignty-protective officials who are oblivious to the great grandchildren of publics other than their own, NGOs that put their narrow interests ahead of collective policies, the United States that withdraws from treaties, individuals whose corrupt practices undermine efforts to hasten economic development, or bureaucrats and analysts mired in conceptual confusion who do not fully appreciate the numerous local foundations of global structures – to mention only a few of the ways in which the diverse actors on the global stage can divert movement toward a sane world – the coordination needed to implement GG seems unlikely to surmount the disaggregated authority structures on which GG rests.

This is not to suggest that GG accords all actors a veto over the pace of reform and progress. Rather, it is to highlight the extraordinary complexity and barriers that confront efforts to move a world marked by highly disaggregated SOAs in meaningful and desired directions.

Nor is it to suggest that no progress toward effective GG lies ahead. In the environmental field, for example, there has already been a proliferation of environmental regimes: "fourteen different global environmental agreements [were] concluded in the rather short period between 1985 and 1997,"[22] though, to be sure, the record of compliance with these treaties has been, at best, spotty. Equally relevant, there is no lack of good, knowledgeable leaders and activists who expend a lot of energy on behalf of decent goals. Pockets of progress will thus doubtless occur as some countries, corporations, and NGOs sign on to constructive rule systems designed to advance GG as the skill and organizational revolutions lead to public pressures on recalcitrant collectivities. One observer expresses the difficulty of coming to a conclusion on whether progress or decline lie ahead by asking an upbeat question and then offering a downbeat answer relative to the environment:

> Is the world witnessing the beginning of such a phase shift [toward GG] in the antiglobalization protests, in the unprecedented initiatives undertaken by both private corporations and local communities, in the growth of NGOs and their innovations, in scientists speaking up and speaking out, and in the outpouring of environmental initiatives by the religious community? We must certainly hope so. The alarms sounded 20 years ago have not been heeded, and soon it will be too late to prevent an appalling deterioration of the natural world.[23]

My own view is that, on balance, the dynamics that underlie the disaggregated character of GG seem likely to thwart movement toward a viable and worldwide coherence. It was neither an accident nor pervasive malevolence that prevented earlier treaty commitments from being implemented. The pervasive inaction appears, rather, to be inherent in the structural constraints and conceptual blocks that currently prevail in the global system.

Yet, I am inclined to cling to my inveterate optimism by noting three aspects of an upbeat answer that may prove operative if one is willing to look beyond the immediate present. In the first place, more than a little truth attaches to the aphorism that there is safety in numbers. That is, the more pluralistic and crowded the global stage gets with SOAs and their diverse steering mechanisms, the less can any one of them, or any coalition of them, dominate the course of events and the more will all of them have to be sensitive to how sheer numbers limit their influence. Every rule system, in other words, will be hemmed in by all the others, thus conducing to a growing awareness of the virtues of cooperation and the need to contain the worst effects of deleterious fragmegration.

Second, there is a consciousness of and intelligence about the processes of globalization that is spreading widely to every corner of the earth. What has been designated as "reflexivity"[24] and what I call "the globalization of globalization" (see Chapter 8) is accelerating at an extraordinary rate – from the ivory towers of academe to the halls of government, from the conference rooms of corporations to the peasant homes of China (where the impact of the WTO is an intense preoccupation), people in all walks of life have begun to appreciate their interdependence with others as time and distance shrink. For some, maybe even many, the rush into a globalized world may be regrettable, but few are unaware that they live in a time of change and thus there is likely to be a growing understanding of the necessity to confront the challenges of fragmegration and of being open to new ways of meeting them. Put more positively, and as indicated earlier, an endlessly explosive literature on globalization reflects substantial evidence that good minds in government, academe, journalism, and the business community in all parts of the world are turning, each in their own way, to the task of addressing the questions raised above. It is difficult to recall another period of history when so many thoughtful people concentrated their talents on the human condition from a worldwide perspective.

Third, the advent of networks and the flow of horizontal communications has brought many more people into one or another aspect of the ongoing dialogue. The conditions for the emergence of a series of global consensuses never existed to quite the extent they do today. The skills of individuals and the orientations of the organizations they support are increasingly conducive to convergence around shared values. To be sure, the battle of Seattle and subsequent skirmishes between advocates and critics of globalization – quintessential instances of fragmegration – point to a polarization around two competing consensuses, but aside from those moments when their conflicts turn violent, the very competition between the opposing camps highlights a potential for dialogue that may lead to compromises and syntheses. Already there are signs that their critics have arrested the attention of international institutions such as the World Bank, the World Economic Forum, the WTO, and the IMF and that they are pondering the challenges posed by the growing gap between rich and poor people and nations.

Perhaps these conflicting downbeat and upbeat conclusions are another way of saying the future hangs in the balance. Still unforeseen events and trends will determine how the balance tips.

16 Change, complexity, and governance in globalizing space[1]

> Now that we have a global world with global institutions, the question of institutional reform takes on a larger meaning. We know very little and understand next to nothing about "globalization." All we have so far is slogans and anecdotes. But we do know that the supra-national question is alarming from the point of view of democratic theory. We have these bodies that are not accountable to anybody, anywhere. This is the sort of thing we are going to be thinking about.[2]

Well, yes and no. Yes, the world is globalizing and yes, the lack of accountability at the global level is alarming; but no, our knowledge of globalization is not inconspicuous. And yes, the question of institutional reform is urgent; but no, our comprehension is not confined to slogans and anecdotes. Before the question of institutional reform can be faced, however, the challenges globalization poses for democratic governance need to be identified and the variety of ways in which the challenges are addressed need to be clarified. Such is the purpose of this inquiry. I am less interested in suggesting institutional reforms than in clarifying the problems reformers will have to confront. I assume that the tasks of reformers will be greatly eased if the obstacles they must surmount are better understood.

The limits of IR theorizing

Comprehension of these matters is not easily developed. The dynamics of globalization are complex and the pace of change renders them all the more elusive. And for a variety of reasons, only some of which are noted below, political scientists in the United States who probe the subfield of international relations (IR), unlike many (though not all) counterparts elsewhere in the world, tend either to ignore the dynamics of globalization or to treat them as secondary to the behavior of states. Consequently, they are for the most part ill-equipped to focus on the forces and dialectics of change and complexity through which globalizing processes unfold. Rather, often unwilling to acknowledge the diverse ways in which the authority and power of states have been undermined by the transforming and de-territorializing processes wrought by globalization, the IR mainstream tends to focus on the activities of governments and, in so doing, to investigate the sources of war as the central interstate phenomenon or otherwise to posit states as rational actors and presume that their choices underlie the continued viability of the international system and its ability to maintain control over the pace and direction of change. Whether they adhere to realist or liberal theory, IR scholars are thus disinclined to attach relevance to restless publics, to ignore the deleterious potential of income disparities and poverty conditions, to assess the consequences of dynamic microelectronic technologies, or to allow for the possibility that nongovernmental actors shoulder some of the crucial tasks of governance – to mention only a few of the glaring gaps in IR studies.[3] Thus it is not far-fetched to observe that the concepts of change, complexity, and dialectics lie beyond the concern of numerous IR scholars, that such concepts do not pervade their literature, formulations, or footnotes.[4] It is as if constancy and not change is the world's primary pattern, as if history knows no breakpoints, no reorganization of the values and priorities through which peoples ponder their circumstances, frame their aspirations, and conduct their lives.

Not surprisingly, it follows that most IR scholars have not developed broad-gauged approaches to the concept of governance, much less schema and data linked to theories of governance. Persuaded that the world is anarchical in the sense that it is dominated by sovereign states who answer to no higher authority, most practitioners in the field are disposed not to posit authority as located outside the reach of states and their international system. For them governance in global-ized space tends to connote world government, an arrangement that they dismiss as so naive and far-fetched that they seem unable to envision the possibility of governance outside the domestic realm. Consequently, most IR practitioners view governance as what governments do, whereas transnational processes and actors tend to be seen as relevant only as they make inputs into the work of governments. To be sure, theories about international organizations and regimes mark the IR literature, but such actors are seen as engaging in cooperation rather than govern-ance, in cooperative acts to which authority may be attached but which can also be withdrawn if states so wish. Thus, convinced that the only authority that exists in the international realm is possessed or delegated by states and that it can readily be retrieved by states, a vast majority of IR scholars have had no need to develop or use the concept of governance in the analysis of world affairs.[5] For them "a new world order" would rest not on processes of governance but on little more than a realignment of the pecking order among states. Hence, they tend to scoff at the notion that a global civil society may eventually emerge as the basis for global governance.[6]

On the other hand, if one proceeds from a perspective that allows for govern-ance occurring apart from what governments do, governance can be conceived as systems of rule, as the purposive activities of any collectivity that sustain mechan-isms designed to insure its safety, prosperity, coherence, stability, and continu-ance.[7] Governments specialize in such mechanisms, but they are also found in a variety of other types of collectivities, from states that form issue regimes to crime syndicates that circumvent national boundaries, from groups who seek to promote a new world order to those concerned with particular issue-areas, from formal international organizations or informal coalitions of the willing that intervene to prevent or end domestic violence to debt-rating agencies that monitor financial markets, from nongovernmental organizations (NGOs) that highlight the failings of governments to social movements that launch protests against corporate practices, from organized ethnic groups to corporations, from nonprofit associations to epistemic communities, from economic zones to professional societies, and so on across the vast array of organizations that people form to protect their interests and enhance their well being. It is possible, in short, to conceive of governance without government.[8]

The focus here on global governance is not in any way to imply a concern with some form of world government. Quite the contrary, I too assume that the prospects for a world government in the foreseeable future are nil, but at the same time I conceive of governance as occurring on a global scale in the sense that there are worldwide problems – e.g. environmental pollution, currency crises, corruption, AIDS, terrorism, mass migrations, and the drug trade – crying out for amelioration and that while these problems cannot be addressed by states alone or by a single agency of governance, they will be confronted piecemeal and incrementally by diverse types of collectivities. In other words, governance occurs on a global scale through both the coordination of states and the activities of a vast array of rule systems that exercise authority in the pursuit of goals and that function outside national jurisdictions. Some of the systems are formalized, many consist essentially of informal structures, and some are still largely inchoate, but taken together they cumulate to governance on a global scale.

In short, my conception of global governance is a broad one. The analysis focuses on governance in – and not of – the world. It posits authority on a global scale as highly disaggregated, as dispersed across a densely populated globalized space in which territoriality has been supplemented – and in some instances replaced – by autonomy as a pillar of governance processes. As indicated, it is a formulation that encompasses a variety of rule systems that frame their goals, accumulate their authority, generate their resources, recruit their personnel, and mobilize their followers through diverse procedures across every sphere of human endeavor in every part of the world.

Stated differently, I treat the world not as national and international arenas, but as a globalized space – a space that is not disaggregated in terms of specified geographic territories so much as it consists of a wide range of fast-moving, boundary-spanning actors whose activities cascade erratically across amorphous ethnoscapes, mediascapes, ideoscapes, technoscapes, and financescapes.[9] For the foreseeable future, therefore, I view this disaggregated system of diverse transnational collectivities as a multi-centric world that competes, cooperates, or otherwise interacts with the state-centric world and, as such, constitutes the new world order, an order that is so decentralized that it does not lend itself either to hierarchy or coordination under hegemonic leadership.[10]

The dynamics of change and complexity

Whatever level and forms of governance analysts seek to clarify, they must confront two underlying forces at work in human affairs: one is the dynamics of change and the other concerns the ever greater complexity that the changes are fostering. Whether it involves a local community, a national state, a developing society, a geographic region, or the global system, comprehension of the goals, processes, and institutions of governance cannot be advanced unless they are assessed in a transformative context marked by increasingly complex actions and interactions among public and private organizations. This is no easy task inasmuch as governance, however defined, is centrally concerned with the management of change and the reduction of complexity.

And the task is made all the more difficult by the ambiguities and controversies that surround the concepts of change and complexity. Not only has the literature of political science yet to focus on the concepts in any meaningful or consensual way, but their relevance has been subjected to serious challenges. Some observers, for example, contend that key changes in the world have come to an end and settled into predictable regularities, just as others argue that the presence of complexity has been exaggerated and that simplicity is the more dominant characteristic of the human condition.

If governance is about the maintenance of collective order, the achievement of collective goals, and the collective processes of rule through which order and goals are sought – as the ensuing inquiry presumes – then analysts need to be clear about their use of the concepts of change and complexity before proceeding to explore the substantive problems posed by governance. It matters, for example, whether one views the transformations that underlay and accompanied the end of the Cold War as continuing to unfold or as having settled into routinized arrangements. As one observer put it with respect to eastern Europe,

> . . . barring some sort of extraordinary, and probably violent, upheaval, the time of fundamental change is substantially over: further developments will take place in environments that are essentially democratic and capitalistic. The societies may become more or less efficient, humane, responsive, productive, corrupt, civil, or effective, but these changes probably will have to come about within (or despite) the present political and economic framework, not through further fundamental institutional transformation. In consequence, it may be sensible now to decrease the talk of "transition" and to put a quiet, dignified end to the new field of transitology.[11]

Likewise, substantial analytic consequences follow from whether one regards the pervasive processes of globalization as heightening the interdependence of peoples, economies, and societies and thus deepening the complexity of modern life, or whether the course of events is seen as increasingly founded on a bumper-sticker logic. In the words of another analyst, it may be erroneous to conceive of the present era as one of unparalleled complexity because

We live in an age of sound bites, from voice mail and E-mail to television advertising and news stories. Complex business and government issues – from workplace reorganization to the megacity – are throttled down to a catchy slogan, symbol, mission statement or stereotype in order to be communicated to, and be accepted by, an ill-informed but information-besieged citizenry. We succumb to fads and false messiahs, eroding our faith in our leaders and our very system of government.[12]

As previously implied, the pages that follow derive from unequivocal premises that reject these quoted observations. Stated most succinctly, the degrees of change and complexity unfolding throughout the world are considered to be so great as to lie beyond our full comprehension. Indeed, not only is the age of transitology conceived to be far from over, but it seems likely that only decades from now will the extent of the present transformations be clearly discernible. More than that, the numerous and diverse changes are seen to be adding to the complexities with which communities and societies must contend. Whether or not linearity was ever the central tendency of human affairs, it is now clear that we live in a nonlinear world in which causes and effects are so inextricably intertwined as to underlie central tendencies consisting of feedback loops, contradictory patterns, anomalous developments, and punctuated equilibria.

A qualification of these premises is in order: the links between change and constancy and between complexity and simplicity are seen as dialectic processes, with the dynamics of change fostering impulses to cling to the constants and with the advances of complexity generating aspirations to simplicity. There are, in other words, times and places when inertia and continuities prevail and when bumper sticker logic seems compelling, but such reversions are regarded not as new patterns, but as reactions against the ever greater changes and complexities. Stasis and simplicity feed off change and complexity, but it is the latter that are the dominant dynamics. Where they are taking the world is not at all evident, but it is clear that they enormously complicate the tasks of governance.

Inasmuch as whole chapters and books have been written on the subjects of change, complexity, and the dialectic processes they encompass, this is not the place to elaborate at length on the conceptual nuances that attach to each of the three.[13] Yet, as the foregoing discussion suggests, the concepts are sufficiently controversial to require at least a brief delineation of how they are used in the ensuing analysis. Much of the controversy stems, I have long been convinced, from temperamental differences among analysts that cannot be bridged no matter how extensive and compelling a conceptual formulation may be. These temperamental differences underlie our paradigmatic orientations and are thus central to our intellectual stances. Where one observer sees change, another sees the recurrence of age-old patterns; where one discerns complex processes, another discerns regression toward a long-standing mean; where one perceives the operation of a dialectic, another perceives independent processes. These fundamental temperamental differences can readily be cast in terms of governance issues: where one analyst cites evidence of the emergence of new institutions, another demonstrates that the evidence merely reflects the adaptation of old institutions; where one treats governments as paralyzed by the growing complexity of globalized societies, another points to the stalemates as products of classic bureaucratic in-fighting; where one regards globalizing and localizing dynamics inextricably linked in deep dialectic processes, another presumes that localization derives from cultural origins unique to those who share a common locale.

The recognition of these inherently unbridgeable differences, however, cannot serve as an excuse for using the concepts loosely. Rather, misunderstanding is best minimized through clarity as to how change, complexity, and their dialectic links are conceived to underlie governance on a global level. The temperament of readers may differ from my own, but at least they will be able to evaluate what follows in the context of explicit premises.

Dialectic processes

It is in the nature of change and complexity that neither unfolds in a linear way. Rather, as already indicated, both evolve along paths marked by reversals, sideward movements, feedback loops, and a variety of other nonlinear dynamics that make it difficult to both practice and trace the exercise of governance. Perhaps most notable in this regard are the worldwide tensions that derive from the simultaneity of dynamics promoting integration, centralization, and globalization on the one hand, and those generating disintegration, decentralization, and localization on the other hand. Not only do the two sets of dynamics unfold simultaneously, but they are also causally linked, with increments of the one often giving rise to increments of the other. The tensions thereby created strike me as so essential that they define the fragmegrative era into which the world is moving as it leaves the post-Cold War era behind.

Fragmegrative dynamics derive their impetus from the many process of globalization that have come to mark the course of events. Localizing and fragmenting reactions to globalization may often seem in the ascendancy in the politics of particular locales, and there may well be periods of time when localizing forces predominate on a global scale, but in the long run it is the globalizing dynamics that are presumed to underlie the nature and processes of change as they erode the capabilities of states, undermine the meaning of territory, and collapse the distances that separate peoples, economies, cultures, and societies.

Change

Whether they result from slow, evolutionary processes or sharp historical breakpoints, the changes of concern here are those which involve differences in kind, rather than in degree, compared to previous decades.[14] The distinction between the two kinds of change are conceived to reflect huge differences in the number, scale, scope, and rapidity through which the affairs of collectivities are conducted and with respect to which governance must contend. Where the differences along these dimensions are regarded as huge and unmistakable, transformative changes in kind are deemed to have taken place. Lesser shifts along these dimensions – differences in degree – may eventually cumulate to differences in kind, but until they do the tasks of governance can be carried out in familiar ways. It is the differences in kind that pose the most severe challenges to those responsible for governance as well as to those who seek to develop adequate theories of governance on a global scale.

For present purposes, four differences in kind require notation. One concerns the structures that sustain the structures of global politics; another involves the structures of the globalized world economy, the third focuses on the time frame within which events and trends unfold, and the fourth pertains to what I call the skill revolution and its consequences for collective action. The first of these differences has been well summarized by David Held:

> [T]here is a fundamental difference between, on the one hand, the develop-
> ment of particular trade routes, and the global reach of nineteenth-century
> empires, and, on the other hand, an international order involving the con-
> juncture of a global system of production and exchange which is beyond the
> control of any single nation-state (even of the most powerful); extensive net-
> works of transnational interaction and communication which transcend
> national societies and evade most forms of national regulation; the power
> and activities of a vast array of international regimes and organizations,
> many of which reduce the scope for action of even leading states; and the
> internationalization of security structures which limit the scope for the
> independent use of military force by states. While in the eighteenth and
> nineteenth centuries trade routes and empires linked distant populations
> together through quite simple networks of interaction, the contemporary
> global order is defined by multiple systems of transaction and coordination
> which link people, communities and societies in highly complex ways and
> which, given the nature of modern communications, virtually annihilate
> territorial boundaries as barriers to socio-economic activity and relations,
> and create new political uncertainties.[15]

As for the structure of the global economy, the differences have been argued in terms of whether it consists of an "extension of the modern international econ-omy into somewhat unfamiliar territory or a systemic transformation which entails both changes in quantity (breadth and depth) and quality, defining new structures and new modes of financing." Having identified this basis for addressing the kind-or-degree question, Kobrin has no difficulty answering it:

> [W]e are in the midst of a qualitative transformation of the international
> world economy. Our argument is based on three related propositions. First,
> dramatic increases in the scale of technology in many industries – in its cost,
> risk and complexity – have rendered even the largest national markets too
> small to be meaningful economic units; they are no longer the "principal
> entities" of the world economy. National markets are fused transnationally

rather than linked across borders. Second, the recent explosion of trans-national strategic alliances is a manifestation of a fundamental change in the mode of organization of international economic transactions from markets and/or hierarchies (i.e. trade and MNEs) to *post-modern* global networks. Last, and related to the second point, the emerging global economy is inte-grated through information systems and information technology rather than hierarchical organizational structures.[16]

Thirdly, the elapse of time in the current period is distinguished by processes of aggregation and disaggregation that are occurring and interacting so rapidly – more often than not instantaneously to the point of being simultaneous – that this difference can readily be viewed as one of kind rather than of degree. One need only compare the dynamics of organizational decision-making, societal mobiliza-tion, and inter-societal relationships in the present and previous eras to appreciate that the differences are not trivial, that they are so substantial as to be far more than merely updated repetitions of earlier patterns. Or, to use a more specific example, a comparison of the collapse of the Roman empire across centuries and of the British empire across decades with that of the Soviet empire across weeks and months will highlight how modern technologies have fostered differences in kind rather than degree.[17]

The fourth set of changes involve a change in the skill level of citizens every-where in the world. As elaborated at length elsewhere, people are considered to have become so much more adept at both emotionally and analytically locating themselves in world affairs than earlier generations that their capacities for collect-ive action amount to a difference in kind than simply one of degree.[18] The implications of this skill revolution for the conduct of public affairs are enormous, highlighting as they do the greater obstacles and opportunities involved in mobil-izing public support by those charged with the responsibilities of governance. No longer can leaders rely on the unthinking compliance of their followers when they engage in governance. In effect, traditional criteria of legitimacy have given way to performance criteria, a transformation that can significantly alter the balance of forces that sustain the dynamics of governance.

Complexity

Faced with all these differences in kind, world affairs today are conceived to be ever more complex. They have never been simple, of course, but the extent of their complexity has reached a point where political analysts are increasingly attentive to a growing body of literature known as "complexity theory."[19] A sum-mary of the essentials of complexity theory can be found in Chapter 13 of Volume I of this collection. In brief, four features of the theory stand out as offering especially useful insights into world affairs even as they also highlight enormous challenges to modern governance at all levels that analysts cannot ignore. First, such systems co-evolve with their environments as they adapt;[20] second, being adaptive, they are able to self-organize into an orderly whole and, as they do, they begin to acquire new attributes (what complexity theorists call "emergent properties"); third, their complexity is such that they are vulnerable to small events resulting in large outcomes (the so-called "butterfly effect"); and fourth, slight changes in their initial conditions can lead to very different outcomes.

Unique challenges to IR theorizing

Although rapid change and great complexity are dynamics with which governance at every level of human organization must contend, the challenges they pose for students of IR are arguably more acute and puzzling than for those who focus on local, urban, regional, and national communities. Why? Because the whole world and its far-reaching globalizing processes defines the theoretical scope and serves as the data base for inquiry, thus compelling the investigator to focus on tasks of governance that perforce must span diverse cultures, confront contradictory authority structures, and cope with interaction patterns in which some actors cling to narrow jurisdictional boundaries while others have long since abandoned notions of territoriality. To assess governance on a global scale is to search for collective order and movement toward collective goals among both firmly bounded polities and transnational entities whose activities are not limited by geographic boundaries.

More than that, since authority in a globalized world is highly decentralized and exercised by a wide variety of collectivities, the processes of governance are necessarily more vulnerable to the dynamics of change and complexity than is the case for formally established local, urban, regional, and national governments. Global politics, in other words, are likely to be more susceptible to the power of small events and the distortive potential of initial conditions than are local or domestic politics.[21] An election, a recession, or a coup d'état can redirect a polity, but the onset and outcomes of such events are more readily anticipated than is case when an embassy is seized, a currency collapses, a migration surges, an Okinawan school girl is raped by American soldiers, or a Philippine maid is hanged at the order of a Singaporean court. Controls are in place with which to address the domestic events, but their absence is often conspicuous insofar as governance in globalized space is concerned.

Indeed, in some instances the unexpected cascades precipitated by a small event can career out of control erratically across months and years. Consider, for instance, the cascades that followed the shooting down of the airplane carrying the president of Rwanda in 1994:

> The Rwandan leader was a Hutu, and his death set off the Hutu massacre of Tutsi in Rwanda. A subsequent Tutsi takeover in Rwanda led to an exodus of more than a million Hutu into Zaire. And it was partly to hound these refugees, and to stop Hutu attacks on Rwanda and Burundi from Zairian territory, that the Tutsi-led Government in Rwanda lent critical support to the Zairian rebellion that is now about to topple Mr. Mobuto.[22]

Control over market forces provides another insightful illustration of the large difference between the exercise of controls in domestic and globalized space. A number of interdependence issues – e.g. migration, monetary flows, and drug trafficking – are driven by supply and demand, by the actions of millions of discrete individuals which, when summed, can pose substantial problems that endlessly criss-cross established national boundaries and thus exacerbate the tasks of rule systems. Market forces within countries can be regulated with relative ease, but the demand of huge numbers of people for drugs, for jobs or safety across borders, and for foreign currencies, along with the supplies that these demands evoke, are not readily controlled by states. Consequently, the persistence of such patterns as global challenges configure analytic problems that most subfields of political science never need confront. For students of governance on a global scale, however, these varied market forces are unavoidable. Analysts are compelled to trace and assess whatever rule systems, if any, may be operative as mechanisms of governance when the flows of people, money, or drugs reach crisis proportions.

Of course, not all interdependence issues are founded on the laws of supply and demand. Environmental pollution, human rights, terrorism, and crime are no less boundary-spanning and no less resistant to regulation, but their roots lie not so much in the dynamics of the workplace as in normative concerns. These norm-driven interdependence issues are so potentially capable of causing individual and societal damage that, like migration, currency crises and the drug trade, their governance is necessarily preoccupying for students of world affairs. Unlike the supply-and-demand issues, however, those deriving from global norms are relatively subject to controls because those who violate the norms are relatively few in number and their identity is readily identifiable. Indeed, each norm-driven issue has become the focus of a large literature that focuses on the clash between the resistance to regulation and the various control mechanisms that NGOs, international regimes, the United Nations, and subnational groups have evolved to overcome the resistance.[23] In two of these issue areas – the environment and human rights – moderate records of successful governance have been recorded, whereas the resistances to control are still dominant with respect to transnational crime and terrorism, and in all of the areas there remains much to be done if the normative concerns are to be fully met.

The variability of control mechanisms suggests another, equally crucial reason why the tasks of IR analysts are considerably more difficult than those facing their non-IR counterparts. The distinction can be summarized as a difference in pattern recognition. National and subnational spaces, while no less subject to the dynamics of change and complexity than globalized space, are nonetheless pervaded with recognizable and long-standing patterns. They encompass patterns marked by authority structures that are in place rather than in flux, by deep-seated habits of compliance, by well-worn techniques for mobilizing support, and by established mechanisms for insuring that officials are accountable. To be sure, the patterns that sustain national and subnational processes are not so firmly rooted as to be immune to the dynamics at work in globalized space; and it is also the case, as previously noted, that the demarcation between domestic and foreign affairs has become increasingly porous; but relative to globalized space, the patterns through which governance is sustained in national and subnational spaces are clearly discernible and tied to easily traced territorial boundaries. In globalized space, however, discernible patterns are still very much in formation. The changes initiated by the acceleration of globalization in the last several decades have yet to settle into apparent regularities, thus leaving IR specialists with the difficult challenge of seeking to grasp unfamiliar patterns and elusive structures.

Finally, and relatedly, IR analysts are at a disadvantage relative to their non-IR colleagues because of a bewildering array of agents whose actions are consequential for the course of events. The identities of the relevant actors in other subfields of political science present no analytic problems. They are governments and the groups and parties that seek to affect the policies of the officials, bureaucracies, legislatures, or courts that act on behalf of governments. To be sure, both the governments and the groups seeking to affect their policies divide into supporters and adversaries in ways that may sometimes obscure the loci of control, but such factional obscurities are models of clarity compared to those created by the agents vying for control in globalized space. In the absence of any centralized authorities that can serve as focal points around which conflicting actors can converge, students of IR must not only confront diverse collectivities, but they are also endlessly faced with the perplexing problem of how to classify the various agents so that their conduct can be cogently analyzed and explained. There is no established actor typology around which the IR subfield has formed a widely shared consensus. Rather, a multiplicity of collectivities varyingly and contradictorily serve to organize inquiry.

Furthermore, although the need for more adequate classsificatory schemes has been fully appreciated,[24] most efforts at classifying actors tend to slip back into framing categories that reflect the very distinction the new typologies are intended to avoid, namely, the distinction between states and their intergovernmental organizations (IGOs) on the one hand and all types of NGOs on the other hand. Not only does the NGO category embrace numerous unalike organizations, but it also privileges states by being a residual category for any agent that is not a state. No matter that the boundary between foreign and domestic affairs is porous and eroding. No matter that states are increasingly unable to exercise control over increasing numbers of complex and change dynamics unfolding in globalized space. No matter that a wide variety of rule systems have evolved in globalized space independently of the interstate system. Such developments tend to be downplayed, if not ignored, by the unremitting tendency to differentiate between states and an amorphous cluster of agents grouped together as NGOs.

The tendency to cluster and classify in this way is, of course, not surprising. In the absence of an agreed upon nomenclature for all the diversity that marks the agents occupying one or another part of globalized space, it is perhaps natural to fall-back on an overly simple dichotomy. Consider, for example, the challenge of framing a more elaborate and viable typology for the following: states;

insurgents ("aspiring states"); warring factions ("failed states"); diasporas; terrorists (state-, insurgent-, and crime-sponsored); nonprofit interest groups such as political parties, unions, and religious organizations; IGOs; domestic political and administrative entities (DGOs?); firms and corporations; crime and drug syndicates; nonprofit advocacy groups; for-profit service groups such as media organizations; transnational regimes comprised of both public and private participants; donor communities; coalitions of the willing; civil associations; business alliances; and private voluntary organizations (PVOs).[25]

If governance on a global scale involves the norms and practices that constrain and empower social, economic, and political entities engaged in collective behavior in globalized space, then all of these agents – and many more too numerous to list here[26] – need to be sorted out. IR analysts have yet to take on this task not only because of their state–nonstate orientations, but also because none among us has been able to frame a theory of globalized space amenable to the generation of an appropriate actor typology. Obviously, an understanding of governance on a global scale is bound to be hampered until it yields an incisive conception of the agents that sustain it.

While change and complexity dynamics render the challenges confronting students of IR especially difficult, none of the foregoing is to suggest that globalized space is a jungle, an arena in which collectivities compete so ferociously for influence, market shares, or mere survival that the result is an unrestrained free-for-all. Conflict is a recurrent pattern, but complexity theory tells us that there are other, equally important patterns through which conflicts get ameliorated. That is, while the collectivities in globalized space are not responsive to a common authority, they all are complex adaptive systems, which means that they tend to adjust to each other in ways that allow for movement toward their respective goals and to co-evolve as the movement occurs. Thus has it become commonplace and acceptable for competitive multinational corporations to form alliances[27] even though in earlier times they would have been condemned for engaging in collusion. Thus has it become customary for nonprofit transnational organizations with, say, similar environmental or human rights concerns to join together to press for progress on their issues.[28] And thus, too, have states and their international organization joined with humanitarian agencies to form coalitions of the willing to intervene in collapsed societies such as Albania, Rwanda, or El Salvador.[29] Viewed from the perspective of complexity theory, arrangements such as these are not as ad hoc as they may seem. Rather they reflect the shared need to address common problems in the absence of higher authorities. More than that, since globalized space is a dense and still uncharted political landscape, it is hardly surprising that innovative mechanisms for developing rule systems have become so pronounced in so many different fields of endeavor. Authority remains highly disaggregated in globalized space, but it is by no means in sheer disarray; rather, it has congealed in a variety of ways and in disparate locales.

Governance in globalized space

How, then, to comprehend the order and disorder, the stabilities and instabilities, that mark world affairs? Given the pervasive changes, the deepening complexities, the perplexing dialectics, and the innumerable collectivities that sustain the dynamics of fragmegration, how do we go about constructing viable theoretical perspectives that will infuse meaning into the course of events? And, to revert to the opening epigraph, how do we begin to lay the bases for thinking creatively about institutional reforms which can reduce the lack of transparency and democratic deficit that mark so many collectivities in globalized space?

Full responses to these questions require more time and space than is available, but a few lines of theoretical development are plainly suggested by the foregoing analysis. First and foremost perhaps, it seems clear that we need to abandon the long-standing and conventional approaches to IR that locate states at the analytic epicenter of our inquiries. States remain important agents of both change and constancy in world affairs, but so many new collectivities and structures have emerged as equally important that keeping states exclusively at the epicenter tends to blind us to the underlying forces and processes that sustain the evolution of global politics. Put differently, while states continue to be vital and active participants at the core of public affairs, they are no longer the only actors who initiate and dominate the cascades which radiate out from the epicenter.

Second, theory needs to be developed that treats globalized space as the locale of the epicenter, as a vast arena composed of actors and processes that are not limited by territorial boundaries or sovereign rights, as a bifurcated system composed of both state-centric and multi-centric worlds. But how to approach this emergent space in a systematic way that can trace its underlying patterns? The answer lies in the concept of governance. We need to place rule systems at the heart of our theoretical formulations. By doing so, we will not be confined to the world of states and will be empowered to explore issues and processes in terms of the way in which authority is created and control is exercised wherever such dynamics are operative. A governance perspective will enable us to identify the challenges embedded in globalization and its corollary, localization, and to be sensitive to the fragmegrative dialectics whereby globalizing and localizing forces are inextricably linked.

Third, it follows that a governance perspective necessitates an elaboration of the concept of authority in such a way that it is not confined to vertical hierarchical structures in which subordinates comply with the directives of superiors. Rather, allowance must be made for authority that is embedded in horizontal networks and nongovernmental collectivities.

Fourth, if globalized space is as heterogeneous as it appears to be, innovative ways of theorizing about accountability are needed. The democratic deficit that marks the multi-centric world needs to be approached in terms of rule systems that are not constrained by the domestic–foreign dichotomy. Having already touched on the changing relevance of states, the nature of globalized space, and the concept of governance, let us conclude by looking briefly at the third and fourth of these theoretical necessities.

The creation and implementation of authority structures

At the core of rule systems are authority structures that enable them to generate compliance on the part of persons and organizations in their domains. Often collectivities establish their authority structures through a legal enactment, be it a constitution, a law, a court decision, by-laws, or any other authority-granting mechanism that conveys legitimacy upon the roles or offices occupied by the authorities. But the key to the effectiveness of an authority structure does not lie in its formal documents. It is to be found, rather, in the readiness of those toward whom authority is directed to comply with the rules and policies promulgated by the authorities. Formal authority is vacuous if it does not evoke compliance, whereas informal authority not backed by formal documentation can be stable and effective if its exercise produces compliance. This is especially so for rule systems in the multi-centric world where hierarchy is less important than non-linear feedback processes as the basis for coherence among those who make and implement decisions. Where hierarchy is minimal, as is the case for numerous collectivities in globalized space, compliance derives more from shared aspirations and cooperative practices than from felt obligations or coercive threats that foster an unthinking acceptance of directives.

In short, authority structures are essentially and profoundly relational in character. The recurrent patterns that sustain them are continuously fashioned by the interactions between the holders and the targets of authority. The more habitual the participation of the latter in authority relationships, of course, the stronger and the more enduring is the structure likely to be. Contrariwise, the more the authorities fail to adhere to minimal performance criteria of legitimacy, the more are the targets likely to question and challenge the authorities and thus the less viable will be their compliance habits and the greater will be the fragility and vulnerability of the structured relationship. Put differently, any authority structure derives from underlying (and often unrecognized) bargaining processes between those who preside over it and those who are subject to its directives.

Authority structures can thus be viewed as located on a compliance–defiance continuum in which at the compliance extreme the relational patterns that link authorities to their followers are recurrent and stable, while at the defiance extreme the performance of the authorities and/or the consent of their followers is problematic and unstable. The more a particular authority structure moves toward the defiance extreme, and the longer its patterns of interaction are ensconced in unstable circumstances, the more is the existence of such a structure jeopardized.

Conceiving of authority structures in a compliance–defiance context serves well the task of tracing authority in globalized space. For it is a conception that can be applied equally to states and to collectivities in globalized space as diverse as crime syndicates, financial markets, nonprofit organizations, multinational corporations, coalitions of the willing, issue regimes, and so on. In the case of sovereign states, most possess both the formal and informal authority that enables them to compel compliance in their domains, but in the case of some states authority is fragile as developments undermine the habitual readiness of their citizens to comply. Likewise, the collectivities active in globalized space are located at various points along the compliance–defiance continuum, with a few (such as the European Union) having successfully created both formal and informal authority that can be effectively exercised, while some (such as Greenpeace) have evolved informal authority that evokes compliance on the part of their members and still others (such as crime syndicates) that are located more toward the defiance extreme of the continuum insofar as the reliability of their members is concerned. In short, wherever collectivities persist in globalized space, they have authority structures that enable them to mobilize and give direction to their memberships on behalf of their policies.

It should be emphasized that since the authority of most of the collectivities in globalized space derives from informal rather than formal sources, the nature of their capacity to evoke compliance can vary substantially. For some collectivities – say, epistemic environmental communities or credit-rating agencies – their capacity to evoke compliance is rooted in knowledge that appears to be so authoritative that defying it entails undue risks.[30] Consider, for example, this assessment of one credit-rating agency:

> Moody's is the credit rating agency that signals the electronic herd of global investors where to plunk down their money, by telling them which countries' bonds are blue-chip and which are junk. That makes Moody's one powerful agency. In fact, you could almost say that we live again in a two-superpower world. There is the US and there is Moody's. The US can destroy a country by leveling it with bombs; Moody's can destroy a country by downgrading its bonds.[31]

For other collectivities – such as coalitions of the willing that intervene in the domestic affairs of collapsing countries – their authority derives from the moral imperatives and self-interest claims that are served by coalescing for humanitarian purposes.[32] For still others – such as NGOs and social movements held together by common ideals – their authority derives from a shared recognition that goals can only be achieved through cohesive policies and collective actions.[33] Then there are many profit-making corporations wherein authority tends to be hierarchically arrayed and chief executive officers accorded the right to make final decisions that shape their organizations and frame policy directions; on the other hand, there are also increasing numbers of corporations that have decentralized their authority structures to the point where networks serve as the channels through which compliance flows (see below).

Networks

As a consequence of the Internet and other products of the microelectronic revolution as well as the requirements imposed by the rapidity of change on social movements, transnational corporations, business alliances, and a host of other collectivities that need to adapt to fast-moving situations, horizontal networks have become increasingly salient as organizational forms endowed with authority that can be effectively exercised in ways that appear to defy conventional notions about hierarchical sources of control. The story of Visa International's evolution as a company without central authority or a pyramidal structure is illustrative in this regard. The company has expanded its operations and profits enormously in the last thirty years and has done so by eschewing conventional organizational arrangements in favor of loose networks that maintain standards and cooperative practices without resort to top-down directives. Nor does it rely on bottom-up procedures. Rather horizontality has become its operative mode of conduct, with authority being embedded in the informal rules through which its networks conduct their affairs.[34] In effect, networks have taken on the nature of rule systems. And Visa International is now being replicated in a variety of lines of endeavor.[35] "A group of fishermen and environmentalists in New England, an association of community colleges, and the National 4-H Council are all looking into changing their organizations to be, well, disorganized."[36]

And where is the authority located in networks? As the chief scientist of a major computer company, Sun Microsystems, put it, "Your e-mail flow determines whether you're really part of the organization," that is, "The people who get the most messages and who participate in the most important exchanges are the people [in the organization] with the most power, regardless of what the official chart may say."[37]

When it is appreciated that the world is experiencing an organizational explosion[38] that, in turn, is proliferating networks as major organizational structures, and when these developments are viewed as prime consequences of the rapidity of the fragmegrative dynamics that sustain globalization, it becomes clear that students of IR will have to rethink their grasp of the nature of the authority and the relevance of hierarchy in the conduct of world affairs.[39] And it won't be easy. We are so accustomed to thinking in terms of pyramidal organizations with clear lines of command, that it may be very difficult to adjust our conceptual perspectives to a world in which systems rule in the absence of conventional mechanisms for exercising authority.[40]

The accountability deficit

Notwithstanding the important ways NGOs have created authority for themselves and thereby served as a check on the activities of states as well as each other, most collectivities in globalized space are not accountable for their actions in the sense required by even a minimalist theory of democratic governance. Indeed, from this perspective the prevailing practices whereby authority is exercised is "alarming" (to quote the foregoing epigraph). Quite aside from the fact that international organizations are responsible to their states rather than to publics, the lack of accountability is conspicuous. Many NGOs do not expose their decision-making processes to their members or maintain procedures for electing their leaders. Some do not even have members. And for many, especially multinational corporations, the electoral procedures they do maintain are largely ritualistic formalities in the sense that stockholders are too numerous and too unorganized for their votes to have any consequence.

Yet, it can be misleading to treat the domestic analogy of open and representative procedures as a minimalist theory applicable to globalized space. The theoretical need is to focus on functional equivalents of domestic procedures, and in this respect the present circumstances, while surely a matter worthy of intense concern, may not be as alarming as they seem at first glance. In the first place, there is at least one NGO – Transparency International (TI) – that seeks to expose and contest the widespread corruption that undermines governments and corporations as well as fosters alienation among citizenries. Its programs have been extensive, ranging from the formation of more than fifty-eight national TI chapters to the publication and wide distribution of an annual Corruption Perception Index to support for international anticorruption conferences.[41] Uninhibited by the constraints that limit the anticorruption efforts of governments, TI has increasingly acquired an authoritative voice in this arena of globalized space. It can even be regarded as a nascent rule system in the sense that its activities and publicity have exposed corruptive practices in all parts of the world.

Secondly, the very dynamics of fragmegration have embedded within them one major functional equivalent of democracy. By decentralizing authority in disparate and localized sites, fragmegration has greatly inhibited the coalescence of hierarchical and autocratic centers of powers. It is as if the politics of globalized space, through having both integrative and fragmented components, mimics the global market with its shifting loci of limited decision-making authority and its subservience to macro tides of inflation, currency swings, and productivity breakthroughs.[42] In globalized space no collectivity can exercise extensive control over people and policies outside their own limited jurisdictions. To be sure, many collectivities still maintain authoritarian structures in which individual's rights are denied. And certainly it is the case that numerous transnational corporations still cling to hierarchical forms of organization and make decisions without concern for whether they disempower people or do ecological harm.[43] It was estimated, for example, that the number of transnational corporations exceeded 35,000 and that, in turn, these had over 200,000 subsidiaries.[44] While these figures indicate that sizable areas of global life rest on a form of governance that lacks democratic accountability, they also suggest that the dispersal of authority in globalized space is so widespread that severe violations of democratic values cannot be readily concentrated in hegemonic hands.

Moreover, in some cases public pressure and boycotts do get corporations to alter their practices;[45] and in the case of South Africa, the disinvestment campaign against corporations contributed to the abandonment of apartheid.[46]

Equally important, some NGOs and social movements do exert pressure in globalized space for greater transparency and access on the part of hierarchical organizations, pressures that are in some respects functional equivalents of the various electoral, legislative, and journalistic checks that sustain a modicum of democracy in territorial polities. Indeed, some NGOs face the danger of too much democracy, of multiple accountabilities – " 'downward' to their partners, beneficiaries, staff, and supporters; and 'upward' to their trustees, donors, and host governments"[47] – that foster indecisive policy making and stalemate. Put differently, just as markets are not democratic in their functioning, and just as they are impervious to any damage they may do, so are they not systematic in any harm they cause, all of which can also be said about the fragmegrative dynamics that underlie the disaggregation of globalized space.

Although a stretch of the imagination is required to appreciate its functional equivalency, the widespread growth of the Internet, the World Wide Web, and the other electronic technologies that are shrinking the world offers considerable potential as a source of democracy to the extent wiring for such technologies is available. More accurately, by facilitating the continued proliferation of networks that know no boundaries, these technologies have introduced a horizontal dimension to the politics of globalized space. They enable like-minded people in distant places to converge, share perspectives, protest abuses, provide information, and mobilize resources – dynamics that seem bound to constrain the vertical structures that sustain governments, corporations, and any other hierarchical organizations. As one observer put it, "Anyone with a modem is potentially a global pamphleteer,"[48] while another admitted finding "electrons more fascinating than elections."[49] In other words, since these technologies have the potential "of bringing information directly into our homes any time we want it," they could render

> political institutions (*all institutions*) . . . far less important. . . . Computers could displace schools, offices, newspapers, scheduled television and banks . . . Government's regulatory functions could weaken, or vanish. It's already a cinch on the Internet to get around the rules; censorship, telecommunications restrictions and patent laws are easily evaded.[50]

Nor can it be argued that this line of reasoning is misguided because the computer is available only to a relatively small stratum of the world's population. To be sure, huge numbers of people still do not have access to computer networks, but this circumstance seems likely to undergo alteration as "[c]omputers keep getting faster, cheaper, and smaller."[51] Indeed, the decline in the cost of computer equipment is matched only by the acceleration of its power to process information: "The number of components that engineers could squeeze onto a microchip has doubled every year since 1959, [with the result that [t]wenty years from now, a computer will do in 30 seconds what one of today's computers takes a year to do."[52] Accordingly, it is hardly surprising – to cite but two of myriad examples – that geographically remote Mongolia is now wired into the Internet[53] and that its use is spreading so rapidly in China that the Internet "can be accessed in 700 cities via local dial-up calls."[54]

In short, as it continues to decentralize into a "pluralism of authorities,"[55] the multi-centric world of diverse nongovernmental actors is increasingly pervaded with checks and balances. These constraints are not formalized as they are in territorial polities, and they operate unevenly in various segments of the multi-centric world, but more often than not they tend to inhibit unrestrained exercises of power and to subject unfair or criminal practices to the glare of publicity. The lack of accountability remains an alarming problem – even TI does not focus on the transparency of NGOs – but at the same time it can be said that nascent forms of democratic governance can be discerned in the labyrinths of globalized space.

Conclusion

In sum, the contradictions and dialectics of today's world need to be taken far more seriously than they have been if the challenges of governance on a global scale are to be rendered more comprehensible. The complexity and pervasiveness of cascading sequences of interaction that spill across national and issue boundaries need theoretical attention rather than being dismissed as too erratic to be understood. Governance of these sequences may prove to be minimal as they run their course, but a deeper understanding of their dynamics as complex adaptive systems will surely enhance the prospects for coping with the new circumstances created when the cascades begin to peter out.

In addition, given the variability of authority structures in globalized space, it follows that attempts to achieve governance over worldwide problems are likely to be piecemeal and partial. Coordination among rule systems does occur, but more often than not the differences in authority structures, and especially the scarcity of central authorities with whom agreements can be made, limit the extent to which collectivities can concert their efforts. On the other hand, since complex adaptive systems tend to acquire emergent properties, it may just be that at least some collectivities will be able to converge around common endeavors.

But to recognize the obstacles to governance on a global scale is not to say that the concept of governance lacks utility and is no more useful than a state-centric perspective. Quite to the contrary, by focusing on the presence of rule systems wherever and however they may come into being, the concept of governance provides an opportunity for discerning trendlines indicative of whether the dynamics of change and complexity are leading the world along paths that may culminate in greater degrees of order or whether they are fostering ever wider pockets of disorder.

17 Strong demand, huge supply

Governance in an emergent epoch[1]

In a world where groups, organizations, and countries are simultaneously fragmenting and integrating, where the two contrary forces are pervasive, interactive, and feed on each other, are the resulting tensions subject to governance? If the deaths of time, distance, and sequentiality are taken seriously, can they operate as stimuli to a renewal of creative thought about what governance may mean in the twenty-first century? Can multi-level governance serve as a prime mechanism to steer the tensions in constructive directions? Except for qualifying the "multi-level" concept, the ensuing paper answers these questions in the affirmative and addresses them in the context of continuing processes that are disaggregating authority, rendering traditional boundaries increasingly obsolete, and fostering strong and widespread demands for governance.

To understand the extensive demands for governance one needs to appreciate the distinction between governance and government. Both governance and government consist of rule systems, of steering mechanisms through which authority is exercised in order to enable the governed to preserve their coherence and move toward desired goals. The rule systems of governments can be thought of as structures, as institutions for addressing diverse issues that confront the people within their purview. Governance, on the other hand, "is a broader concept . . . [that involves] a collective act encompassing the ability to create and maintain the delicate balance necessary to act, process, and govern through, for, and with the needs and voices of [a membership or constituency]."[2] Thus governance consists of rule systems that perform or implement social functions or processes in a variety of ways at different times and places (or even at the same time) by a wide variety of organizations. Unlike governments, governance is not obliged to range across a wide variety of issues; often it does, but there are many governance processes that are single-issue in scope.[3]

To govern, whether as structure or function, is to exercise authority. To have authority is to be recognized as having the right to govern, to issuing directives or requests that are heeded by those to whom they are addressed. Rule systems acquire authority in a variety of ways. These range from steering mechanisms that are structures endowed with authority through constitutions, by-laws, and other formally adopted instruments of rule to those that are processes informally created through repeated practices that are regarded as authoritative even though they may not be constitutionally sanctioned. Both the formal and informal rule systems consist of what I call "spheres of authority" (SOA)[4] that define the range of their capacity to generate compliance on the part of those persons toward whom their directives are issued. Compliance is the key to ascertaining the presence of an SOA.

Viewed in terms of their compliance-generating capacities, the steering mechanisms that undertake governance may be just as effective (or ineffective) as those of governments. While governments generate compliance through formal prerogatives such as sovereignty and constitutional legitimacy, the effectiveness of governance rule systems derives from traditional norms and habits, informal agreements, shared premises, and a host of other practices that lead people to comply with their directives. Thus, as the demand for governance increases with the proliferation of complex interdependencies, rule systems can be found in nongovernmental organizations, corporations, professional societies, business associations, advocacy groups, and many other types of collectivities that are not considered to be governments.

It follows that world affairs can be conceptualized as governed through a bifurcated system – what can be called the two worlds of world politics – one a system of states and their national governments that has long dominated the course of events and the other a multi-centric system of diverse types of other collectivities that have lately emerged as rival sources of authority that sometimes cooperate with, often compete with, and endlessly interact with the state-centric system.[5] Viewed in the context of proliferating centers of authority, the global stage is thus dense with actors, large and small, formal and informal, economic and social, political and cultural, national and transnational, international and subnational, aggressive and peaceful, liberal and authoritarian, who collectively form a highly complex system of governance on a global scale.

Does the advent of a bifurcated system imply that states are in a process of disintegration? Not at all. Doubtless the interstate system will continue to be central to world affairs for decades and centuries to come. To stress that collectivities other than states have emerged as important SOAs is not in any way to suggest that states are headed for demise. Analysts differ over the degree to which the national state has been weakened by the dynamics of present-day transformations, but few contend that the weakening amounts to a trend line that will culminate in total collapse. States are still among the main players on the global stage, but they are no longer the only main players. Many of them are ensconced in paralyzing authority crises that inhibit their governing capacities. This is not to refer to those states plagued with internal wars (e.g. Colombia) or to rioting protesters in the streets of national capitals. Some do experience such moments on occasion (e.g. Yugoslavia or the Philippines), but more often than not authority crises involve stalemate, an inability to frame, implement, and realize goals, an avoidance of decisions that would at least address the challenges posed by a world undergoing vast and continuous changes. Many governments, from Russia to Israel, from Peru to China, from the Congo to Indonesia, from the United States to Belgium, are riven by deep divisions and thus often have difficulty raising taxes, preserving societal harmony, ameliorating deep-seated conflicts, expanding their economies, recruiting or retaining members of their armed forces, or otherwise maintaining a level of compliance that sustains their effectiveness. Despite their difficulties, however, most states still control their banking systems and maintain legitimate monopoly over the use of force. Yes, states have undergone transformation into managerial entities and are thus still able to exercise a measure of control over the course of events. And yes, the aspiration to statehood is still shared widely in many parts of the world. But for all its continuing authority and legitimacy, key dimensions of the power of the modern state have undergone considerable diminution. In the words of one analyst, "As wealth and power are increasingly generated by private transactions that take place across the borders of states rather than within them, it has become harder to sustain the image of states as the preeminent actors at the global level."[6]

While present-day demands for both government and governance are extensive in the bifurcated system, they differ in one key respect. The demands for government are qualitative, while those for governance are quantitative as well as qualitative. People throughout the world are restless and unhappy over the quality of their governments, cynical about – and often alienated from – the effectiveness and integrity of the procedures whereby governments frame and implement their policies. Except in those rare cases where statehood is sought, their demands are not for more governments; rather they want their governmental rule systems to be less corrupt, more streamlined, more ready to serve their needs. Indeed, in those instances where classical economic policies have come to prevail, some of the demands are for a diminution of government, for less intrusiveness in the market place and other routines of daily life.

The demands for governance, on the other hand, are also quantitative: innumerable rule systems are sought where none existed before because steering mechanisms have not previously operated to perform the desired social processes. Only recently, for example, an International Accounting Standards Board was created to coordinate what previously had been unregulated practices by diverse accounting firms.[7] As will be seen, this is only one example of literally millions that could be cited. It is the vast proliferation of SOAs in the multi-centric world that underlies the conception of our emergent epoch as marked by both a strong demand for and a huge supply of governance.

The sources of strong demands

There are several compelling reasons why the demand for governance is so strong and pervasive. One is essentially normative: we live in a messy world. There are far too many people who survive on or below the poverty line. There are far too many societies paralyzed by division. There is too much violence within and between countries. In many places there is too little water and too many overly populated, pollution-ridden cities. And, most conspicuously, there is all too little effective governance capable of ameliorating, if not resolving, these and numerous other problems that crowd high on the global agenda. Stated even more forcefully,

Global warming is getting worse. The destitute countries of Africa are becoming poorer and more disease-ridden. The digital gap between the wired "haves" and the unwired "have-nots" is growing. . . . Not only are the problems getting worse, but it's increasingly clear that the mechanisms traditionally advanced for solving them won't work. Environmental treaties, multilateral organizations, UN agencies – none of them stands a prayer.[8]

Hardly less troubling, the demands for governance are accompanied by a generational lack: even the most thoughtful analysts today are short of the orientations necessary to sound assessments of how the authority of governance can be brought to bear on the challenges posed by the prevailing disarray. Wendt provides a succinct statement of this limitation:

So dominant in contemporary consciousness is the assumption that authority must be centralized that scholars are just beginning to grapple with how decentralized authority might be understood. . . . [T]he question of how to think about a world that is becoming "domesticated" but not centralized, about a world after "anarchy," is one of the most important questions today facing not only students of international relations but of political theory as well.[9]

A second source of the swelling demands for governance derives from the extent to which the emergent epoch has unleashed simultaneous, diverse, and contradictory forces that can be summarized in the clash between globalization, centralization, and integration on the one hand and localization, decentralization, and fragmentation on the other. The clashes between these forces – what I call "fragmegration" in order to capture the intricate links between the polarities[10] – underlie the many huge challenges to humankind's capacity to lessen the messiness unfolding throughout the world and to meet the intensifying demands for new and relevant forms of governance that can exercise authority over the proliferating fragmegrative dynamics. Indeed, one way to understand any issue on governance agendas is to assess it through fragmegrative lenses and trace how the local and global forces that interactively sustain it both generate and complicate the need for new and more extensive governance.

Another source of the demands for more governance stems from the aforementioned changing capacities of states. Beset by the acceleration of fragmegrative dynamics and committed to neoliberal economic policies that highlight the centrality of markets, states are less and less able to control the flows of goods, money, pollution, people, ideas, drugs, and crime across their borders. And most important for present purposes, the lessened ability to control the course of societal and international life has reduced the capacity of governments to keep abreast of the proliferating SOAs and to cope with the new and myriad social functions to which the multiplying interdependencies of the fragmegrative epoch is heir. It could well be said that the burgeoning demands for governance bear an inverse relationship to the competence of governments.

Still another reason for the mushrooming of demands for governance concerns the ever-greater interdependence and complexity that new electronic and transportation technologies have induced and that marks the emergent epoch. What happens in one part of the world can now have consequences in remote places, thus leading to the rapid shrinking of time and distance and to what has been called a relationship revolution.[11] Today people are so fully and frequently in contact with like-minded others – and their interests so fully and frequently overlap – as to engage in organization-building and networking processes that call for at least a modicum of governance.[12] The relationship revolution is founded on an organizational explosion that is staggering in its scope. In all parts of the world and at every level of community people – ordinary folk as well as elites and activists – are coming together to concert their efforts on behalf of shared needs and goals. In addition, SOAs proliferate because increasingly people are capable of shouldering and managing multiple identities that lessen their allegiance to their states. As they get involved in more and more networks in the multi-centric world, so may their loyalties fractionate and become issue- and object-specific.

Exact statistics on the extent of the organizational explosion do not exist (largely because so much of it occurs at local levels and goes unreported), but few would argue with the proposition that the pace at which new associations are formed and old ones enlarged is enormous, so much so that to call it an explosion is almost to understate the scale of growth. It has been calculated, for example, that Indonesia had only one independent environmental organization twenty years ago, whereas now there are more than 2,000 linked to an environmental network based in Jakarta. Likewise, registered nonprofit organizations in the Philippines grew from 18,000 to 58,000 between 1989 and 1996; in Slovakia the figure went from a handful in the 1980s to more than 10,000 today; and in the US 70 percent of the nonprofit organizations – not counting religious groups and private foundations – filing tax returns with the Treasury Department are less than thirty years old and a third are less than fifteen years old.[13]

The link between the organizational explosion and the relationship revolution is easily explained by the shifting balance between hierarchical and network forms of organization, between vertical and horizontal flows of authority. Greatly facilitated by the Internet, people now converge electronically as equals, or at least not as superiors and subordinates. They make plans, recruit members, mobilize support, raise money, debate issues, frame agendas, and undertake collective action that amount to steering mechanisms founded on horizontal rather than hierarchical channels of authority. Indeed, it has been argued, with reason, that

> The rise of network forms of organization – particularly "all channel networks," in which every node can communicate with every other node – is one of the single most important effects of the information revolution for all realms: political, economic, social, and military. It means that power is migrating to small, nonstate actors who can organize into sprawling networks more readily than can traditionally hierarchical nation-state actors. It means that conflicts will increasingly be waged by "networks," rather than by

"hierarchies." It means that whoever masters the network form stands to gain major advantages in the new epoch.[14]

In other words, not only has the advent of network forms of organization under-mined the authority of states, but in the context of our concern with increasing demands for governance, it has also had even more important consequences. Most notably, networks have contributed to the disaggregation of authority as well as the formation of new collectivities not founded on hierarchical principles.

If the notion that new rule systems can be founded on horizontal as well as vertical structures of authority seems awkward, it warrants reiterating that the core of effective authority lies in the compliance of those toward whom it is directed. If people ignore, avoid, or otherwise do not heed the compliance sought by "the" authorities, then it can be said that for all practical purposes the latter are authorities in name only, that their authority is more fiction than fact. In short, as noted in Chapter 11, authority is profoundly relational. It links – or fails to do so, or does so somewhat – those who issue directives and those for whom the direct-ives are intended. Stated more elaborately, authority needs to be treated as a continuum wherein at one extreme full compliance is evoked and at the other extreme it is not. The viability of all collectivities can be assessed by ascertaining where they are located on the continuum. The closer they are to the compliance extreme, the greater will be their viability and effectiveness, just as the nearer they are to the noncompliance extreme, the greater is the likelihood that they will be ineffective and falter. Accordingly, it becomes possible to conceive of collectivities held together through horizontal flows of authority – exercised through either face-to-face or electronic messages that initiate bargaining and culminate in com-pliance resulting from negotiated requests rather than authorized directives[15] – and it is precisely the possibility of nonhierarchical authority that underlies the bifurcation of global structures into state- and multi-centric worlds, the prolifer-ation of SOAs, the growing relevance of NGOs, and the widespread demands for governance.

In sum, reinforced by the collapse of time and distance, the weaknesses of states, the vast movements of people, the proliferation of networks, and the ever-greater complexities of modern life, the question of how to infuse a modicum of order, a measure of effective authority and governance into the course of events looms as increasingly urgent. It is being asked within and among states as well as within and among associations and organizations at every level of community and in every walk of life as fragmegrative tensions intensify and as citizens and leaders alike ponder how to better govern their affairs in the face of transformative dynamics that are often bewildering and seemingly out of control.

Much of the bewilderment derives from the fast-paced dynamics of fragmegra-tion. As suggested by linking, in a single phrase, the interactions between world-wide forces pressing for fragmentation and those exerting pressure for integration, fragmegrative dynamics are pervaded with contradictions and tensions. They tug people and institutions in opposite directions, often forcing choices between localizing or globalizing goals. Indeed, it is almost as if every increment of fragmentation gives rise to an increment of integration, and vice versa. This pervasiveness of fragmegrative dynamics is readily traceable in a wide variety of situations, from cultural sensitivities to inroads from abroad to fears of jobs lost through the lowering of trade barriers, from linguistic distortions fostered by the Internet to environmental degradation generated by expanded productive facilities, and so on across all the situations that mark our transformative epoch. To repeat, there is considerable clarity to be had in viewing all the issues of modern life through fragmegrative lenses.

The consequences of strong demands

In view of the foregoing analysis, it is hardly surprising that the major consequence of the unceasing demands for more governance is a vast disaggregation of authority. At every level of community and in every issue-area that comprises their agendas SOAs have come into being, some highly effective and some only nascent in their ability to evoke compliance, but altogether the world's population of SOAs is so great as to render the global stage extremely crowded and dense. Indeed, it is difficult to underestimate how crowded the global stage has become as the world undergoes a multiplication of all kinds of governance, from centralized to multi-level governments, from formally sanctioned entities such as arbitration boards to informal SOAs, from emergent supranational entities such as the European Union to emergent issue regimes, from regional bodies to international governmental organizations (IGOs), from transnational corporations to neighborhood associations, from humanitarian groups to ad hoc coalitions, from certifying agencies to social movements, from truth commissions to private regulatory agencies, and so on across an ever-widening array of activities and concerns.

In short, the strong demand for governance has been and is being met. The supply of governance has been huge. But has the supply been adequate? Is the quality of disaggregated governance and proliferating SOAs sufficient for the needs of a fragmegrative epoch? Is the balance of supply and demand different for governance than it is in the market place? Is there a possibility that our messy world will become increasingly messier? Or is there reason to hope that the sheer number of SOAs will foster a trend toward coherence through multi-level governance within and among states and within and among organizations and associations in the diverse walks of life that comprise the private worlds of people? Does the bifurcation of global structures and processes contain the seeds of a sane and decent adaptation to our fragmegrative epoch?

Time and space do not permit an attempt to respond to such questions. But raising them has the advantage of more precisely specifying the normative and empirical concerns on which inquiries into governance and governability need to focus. The questions highlight the dangers of conventional analysis and the need for renewal in the ways we think about governance. For it is not a simple matter to grasp governance as congeries of diverse collectivities in the two worlds of world politics, as rooted in a vast array of private as well as public SOAs. Such a perspective requires one to wrench free of the long-standing and unquestioned premise that the boundaries separating countries are firm and impassable without permission of the states that preside over them. It also necessitates straining to overcome the premise that governments are the prime source of governance.

These wrenching tasks are not easily accomplished. Our analytic capacities are rooted in methodological territorialism,[16] in a long-standing, virtually unconscious habit of probing problems in a broad, geographic framework. This habit poses an acute problem because of the ever-growing porosity of domestic–foreign boundaries[17] that has rendered territoriality much less pervasive than it used to be even as all the social sciences continue to construct their inquiries, develop their concepts, formulate their hypotheses, and frame their evidence-gathering procedures in spatial contexts. Nor are officials free to think in alternative contexts: as one analyst put it, "Trapped by the territoriality of their power, policy makers in traditional settings often have little choice but to address the symptoms rather than the causes of public problems."[18]

Yet, breaking out of the conceptual jail imposed by methodological territorialism is imperative because prime characteristics of fragmegration are that its processes readily span foreign–domestic boundaries and that its structures are not confined to governments. Fragmegrative dynamics – the microelectronic technologies that have rendered what used to be remote ever more proximate, the continuing proliferation of networked organizations, the variety of incentives that lead huge numbers of people, everyone from the tourist to the terrorist, to move widely around the world, the globalization of national economies and the neo-liberal economic policies that have enhanced the relevance of markets and the power of multinational corporations, the skill revolution that has everywhere linked people ever more closely to the course of events, and the divisive politics that have fostered authority crises which inhibit many states from framing and implementing goals appropriate to the dilemmas they face[19] – have greatly increased transborder flows and rendered domestic–foreign boundaries ever more porous. With the death of time and distance, subnational organizations and governments that once operated within the confines of national boundaries are now so inextricably connected to far-off parts of the world that the legal and geographic jurisdictions in which they are located matter less and less. What matters, instead, are the spheres of authority to which their members are responsive.

The need to move beyond conventional analysis involves recognizing that the concept of multi-level governance can also be misleading and imprisoning. For all its virtues in capturing the complexities of modern-day governance – and I do not underestimate the clarity and utility inherent in the concept[20] – multi-level governance does not allow for a full analysis of the complexity of the emergent political world. Most notably, its scope does not encompass the diverse array of SOAs that are crowding the global stage. As indicated earlier (Note 3), the notion of multi-levels suggests governmental hierarchies and explicitly posits the various levels as vertically structured in layers of authority, whereas the mushrooming demands for governance are also being met in a host of horizontal ways, through SOAs that may be widely dispersed and not necessarily linked to each other through layered hierarchies. Put differently, many of the demands for governance involve an insistence on autonomy that may or may not be operative within hierarchical structures.

Since governance involves the exercise of authority and the necessity of people looking "up" to, and complying with, the authorities to which they are responsive, it is understandable that the multi-level governance concept connotes hierarchy. But once one broadens one's analytic antennae to encompass networking processes and a variety of dissimilar SOAs, it becomes clear that authority relations have to be reconceived. As noted above, at the very least requests for compliance within effective SOAs have to be treated as exercises of authority in the same way directives and commands are seen as authoritative. "That's not possible," some might say, "behind every request under such circumstances is an appreciation that at some higher level there are authorities who have the ultimate sanctions even if compliance at lower levels is achieved through negotiated requests couched in harmonious language." Such reasoning is as faulty as that which posits sovereignty as dichotomous and does not allow for variation within the extremes of having and not having sovereignty. SOAs can rule through requests if the consensus of those within their realm is extensive. Such an expansion of the authority concept ought not be difficult for those who analyze harmonious multi-level governance phenomena inasmuch as the interlinked and negotiated harmony across the levels reflects a consensual understanding of the responsibilities and obligations of officials at the several levels. Stated differently, "authority cannot always be equated with domination." Rather, it can be

> rational-voluntaristic authority . . . in which fundamentally equal individuals reach collective decisions through rational deliberations that are open to all. . . . [This conception] assumes that the interests of the individuals involved are not ultimately irreconcilable, that the rational process itself can lead to a shared understanding of the coincidence of interests once the latter are properly conceived.[21]

A typological scheme

The vast proliferation of rule systems calls for a sorting out, for typological clarification that will enable us to more clearly trace multi-level governance in the welter of SOAs. While the great number and variety of governance entities suggests parsimonious classification is a daunting task, more than a few analysts have undertaken to develop simplifying typologies. Indeed, the very concept of multi-level governance rests on a typological foundation. Unfortunately, none of the classifying efforts fully breaks with the practice of locating the state at the center of the scheme. Different levels of government and different types of issues, for example, have been offered as typological schemes,[22] but in each case they are amplified in the context of states. In order to account for the diversity, the horizontality, and the sheer number of steering mechanisms in addition to states that now crowd the global stage, here the typological focus is on the structures and processes that sustain the flows of authority, whether they be in the form of commands or requests for compliance.

A six-governance typology

For analytic purposes such a focus points to six general forms of transnational governance. Three of these reflect the complex and extensive nonlinear feedback processes that have accompanied the advent of fragmegration: one can be called "network" governance, another labeled "side-by-side" governance, and still another designated as "mobius-web" governance. These three can, in turn, be distinguished from three other, more straightforward forms that are less complex and more linear and familiar sources of governance: those that can be traced so fully to the cajoling, shaming, noisy pressures, or other activities of NGOs and transnational advocacy groups that the governments of states are, in effect, mere policy ratifiers at the receiving end of the flow of authority (the governance-with-out-government or bottom-up model); those that derive from the downward flow of authority originating within corporations or among national states and their bureaucracies (the governance-by-government or top-down model); and those that stem from the informal horizontal flows whereby economic exchanges occur in the framework of formal regulatory mechanisms (the governance-by-market model).

These six forms of governance come more fully into focus if a key structural attribute of the governance system (the degree to which authority is formally established) and a key process attribute (the degree to which authority flows in vertical or horizontal directions) serve as analytic bases for classifying the various collectivities active on the global stage. More precisely, the structural attribute can usefully be trichotomized, with governance arrangements consisting of (1a) formal, (1b) informal, or (1c) both formal and informal (mixed) structures, while the process attribute can be dichotomized in terms of whether authority flows in a (2a) single direction (up or down) or (2b) multiple directions (both up and down as well as back and forth horizontally). The resulting 3×2 matrix (see Table 17.1) serves to distinguish the six forms of global governance.

Before differentiating more fully among the forms of governance, let us specify the eight types of collectivities that crowd the global stage. These consist of (1) public subnational and national governments founded on hierarchical structures formally adopted in constitutions; (2) for-profit private transnational corporations (TNCs) formally and hierarchically structured by articles of incorporation; (3) international governmental organizations (IGOs) based on formal treaties and charters; (4) subnational and national not-for-profit nongovernmental organizations (NGOs) sustained by either formal by-laws or informal, undocumented arrangements; (5) international or transnational not-for-profit nongovernmental organizations (INGOs) either formally structured as organizations or informally linked together as associations or social movements; and (6) markets that have both formal and informal structures which steer horizontal exchanges between buyers and sellers, producers and consumers. In addition to the variety introduced by different degrees of formal or informal organization, note needs to be taken of

Table 17.1 Six types of governance

		PROCESSES	
		unidirectional *(vertical or horizontal)* *(type of collectivities involved in this form of governance)*	*multidirectional* *(vertical and horizontal)*
S T R U C T U R E S	formal	**Top-Down Governance** *(governments, TNCs, IGOs)*	**Network Governance** *(governments, IGOs, NGOs, INGOs–e.g., business alliances)*
	informal	**Bottom-Up Governance** *(mass publics, NGOs, INGOs)*	**Side-by-Side Governance** *(NGO and INGO, governments)*
	mixed formal and informal	**Market Governance** *(governments, IGOs, elites, markets, mass publics, TNCs)*	**Mobius-Web Governance** *(governments, elites, mass publics, TNCs, IGOs, NGOs, INGOs)*

unorganized (7) elite groups or (8) mass publics that form briefly in response to specific issues and then disband when the issue is settled.

Unlike top-down, bottom-up, and market governance, the other three forms are not marked by processes that flow in essentially one direction. The fourth form (the governance-by-network model) involves bargaining among equal (i.e. nonhierarchical), formally organized collectivities – between governments, within business alliances, or between NGOs and INGOs – that ensues when the impetus for governance stems from common concerns about particular problems. The fifth form (the side-by-side model) arises not out of the noisy pressures, internal deliberations, or horizontal bargaining that respectively mark bottom-up, top-down, or network governance, but out of cooperative interchanges among transnational nongovernmental elites and state officials, interchanges that are so thorough and effective that the distinction between formal and informal inputs breaks down and the two become fully intertwined and indistinguishable. The sixth form (the mobius-web model) occurs when the impetus to steer a course of events derives from networked interactions across levels of aggregation among TNCs, INGOs, NGOs, IGOs, states, elites, and mass publics, interactions that are elaborate and diverse enough to constitute a hybrid structure in which the dynamics of governance are so overlapping among the several levels as to form a singular, web-like process that, like a mobius, neither begins nor culminates at any level or at any point in time.

It is important to reiterate that all six models involve governance and government on a transnational or global scale. One cannot rely upon the literature on state–society relationships to distinguish these models, since this literature focuses on national governance and does not allow for transnational processes and structures of governance that transcend societal and state boundaries. National and subnational actors may be participants in any or all of the six processes, but their participation stems from their interdependence with issues and developments that unfold beyond their national or subnational jurisdictions.

It should also be stressed that while the labels used to designate the different forms of governance are descriptive of hierarchy or its absence, they do not preclude occasional fluctuations and reversals in the patterns of interaction. The labels are shorthand ways of referring to central tendencies, to the nature and essential direction of the paths along which authority and the impetus for govern-ance flows. But they also allow for nuance. Top-down governance, for example, originates mainly within the halls of state governments, but corporations that dominate an industry can also initiate it. The campaign to get Yugoslavia to desist from ethnic cleansing in Kosovo is illustrative in this regard. Both during its diplomatic and military phases, the campaign was sustained exclusively by gov-ernments. To be sure, NATO's efforts were energized and supported by public shock over the scenes of cleansing depicted by the television media, but the origins and impetus for governance in that situation can be traced readily to the authority exercised by governments. On the other hand, bottom-up governance refers to policies that may be ratified by governments but that are propelled and sustained mainly outside the halls of governments. The processes in which governments eventually yielded to pressures from NGOs to approve a land-mine treaty are a quintessential example of bottom-up governance. The setting of standards for commodities and productive processes is no less a striking example of bottom-up governance. Thousands of standards were authorized for thousands of commod-ities and productive processes by autonomous and nongovernmental organizations well before quasi-state bodies became involved in monitoring and implementing the standards.[23] As for market governance, its processes are horizontal in the sense that they involve the day-to-day interactions of traders and investors, and they are both formal and informal in the sense that governments and market officials exercise a modicum of formal regulation over the informal flows of trade and investment. In contrast to the three unidirectional types of governance, the net-work, side-by-side, and mobius-web forms of governance are pervaded with nuance, by interactive and multiple flows of influence in which authority may be exercised horizontally as well as vertically. The three types of governance in the right-hand column of Table 17.1 are too complex and overlapping to justify an essentially unidirectional presumption.

The existence of six discernible and meaningful forms of transnational gov-ernance speaks to the continuing expansion of complexity in the evolving fragmegrative epoch. If the statics of continuity rather than the dynamics of transformation prevailed today, it would be unnecessary to enlarge our analytic antennae beyond the long-standing conceptions in which the boundaries between domestic and foreign affairs are firmly in place and top-down and bottom-up governance serve as the prime means for framing and implementing policies both at home and abroad. As stressed throughout, however, such conceptions are no longer sufficient. More often than not, the global stage is witness to situations unfolding in ways that call for supplementing linear models with models rooted in nonlinear feedback and network processes.

The nonlinearity of network, side-by-side and complex-web governance derives from the nature of the issues that each, respectively, undertakes to resolve. In the case of network governance, it occurs when interactions take place exclusively among formal actors such as states, NGOs, or business alliances (as distinguished from informal aggregations such as social movements) that form feedback loops to address and solve common problems. The 1992 summit meeting on the environment and the parallel and simultaneous, down-the-street meeting of established INGOs and NGOs was marked by extensive feedback loops between leaders at the two meetings – as also occurred at subsequent meetings on human rights, population, habitat, and women's rights – and exemplify network governance in the sense that all the participants who interacted at the meetings held posts in either governmental or nongovernmental organizations.[24]

Side-by-side governance, on the other hand, emerges and is sustained in issue areas where the loci of action are so widely dispersed, unrelated, and situation-specific that neither the relevant governmental officials nor their nongovernmental counterparts can usefully resort to mass mobilization and, instead, must rely on nonconfrontational cooperation to achieve control over the diverse and unrelated situations. The global effort to combat corruption is a classic example in this regard. A major INGO devoted to waging this fight, Transparency International (TI), has self-consciously avoided provoking mass publics and confined its efforts to working closely with the officials of both states and IGOs in the hope of persuading them to adopt anti-corruption policies. The efforts would appear to have been successful: eight years of TI's short life has witnessed the World Bank, the OECD, the International Monetary Fund (IMF), several regional IGOs, and many states formally explicate goals and strategies for reducing corrupt practices within their realms of authority.[25]

In a sense mobius-web governance would seem to amount to a vast elaboration of side-by-side governance. The major difference involves resort to mass mobilization. As noted, such processes are unlikely to occur in side-by-side governance. In the case of mobius-web governance, however, the relevant actors are closely linked and neither widely dispersed nor situation-specific, with the result that the relevant agencies are prone to cross the private–public divide by mobilizing mass publics as well as elites on behalf of the values at stake. The human rights issue-area is illustrative. It encompasses intricate networks of actors at subnational, national, transnational, and international levels who interact in such diverse ways as to render difficult, perhaps even fruitless, any attempt to tease out the direction of causal processes. That is, IGOs and most states tend to yield to the pressures of NGOs and INGOs on issues pertaining to human rights and, in so doing, have cooperatively formed both formal and informal networks through which the spreading norms get translated into mechanisms of governance.[26] Indeed, mobius-web governance may be marked by a cumulative sequencing in which the pressures generated by bottom-up governance give rise to top-down and side-by-side governance that, in turn, becomes a vast network encompassing all levels of governance and diverse flows of authority. Given the ever-greater complexity of our fragmegrative epoch, mobius-web governance may well supersede the other five forms and become the dominant form of governance in the future.[27] Presumably it would also embrace multi-level governance, however that form may be defined.

Admittedly this six-governance typology is complicated and not lacking in overlaps among the types. Given the diversity of new forms of horizontal governance, however, the typology helps bring a modicum of order to the subject even as it highlights the complexity of our fragmegrative epoch. No less important, the typology allows for seemingly similar types of collectivities to be analyzed differently to the extent their structures and processes vary. Indeed, as indicated in Table 17.1, each of the various types of collectivities involved in governance can engage in more than one form of governance if different situations evoke their participation and authority in different ways. In other words, conceived on a global scale, governance is much too convoluted for there to be a perfect fit between the six forms of governance and the eight types of collectivities.

Conclusions

Of course, typologies are only aides to organizing thought. They do not in any way come close to resolving the problems of legitimacy, accountability, transparency, and effectiveness that loom large in the conduct of multi-level governance. Presumably other papers presented at this conference will serve to clarify whether such problems will prove manageable or insurmountable in the long run. To a large degree, however, much depends on one's temperament – on whether one pessimistically stresses the disarray inherent in weakened states or optimistically focuses on humankind's capacities for innovation and adaptation. Will the proliferation of rule systems, the disaggregation of authority, and the greater density of the global stage enhance or diminish the effectiveness of the various systems of governance? While there doubtless will be pockets of ineffectiveness and breakdown, will the emergent system, on balance, make for more humane and sensitive governance? Are the tensions and conflicts fostered by the deleterious aspects of fragmegration likely to prove ungovernable? If it is the case, as previously indicated, that none of the extant governmental mechanisms "stand a prayer" of solving such global problems as environmental degradation, spreading poverty, and a widening digital gap, can a renewal of creative thought yield the outlines of new solutions?

As an optimist, I am inclined to note four aspects of an upbeat response if one is willing to look beyond the immediate present. In the first place, more than a little truth attaches to the aphorism that there is safety in numbers. That is, the more pluralistic and crowded the global stage gets with SOAs and their diverse steering mechanisms, the less can any one of them, or any coalition of them, dominate the course of events and the more will all of them have to be sensitive to how sheer numbers limit their influence. As is the case in multi-level systems of governance, every rule system will be hemmed in by all the others, thus conducing to a growing awareness of the virtues of cooperation and the need to contain the worst effects of deleterious fragmegration.

Second, there is a consciousness of and intelligence about the proliferation of SOAs that is spreading widely to every corner of the earth. What has been designated as "reflexivity"[28] and what I call "the globalization of globalization"[29] is accelerating at an extraordinary rate – from the ivory towers of academe to the halls of government, from the conference rooms of corporations to the peasant homes of China (where the impact of the WTO is an intense preoccupation), people in all walks of life have begun to appreciate their interdependence with others as time and distance shrink. For some, maybe even many, the processes underlying ever-greater complexity may be regrettable, but few are unaware that they live in a time of change and thus there is likely to be a growing understanding of the necessity to confront the challenges of fragmegration and of being open to new ways of meeting them. Put even more positively, an endlessly explosive literature on governance and globalization reflects substantial evidence that good minds in government, academe, journalism, and the business community in all parts of the world are turning, each in their own way, to the task of addressing and constructively answering the questions raised above. It is difficult to recall another period of history when so many thoughtful people concentrated their talents on the human condition from a worldwide perspective.

Third, the advent of networks and the flow of horizontal communications has brought many more people into one or another aspect of the ongoing dialogue. The conditions for the emergence of a series of consensuses within and between societies never existed to quite the extent they do today. The skills of individuals and the orientations of the organizations they support are increasingly conducive to convergence around shared values. To be sure, the battle of Seattle and subsequent skirmishes between advocates and critics of globalization – quintessential instances of fragmegration – point to a polarization around two competing consensuses, but aside from those moments when their conflicts turn violent, the very competition between the opposing camps highlights a potential for dialogue that may lead to compromises and syntheses. There are signs already, for example, that the attention of international institutions such as the World Bank, the World Economic Forum, the WTO, and the IMF has been arrested by the complaints of their critics and that they are pondering the challenges posed by the growing gap between rich and poor people and nations.

Lastly, the aforementioned likelihood that mobius-web governance will become the dominant mode through which rule systems generate compliance in the years ahead points to opportunities for creative solutions to both local and global problems. It is a form of governance that can cope with deepening complexity, that in its lack of chains of command facilitates innovative feedback mechanisms for addressing the deeply entrenched problems that have long resisted solution, that enables the poor and the digitally-deprived to seek redress through horizontal channels, that provides all the diverse actors that crowd the global stage access to governance processes, that allows for coalitions within and among public and private collectivities, and that is rooted in the interdependencies that mark life in our fragmegrative era.

For example, one creative solution to many of the challenges of our time closely resembles the formulation here of mobius-web governance and highlights its potential. It has been proposed by Jean-Francois Rischard, who is vice-president for Europe of the World Bank. He suggests that

> The only models that have a chance in the 21st century will be ones that share the network effects of the New Economy. They'll be coalitions of interested nations, private companies and non-governmental organizations. They'll use online polling to speed their work along. And they'll focus on setting standards or norms – much like the informal bodies that built out the Internet without treaties or legislated rules and regulations.

> Rischard calls them "Global Issues Networks." And he hopes that, over time, they'll issue ratings that measure how well countries and private businesses are doing in meeting specified norms on the environment and other issues that affect the welfare of the planet.

> The process will be quick and non-bureaucratic. The premise will be that if you don't meet the agreed-upon norms, you will be exposed as a rogue player in the global economy.

> Evidence that this approach can work comes from the recent success of the Group of Seven nations against money laundering. All it took was publishing a list of countries that are havens for global criminals – and threatening to blacklist these countries from the process of international financial transfers that runs the global economy. Really, that's all it took! Within six months, some of the most notorious offshore havens had rewritten their laws.[30]

To express a measure of optimism, however, is not to assert that nirvana lies ahead. Surely it does not. Surely fragmegration will be with us for a long time and surely many of its tensions will intensify and disrupt the balance between the strong demand and huge supply that presently sustains the conduct of governance. But the collective will to preserve and use new horizontal forms of authority is not lacking and that is not a trivial conclusion.

Notes

1 Introduction

1 James N. Rosenau, *Distant Proximities: Dynamics Beyond Globalization* (Princeton, NJ: Princeton University Press, 2003), pp. 396–7. For an alternative to a complex approach to the subject, see the simplistic (and erroneous) conception ascribed to thoughtful observers by journalist David Brooks, who either misconstrues or is unfamiliar with the academic literature on global governance when he writes: "The people who talk about global governance begin with the same premises as the world government types: the belief that a world of separate nations, living by the law of the jungle, will inevitably be a violent world. Instead, these people believe, some supra-national authority should be set up to settle international disputes by rule of law" (David Brooks, "Loudly, With a Big Stick," *New York Times*, April 14, 2005, p. A27). I know of no serious scholar who conceives of global governance in these terms.
2 James N. Rosenau, *Distant Proximities: Dynamics Beyond Globalization* (Princeton, NJ: Princeton University Press, 2003), pp. 396–7.

2 The new global order: underpinnings and outcomes

1 This chapter is excerpted from a chapter written for Armand Clesse, Richard Cooper, and Yoshikazu Sakamoto (eds.), *The International System After the Collapse of the East–West Order*, (Dordrecht, The Netherlands: Martinus Nijhoff, 1994), pp. 106–26, and is reprinted here with permission of Brill Academic Publishers.
2 The sources of these six common outcomes are analyzed in James N. Rosenau, "Interdependence and the Simultaneity Puzzle: Notes on the Outbreak of Peace," in C. W. Kegley, Jr. (ed.), *The Long Postwar Peace: Contending Explanations and Projections* (New York: HarperCollins Publishers, 1991), pp. 307–28.
3 Francis Fukuyama, "The End of History?" *National Interest*, No. 16 (Summer 1989), pp. 3–18.
4 John Lukas, "The Short Century – It's Over," *New York Times*, February 17, 1991, sec. 4, p. 13.
5 For a compelling expression of the disappointment that has followed the initial optimism occasioned by the end of the Cold War, see Stanley Kober, "Revolutions Gone Bad," *Foreign Policy*, Vol. 91 (Summer 1993), pp. 63–84.
6 The analysis which concludes that the system's parameters are undergoing their first profound transformation since 1648 can be found in James N. Rosenau, *Turbulence in World Politics: A Theory of Change and Continuity* (Princeton, NJ: Princeton University Press, 1990), Chap. 5.
7 Rosenau, *Turbulence in World Politics*, pp. 10–11. For a formulation that identifies six parameters, see Mark W. Zacher, "The Decaying Pillars of the Wesphalian Temple: Implications for International Order and Governance," in James N. Rosenau and

Ernst-Otto Czempiel (eds.), *Governance Without Government: Order and Change in World Politics* (Cambridge: Cambridge University Press, 1992), Chap. 3.

3 Ominous tensions in a globalizing world

1 From a paper originally presented at the Conference on International Relations, Middle East Technological University, Ankara, Turkey, July 3, 2002.
2 Marcel Larmanou, commenting on the outcome of the vote that propelled Jean-Marie Le Pen into the two-man race for the French presidency. Quoted in Suzanne Daley, "Why Vote for Le Pen? A French Village is Tight-Lipped," *New York Times*, April 25, 2002, p. A3.
3 For an elaboration of this conception of present-day world affairs, see James N. Rosenau, *Distant Proximities: Dynamics Beyond Globalization* (Princeton, NJ: Princeton University Press, 2003).
4 This concept was first developed in James N. Rosenau, " 'Fragmegrative' Challenges to National Security," in Terry Heyns (ed.), *Understanding US Strategy: A Reader* (Washington, DC: National Defense University, 1983), pp. 65–82. For a more recent and elaborate formulation, see James N. Rosenau, *Along the Domestic–Foreign Frontier: Exploring Governance in a Turbulent World* (Cambridge: Cambridge University Press, 1997), Chapter 6.
5 James N. Rosenau, *Turbulence in World Politics: A Theory of Change and Continuity* (Princeton, NJ: Princeton University Press, 1990), Chap. 2.
6 Max Frankel, "Sound of One Saber Rattling," *The New York Times Book Review* (May 26, 2002), p. 16.

4 Aging agendas and ambiguous anomalies: tensions and contradictions of an emergent epoch

1 This chapter was originally published in Stephanie Lawson (ed.), *New Agenda for International Relations* (Cambridge: Polity Press, 2002), pp. 19–34, and is reprinted here with permission of Polity Press.
2 Václav Havel, "Kosovo and the End of the Nation-State," *The New York Review of Books*, Vol. XLVI (June 10, 1999), pp. 4–6.
3 Office of the Press Secretary, "Remarks by President Clinton at University of Chicago Convocation Ceremonies" (June 12, 1999), p. 2 (http://www.whitehouse.gov/WH/New/html/19990612.html).
4 *Ibid.*, p. 1.
5 John Markoff, "Tiniest Circuits Hold Prospect of Explosive Computer Speeds," *New York Times*, July 16, 1999, p. A1.
6 David Bornstein, "A Force Now in the World, Citizens Flex Social Muscle," *New York Times*, July 10, 1999, p. B7.
7 Shashi Tharoor, "The Future of Civil Conflict," *World Policy Journal*, Vol. XVI (Spring 1999), p. 7.
8 Office of the Press Secretary, "Remarks by President Clinton at University of Chicago Convocation Ceremonies," p. 2.
9 John Boli, "*International Nongovernmental Organizations in World Society: Authority Without Power*," a paper presented at the Conference on International Institutions: Global Processes–Domestic Consequences, Duke University, April 9–11, 1999, pp. 1–2.
10 Susan Strange, *The Retreat of the State: The Diffusion of Power in the World Economy* (Cambridge: Cambridge University Press, 1996), p. 5.
11 Manuel Castells, *The Information Age – Vol. II: The Power of Identity* (Oxford: Blackwell Publishers, 1997), p. 306.
12 Initial efforts to probe the first, second, and fourth questions can be found in James N. Rosenau, *Along the Domestic–Foreign Frontier: Exploring Governance in a Turbulent World*

(Cambridge: Cambridge University Press, 1997). An attempt to explore the third question through survey research is presently underway.

13 For an elaboration of the frontier concept, see Rosenau, *Along the Domestic–Foreign Frontier*, Chaps. 1–3.

14 All but the last of these "scapes" are discussed in Arjun Appadurai, *Modernity at Large: Cultural Dimensions of Globalization* (Minneapolis, MN: University of Minnesota Press, 1996), pp. 33–7. I am indebted to David Earnest for the addition of "identiscapes" as a concept designed to capture that dimension of the emergent epoch that embraces the normative content of transborder affiliations.

15 Ulf Hannerz, *Transnational Connections: Culture, People, Places* (London and New York: Routledge, 1996), p. 19.

16 Castells, *The Information Age – Vol. II*, Chap. 5; David Held, Anthony McGrew, David Goldblatt, and Jonathan Perraton, *Global Transformations: Politics, Economics and Culture* (Cambridge: Polity Press, 1999), pp. 49–52; Strange, *The Retreat of the State, passim.*

17 Castells, *The Information Age – Vol. II*, p. 304 (italics in the original).

18 "I got the clear impression at the . . . conference [on international institutions] that, among the many younger scholars there, the fixation on the state is seen as outmoded and even a little silly. They all assume that there are many sorts of significant actors in the world, and I was struck by how comfortable many people were in talking about the importance of NGOs, the idea of world culture, and so on." John Boli, personal communication, April 30, 1999.

19 For an exception in this regard, see John J. Mearsheimer and Steven Van Evera, "Redraw the Map, Stop the Killing," *New York Times*, April 19, 1999, p. A23.

20 Jan Aart Scholte, "Globalization and Modernity," a paper presented at the Annual Meeting of the International Studies Association, San Diego, April 15–20, 1996, p. 15.

21 The reference here is to "an increasingly pervasive and contentious political struggle between a 'discourse of pace' linked, on the one hand, to accelerating transitions, speeding flows, overcoming resistances, eliminating frictions, and engineering the kinematics of globalization, and, on the other hand, a 'discourse of place' centered upon solidifying porous borders, bolstering breached containments, arresting eroded identities, and revitalizing faded essences." Timothy W. Luke and Gearóid Ó Tuathail, "Global Flowmations, Local Fundamentalism, and Fast Geopolitics: 'America' in an Accelerating World Order," in A. Herod, G. Ó. Tuathail, and S. M. Roberts (eds.), *An Unruly World? Globalization, Governance and Geography* (London and New York: Routledge, 1998), p. 73.

22 Roland Robertson, "Mapping the Global Condition: Globalization as the Central Concept," in Mike Featherstone (ed.), *Global Culture: Nationalism, Globalization, and Modernity* (London: Sage, 1990), p. 19.

23 Other terms suggestive of the contradictory tensions that pull systems toward coherence and collapse are "chaord," a label that juxtaposes the dynamics of chaos and order, and "glocalization," which points to the simultaneity of globalizing and localizing dynamics. The former designation is proposed in Dee W. Hock, "Institutions in the Age of Mindcrafting," a paper presented at the Bionomics Annual conference. San Francisco, CA, photocopy, October 22, 1994, pp. 1–2, while the latter term is elaborately developed in Roland Robertson, "Glocalization: Time-Space and Homogeneity-Heterogeneity," in Mike Featherstone, Scott Lash, and Roland Robertson (eds.), *Global Modernities* (Thousand Oaks, CA: Sage, 1995), pp. 25–44. Here the term "fragmegration" is preferred because it does not imply a territorial scale and broadens the focus to include tensions at work in organizations as well as those that pervade communities.

24 One observer has suggested that the world has entered "the age of deregulation," but this label lacks any hint of the integrative dynamics at work on the world scene, and it too fails to specify a historic landmark, which may be why one reviewer "suspects . . . [the label] will not catch on as the paradigm of the year." The deregulation label is offered in Richard Haas in *The Reluctant Sheriff: The United States after the Cold War*

(New York: Council on Foreign Relations Press, 1997), and the suspicion it will not take hold is expressed in *Foreign Affairs*, Vol. 76 (July/August 1997), p. 155.

25 Harry C. Triandis, *Individualism and Collectivism* (Boulder, CO: Westview Press, 1995), p. xiv.

26 Judith R. Blau, *Social Contracts and Economic Markets* (New York: Plenum Press, 1993), p. 97.

27 James N. Rosenau, "In Search of Institutions," a paper presented at the Conference on International Institutions: Global Processes–Domestic Consequences, sponsored by the Center for International Studies, Duke University, Durham, NC, April 9–11, 1999. This initial formulation was subsequently refined in James N. Rosenau, *Distant Proximities: Dynamics Beyond Globalization* (Princeton, NJ: Princeton University Press, 2003), Chap. 13.

5 Global affairs in an epochal transformation

1 This chapter first appeared in Edward Peartree and Ryan Henry (eds.), *The Information Revolution and International Security* (Washington, DC: CSIS, 1998), and is reprinted here by permission of the CSIS Press.

2 As Cox puts it, "borrowing a philosophical term, . . . each era and each object of interest [has] a relevant ontology. Ontologies tell us what is significant in the particular worlds we delve into – what are the basic entities and the key relationships. Ontologies are not arbitrary constructions; they are the specification of the common sense of an epoch." Robert W. Cox, "Critical Political Economy," in Bjorn Hettne (ed.), *International Political Economy: Understanding Global Disorder* (London: Zed Books, 1995), p. 34.

3 Since repercussions of the end of the Cold War were clearly evident at all levels of organization, it is tempting to treat this development as an epochal turning point. Such an interpretation, however, is misleading; it exaggerates the impact of a single historical moment and does not allow for the possibility that the end of the Cold War was the culmination of underlying and long-standing processes of change which, as stressed here, ushered in a common sense of dynamics and structures that amounted to a new epoch. For an analysis in which the Cold War is seen as having "left so light an impact on the living memory of states and societies that it is already en route to oblivion," see Ian Gambles, "Lost Time – The Forgetting of the Cold War," *National Interest*, Vol. 41 (Fall 1995), p. 35.

4 For a rare effort to come to terms with this problem, see Yale Ferguson and Richard W. Mansbach, *Polities: Authority, Identities, and Change* (Columbia, SC: University of South Carolina Press, 1996).

5 Partial exceptions in this regard can be found in Hans-Henrik Holm and George Sorenson (eds.), *Whose World Order? Uneven Globalization and the End of the Cold War* (Boulder, CO: Westview Press, 1995).

6 Attempts to confront these difficulties are undertaken in Ronnie D. Lipschutz (ed.), *On Security* (New York: Columbia University Press, 1995).

7 For an initial endeavor to focus on this overlap, see James N. Rosenau, *Along the Domestic–Foreign Divide: Governance in a Turbulent World* (Cambridge: Cambridge University Press, 1997).

8 Seyom Brown, *New Forces, Old Forces, and the Future of World Politics* (New York: Harper-Collins, Post-Cold War Edition, 1995), Chap. 8.

9 James P. Sewell and Mark B. Salter, "Panarchy and Other Norms for Global Governance," *Global Governance*, Vol. 1 (September–December 1995), pp. 373–82.

10 P.G. Cerny, "Plurilateralism: Structural Differentiation and Functional Conflict in the Post-Cold War World Order," *Millennium: Journal of International Studies*, Vol. 22 (Spring 1993), pp. 27–51.

11 Andrew Dunsire, "Modes of Governance," in J. Kooiman (ed.), *Modern Governance: New Government–Society Interactions* (Newbury Park, CA: Sage, 1993), p. 31.

12 A measure of this vacuum is suggested by the imprecision of a standard definition of global governance "as better ordered and more reliable responses that go beyond the individual or collective capacities of even powerful states" (from a newsletter of the Academic Council on the United Nations System, February 1966).

13 James N. Rosenau, *Turbulence in World Politics: A Theory of Change and Continuity* (Princeton, NJ: Princeton University Press, 1990), pp. 36–41.

14 Anthony J. N. Judge, "NGOs and Civil Society: Some Realities and Distortions," *Transnational Associations* (May/June 1995), p. 178.

15 Rosenau, *Turbulence in World Politics*, p. 228.

16 For inquiries which, in one way or another, explore the tensions and posit them as central to the course of events, see Joseph A. Camilleri and Jim Falk, *The End of Sovereignty? The Politics of a Shrinking and Fragmenting World* (Aldershot: Edward Elgar Publishing, 1992); Michael Zurn, "The Challenge of Globalization and Individualiza-tion: A View from Europe," in Holm and Sorenson (eds.), *Whose World Order? Uneven Globalization and the End of the Cold War*, pp. 137–64; Antoni Kuklinski (ed.), *Globality versus Locality* (Warsaw: Institute of Space Economy, University of Warsaw, 1990); and Zdravko Mlinar (ed.), *Globalization and Territorial Identities* (Aldershot: Avebury, 1992).

17 In one formulation "complex humanitarian emergencies are defined by five common characteristics: the deterioration or complete collapse of central government authority; ethnic or religious conflict and widespread human rights abuses; episodic food insecur-ity, frequently deteriorating into mass starvation; macroeconomics collapse involving hyperinflation, massive unemployment, and net decreases in GNP; and mass popula-tion movements of displaced persons and refugees escaping conflict or searching for food." Andrew S. Natsios, "NGOs and the UN System in Complex Humanitarian Emergencies: Conflict or Cooperation?" in Thomas G. Weiss and Leon Gordenker (eds.), *NGOs, the UN, and Global Governance* (Boulder, CO: Lynne Rienner, 1996), p. 67.

18 For an extensive survey of findings that highlight the importance of emotional skills, see Daniel Goleman, *Emotional Intelligence* (New York: Bantam Books, 1995).

19 For systematic data on the greater skills of elites across sixty years, see James N. Rosenau and W. Michael Fagen, "Increasingly Skillful Citizens: A New Dynamism in World Politics?" a paper presented at the Joint Conference of the Japan Association of International Relations and the International Studies Association, Makuhari, Japan, September 20–22, 1996.

20 Philip G. Cerny, "Globalization and the Changing Logic of Collective Action," *International Organization*, Vol. 49 (Autumn 1995), pp. 597–98.

6 Material and imagined communities in globalized space

1 This chapter was originally published in Donald H. McMillen (ed.), *Globalization and Regional Communities: Geoeconomic, Sociocultural and Security Implications for Australia* (Toowomba, Australia: USQ Press, 1997), pp. 24–40, and is reprinted here by permission of Donald McMillen.

2 See, for example, John Agnew and Stuart Corbridge, *Mastering Space: Hegemony, Territory and International Political Economy* (New York: Routledge, 1995), and Hugh De Santis, *Beyond Progress: An Interpretive Odyssey to the Future* (Chicago, IL: University of Chicago Press, 1996). Indeed, even bona fide poets have added their voice to the problematic nature of this separation. See, for example, Wislawa Szymborska, *View With a Grain of Sand: Selected Poems* (New York: Harcourt Brace & Co., 1995), pp. 99–100.

3 "While politicians go through the motions of national elections – offering chimerical programs and slogans – world markets, the Internet and the furious pace of trade involve people in a global game in which elected representatives figure as little more than bit players." Roger Cohen, "Global Forces Batter Politics," *New York Times*, November 17, 1996, sec. 4, p. 1.

4 For a discussion of the nature of these diverse "scapes," see Arjun Appadurai,

"Disjuncture and Difference in the Global Cultural Economy," *Public Culture*, Vol. 2 (1990), pp. 1–23.

5 For a similar formulation that focuses on some of the processes considered here to be central to Globalized Space, see Mathias Albert and Lothar Brock, *Debordering the World of States: New Spaces in International Relations* (Frankfurt: World Society Research Group, Working Paper No. 2, 1995). Another formulation that downplays the domestic–foreign boundary – calling it a "nonplace" (p. 260) – is developed in Richard K. Ashley, "Living on Border Lines: Man, Poststructuralism, and War," in James Der Derian and Michael J. Shapiro (eds.), *International/Intertextual Relations* (Lexington, MA: Lexington Books, 1989), pp. 259–321.

6 Since repercussions of the end of the Cold War were clearly evident at all levels of organization, it is tempting to treat this development as an epochal turning point. Such an interpretation, however, is misleading; it exaggerates the impact of a single historical moment and does not allow for the possibility that the end of the Cold War was the culmination of underlying and long-standing processes of change which, as stressed here, ushered in a common sense of dynamics and structures that amounted to a new epoch. For an analysis in which the Cold War is seen as having "left so light an impact on the living memory of states and societies that it is already en route to oblivion," see Ian Gambles, "Lost Time – The Forgetting of the Cold War," *National Interest*, Vol. 41 (Fall 1995), p. 35.

7 Cf. Francis Fukuyama, "Social Networks and Digital Networks" (Washington, DC: RAND Corporation, 1996, photocopy); Dee W. Hock, "Institutions in the Age of Mindcrafting" (San Francisco, CA: Bionomics Annual Conference, 1994, photocopy); David Ronfeldt, "Tribes, Institutions, Markets, Networks: A Framework About Societal Evolution" (Santa Monica, CA: RAND Corporation, 1996, photocopy). For a succinct discussion of the challenges analysts face in studying networks, see Mustafa Emirbayer and Jeff Goodwin, "Network Analysis, Culture, and the Problem of Agency," *American Journal of Sociology*, Vol. 99 (May 1994), pp. 1411–54.

8 For an incisive formulation of this concept, see Benedict Anderson, *Imagined Communities: Reflections on the Origin and Spread of Nationalism* (London: Verso, 1983).

9 Amos A. Jordan and Jane Khanna, "Economic Interdependence Challenges to the Nation-State: The Emergence of Natural Economic Territories in the Asia-Pacific," *Journal of International Affairs*, Vol. 48 (Winter 1995), p. 433.

10 *Ibid.*

11 Recent history offers a quintessential example of the vulnerabilities of established communities: the shared sense of community that bound the people of the Soviet Union together for seventy years collapsed – simply disappeared – over a summer weekend in 1991.

12 See, for example, Kishore Mahbubani, "The Pacific Way," *Foreign Affairs*, Vol. 74 (January/ February 1995), pp. 100–11; Ralph Pettman, "Asian Globalism," a paper presented at the Joint Convention on Globalism, Regionalism and Nationalism: Asia in Search of Its Role in the 21st Century, Makuhari, Japan, September 20–22, 1996; and Johan Saravanamuttu, "ASEAN: A Rejoinder," *Security Dialogue*, Vol. 25 (December 1994), pp. 469–72.

13 For some of the more interesting recent additions to this literature, see Joseph A. Camilleri, Anthony P. Jarvis, and Albert J. Paolini (eds.), *The State in Transition: Reimagining Political Space* (Boulder, CO: Lynne Rienner Publishers, 1995); Yale Ferguson and Richard W. Mansbach, *Polities: Authority, Identities, and Change* (Columbia, SC: University of South Carolina Press, 1996), and David Hooson (ed.), *Geography and National Identity* (Oxford: Blackwell Publishers, 1994).

14 An exception is the debate initiated by Samuel P. Huntington's article, "The Clash of Civilizations?" *Foreign Affairs*, Vol. 72 (Summer 1993), pp. 22–49.

15 See, for example, Richard Robison, "The Politics of 'Asian Values,' " *The Pacific Review*, Vol. 9, No. 3 (1996), pp. 309–27.

16 Andrew Gamble and Anthony Payne, "Conclusion: The New Regionalism," in A. Gamble and A. Payne (eds.), *Regionalism and World Order* (London: Macmillan Press, 1966), p. 250.

17 James C. McKinley Jr., "As the West Hesitates on Burundi, Leaders in Africa Make a Stand," *New York Times*, August 24, 1996, p. 1.

18 Richard Higgott, "Ideas and Identity in the International Political Economy of Regionalism: The Asia Pacific and Europe Compared," a paper presented at the ISA-JAIR Joint Convention on Globalism, Regionalism and Nationalism: Asia in Search of Its Role in the 21st Century, Makuhari, Japan, September 20–22, 1996, pp. 9, 25.

19 James Riker, "NGOs and Transnational Advocacy in Southeast Asia: The Politics of Sustainable and Democratic Development," a paper presented at the ISA-JAIR Joint Convention on Globalism, Regionalism and Nationalism: Asia in Search of Its Role in the 21st Century, Makuhari, Japan, September 20–22, 1996, p. 1.

20 For analyses of the causal links between globalization and localization, see James N. Rosenau, "Distant Proximities: The Dynamics and Dialectics of Globalization," in Bjorn Hettne (ed.), *International Political Economy: Understanding Global Disorder* (London: Zed Books, 1995), pp. 46–64, and James N. Rosenau, "New Dimensions of Security: The Interaction of Globalizing and Localizing Dynamics," *Security Dialogue*, Vol. 25, No. 3 (September 1994), pp. 255–81.

21 For an overview of this literature, see Ronnie D. Lipschutz, *Global Civil Society and Global Environmental Governance: The Politics of Nature from Place to Planet* (Albany, NY: SUNY Press, 1996).

22 I. William Zartman, "Self and Space: Negotiating a Future from the Past," a paper presented at the Annual Meeting of the International Studies Association, San Diego, April 19, 1996, pp. 3–4.

7 Many globalizations, one international relations

1 This chapter was originally published as an article of the same title in the inaugural issue of *Globalizations* (No. 1, 2004), and is reprinted here with permission of Taylor and Francis Ltd, http://www.tandf.co.uk/journals.

2 For a measure of the explosiveness of the literature, see the 713 entries of the bibliography listed in Jan Aart Scholte, *Globalization: A Critical Introduction* (New York: St. Martin's Press, 2000), pp. 318–48.

3 Robert O. Keohane, *Power and Governance in a Partially Globalized World* (London and New York: Routledge, 2002), p. 284.

4 *Ibid.*, p. 14.

5 It is no accident, therefore, that the syllabus for my "Dynamics of Globalization" seminar is the longest I have ever compiled. Since the course seeks to touch upon the many globalizations and cover their literatures, the syllabus is some 48 pages and growing. I would be happy to share it with any readers who contact me at jnr@gwu.edu.

6 *The Information Age: Economy, Society, and Culture* (Oxford: Blackwell Publishers, 1996, 1997, 1998).

7 Arjun Appadurai, *Modernity at Large: Cultural Dimensions of Globalization* (Minneapolis, MN: University of Minnesota Press, 1996); Zygmunt Bauman, *Globalization: The Human Consequences* (New York: Columbia University Press, 1998); Anthony Giddens, *The Consequences of Modernity* (Stanford, CA: Stanford University Press, 1990); David Held *et al.*, *Global Transformations: Politics, Economics and Culture* (Stanford, CA: Stanford University Press, 1999).

8 For one effort to assess world affairs through a lens in which localizing and globalizing dynamics are treated as inextricably interwoven, see James N. Rosenau, *Distant Proximities: Dynamics Beyond Globalization* (Princeton, NJ: Princeton University Press, 2003).

9 See, for example, John Urry, *Global Complexity* (Cambridge: Polity Press, 2003), p. ix.

10 *Ibid.*, p. x.

8 The globalization of globalization

1 This chapter originally appeared in Michael Breecher and Frank Harvey (eds.), *Millennium Reflections on International Studies* (Ann Arbor, MI: University of Michigan Press, 2002), pp. 271–90, © The University of Michigan, and is reprinted here by permission.

2 James N. Rosenau, "Comparative Foreign Policy: Fad, Fantasy, or Field," *International Studies Quarterly*, Vol. 12 (September 1968), pp. 296–329.

3 Among the exceptions are Barry Buzan and R. J. Barry Jones (eds.), *Change and the Study of International Relations: The Evaded Dimension* (London: Pinter, 1981); K. R. Dark, *The Waves of Time: Long-Term Change and International Relations* (London: Pinter, 1998); Joshua Goldstein, *Long Cycles: Prosperity and War in the Modern Age* (New Haven, CT: Yale University Press, 1988); K. J. Holsti, *Change in the International System: Essays on the Theory and Practice of International Relations* (Brookfield, VT: Edward Elgar, 1991); and George Modelski, *Long Cycles in World Politics* (Basingstoke: Macmillan, 1987).

4 See, for example, Stuart Hall, "Old and New Identities, Old and New Ethnicities," in Anthony D. King (ed.), *Culture, Globalization and the World-System: Contemporary Conditions for the Representation of Identity* (Minneapolis, MN: University of Minnesota Press, 1997); Ulf Hannerz, *Transnational Connections: Culture, People, Places* (London: Routledge, 1996); Arjun Appadurai, *Modernity at Large: Cultural Dimensions of Globalization* (Minneapolis, MN: University of Minnesota Press, 1996); and Kevin R. Cox (ed.), *Spaces of Globalization: Reasserting the Power of the Local* (New York: Guilford Press, 1997). For fragmegrative analyses by business executives and journalists, see Dee Hock, *Birth of the Chaordic Age* (San Francisco, CA: Berrett-Koehler Publishers, 1999), and Thomas L. Friedman, *The Lexus and the Olive Tree* (New York: Farrar, Straus and Giroux, 1999).

5 These "scapes" are discussed in Arjun Appadurai, *Modernity at Large: Cultural Dimensions of Globalization* (Minneapolis, MN: University of Minnesota Press, 1996), pp. 33–37.

6 J. David Singer, "The Levels-of-Analysis Problem in International Relations," *World Politics*, Vol. XIV (October 1961), pp. 77–92.

7 See, for example, J. C. Alexander *et al.* (eds.), *The Micro–Macro Link* (Berkeley, CA: University of California Press, 1987), and K. D. Knorr-Cetina and A. V. Cicourel (eds.), *Advances in Social Theory and Methodology: Toward an Integration of Micro- and Macro-Sociologies* (Boston, MA: Routledge & Kegan Paul, 1981).

8 John Markoff, "Tiniest Circuits Hold Prospect of Explosive Computer Speeds," *New York Times*, July 16, 1999, p. A1.

9 (New York: Simon & Schuster), 1992.

9 The complexities and contradictions of globalization

1 This chapter incorporates excerpts from two articles which originally appeared in *Security Dialogue*: "New Dimensions of Security: The Interaction of Globalizing and Localizing Dynamics," Vol. 25 (September 1994), pp. 255–81, © International Peace Research Institute, Oslo (PRIO), 1994, and "The Dynamics of Globalization: Toward an Operational Formulation," Vol. 27 (September 1996), pp. 247–62, © International Peace Research Institute, Oslo (PRIO), 1996. The articles are reused here with permission from SAGE Publications Ltd.

2 For an extensive discussion of the dynamics of fragmegration, see James N. Rosenau, *Along the Domestic–Foreign Frontier: Exploring Governance in a Turbulent World* (Cambridge: Cambridge University Press, 1997), Chap. 6.

3 William W. Lewis and Marvin Harris, "Why Globalization Must Prevail," *The McKinsey Quarterly* (1992), No. 2, p. 115.

4 Barry K. Gills, "Editorial: 'Globalization' and the 'Politics of Resistance,' "*New Political Economy*, Vol. 2 (March 1997), p. 12.

5 Michael Zurn, "What Has Changed in Europe? The Challenge of Globalization and Individualization," a paper presented at a meeting on What Has Changed? Competing Perspectives on World Order, Copenhagen, May 14–16, 1993, p. 40.
6 Zurn, "What Has Changed in Europe?" p. 41.

10 Toward a viable theory of globalization

1 A revised version of this chapter is scheduled to appear in Ino Rossi, *Frameworks for Globalization Research*. It will be reproduced there with the permission of Taylor & Francis.
2 This assumption lies at the core of my book, *Distant Proximities: Dynamics Beyond Globalization* (Princeton, NJ: Princeton University Press, 2003).
3 James N. Rosenau, "Thinking Theory Thoroughly," in K. P. Misra and Richard Smith Beal (eds.), *International Relations Theory: Western and Non-Western Perspectives* (New Dehli: Vikas Publishing House, 1980), pp. 14–28.
4 Ashley Dunn, "Ancient Chinese Craft Reshaping Building Design and Sales in the U.S.," *New York Times*, September 22, 1994, p. 1.
5 Rosenau, *Distant Proximities*, Chap. 3.

11 Democracy and globalization

1 A paper prepared for a roundtable at the Conference on Democracy: New Challenges, Paris: UNESCO, February 4–5, 2003. The conference was cancelled and the paper never delivered.
2 James N. Rosenau, *Along the Domestic–Foreign Frontier: Exploring Governance in a Turbulent World* (Cambridge: Cambridge University Press, 1997).
3 Cf. James N. Rosenau, *Distant Proximities: Dynamics Beyond Globalization* (Princeton, NJ: Princeton University Press, 2003).
4 See, for example, Volker Rittberger (ed.), *Regime Theory and International Relations* (Oxford: Clarendon Paperbacks, 1995).
5 Joseph A. Camilleri, "Major Structural Reform," in Esref Aksu and Joseph A. Camilleri (eds.), *Democratizing Global Governance* (London: Palgrave Macmillan, 2002), pp. 256–71 (the quote is on pp. 257–58). For an even more elaborate set of proposed arrangements that also outlines the role of a second chamber and is rooted in state-based institutions, see David Held's chapter on "Democracy, the Nation-State and the Global System," in his *Models of Democracy*, 2nd ed. (Stanford, CA: Stanford University Press, 1996), pp. 335–60.
6 Camilleri, "Major Structural Reform," p. 258.
7 *Ibid.*
8 *Ibid.*, p. 258–59.
9 *Ibid.*, p. 259.
10 *Ibid.*
11 For extended discussions of the skill revolution and organizational explosion, see James N. Rosenau, *Turbulence in World Politics: A Theory of Change and Continuity* (Princeton, NJ: Princeton University Press, 1990), and Rosenau, *Distant Proximities*.
12 See Ronald J. Deibert, "International Plug 'n Play? Citizen Activism, the Internet, and Global Public Policy," *International Studies Perspectives*, Vol. 1 (2000), pp. 255–72.
13 *Ibid.*, p. 256.
14 *Ibid.*, p. 262.
15 *Ibid.*, p. 263.
16 *Ibid.*, p. 256.
17 *Ibid.*, p. 267.
18 *Ibid.* (italics in the original).

19 See, for example, Thomas Risse, Stephen C. Ropp, and Kathyrn Sikkink (eds.), *The Power of Human Rights: International Norms and Domestic Change* (Cambridge: Cambridge University Press, 1999), which has chapters on the evolution of human rights norms in five regions and nine countries.

12 Think globally, pray locally

1 Jason Horowitz, "Italians Feel They Need the Next Papacy for Themselves," *New York Times*, April 16, 2005, p. A3.

2 For an extensive conceptualization of fragmegration, see James N. Rosenau, *Along the Domestic–Foreign Frontier: Exploring Governance in a Turbulent World* (Cambridge: Cambridge University Press, 1997), Chap. 6.

3 Other terms suggestive of the void in our vocabulary that highlight the contradictory tensions pulling systems toward both coherence and collapse are "chaord," a label that juxtaposes the dynamics of chaos and order, "glocalization," which points to the simultaneity of globalizing and localizing dynamics, and "regcal," a term designed to focus attention on the links between regional and local phenomena. The chaord designation is proposed in Dee W. Hock, *Birth of the Chaordic Age* (San Francisco, CA: Berrett-Koehler Publishers, 1999); the glocalization concept is elaborately developed in Roland Robertson, "Glocalization: Time-Space and Homogeneity-Heterogeneity," in Mike Featherstone, Scott Lash, and Roland Robertson (eds.), *Global Modernities* (Thousand Oaks, CA: Sage, 1995), pp. 25–44; and the regcal formulation can be found in Susan H. C. Tai and Y. H. Wong, "Advertising Decision Making in Asia: 'Glocal' versus 'Regcal' Approach," *Journal of Managerial Issues*, Vol. 10 (Fall 1998), pp. 318–39. Here the term "fragmegration" is preferred because it does not imply a territorial scale and broadens the focus to include tensions at work in organizations as well as those that pervade communities.

4 Craig S. Smith, "Muslim Group in France is Fertile Soil for Militancy," *New York Times*, April 28, 2005, p. 15.

5 Ian Reader, *Religious Violence in Contemporary Japan: The Case of Aum Shinrikyo* (Honolulu: University of Hawaii Press, 2000).

6 One need only tour the monasteries perched on mountainsides in northern Greece to encounter gruesome wall paintings of earlier centuries that avert the eyes and induce wonder that religious conviction can foster such horrid images.

7 For an elaboration of these several dynamics, see my *Distant Proximities: Dynamics Beyond Globalization* (Princeton, NJ: Princeton University Press, 2003), Chap. 3.

8 For an empirical test of the hypothesized skill revolution, see James N. Rosenau and W. Michael Fagen, "Increasingly Skillful Citizens: A New Dynamism in World Politics?" *International Studies Quarterly*, Vol. 41 (December 1997), pp. 655–86.

13 Toward an ontology for global governance

1 This chapter is reprinted by permission from *Approaches to Global Governance Theory* edited by Martin Hewson and Timothy J. Sinclair, the State University of New York Press. © 1999 State University of New York. All Rights Reserved. The chapter appeared as pages 287–301 in that volume.

2 See, for example, a new journal, *Global Governance*, published by Lynne Rienner Publishers in cooperation with the Academic Council on the United Nations (ACUNS) and the United Nations University. The books and study commission reports on the subject include the Commission on Global Governance, *Our Global Neighborhood* (New York: Oxford University Press, 1995); the Commission on Global Governance, *Issues in Global Governance: Paper Written for the Commission on Global Governance* (London: Kluwer Law International, 1995); Meghnad Desai and Paul Redfern (eds.), *Global Governance: Ethics and Economics of the World Order* (London: Pinter, 1995); Jan Kooiman

(ed.), *Modern Governance: New Government–Society Interactions* (London: Sage, 1993); Mihaly Simai, *The Future of Global Governance: Managing Risk and Change in the International System* (Washington, D.C.: United States Institute of Peace Press, 1994); and Yoshikazu Sakamoto (ed.), *Global Transformation: Challenges to the State System* (Tokyo: United Nations Press, 1994).

3 Lawrence S. Finkelstein, "What is Global Governance?" *Global Governance*, Vol. 1 (September–December 1995), pp. 367–72 (the quote is from p. 369).

4 This notion of paradigm extends, but does not contradict, the early specification of the concept set forth in Thomas S. Kuhn, *The Structure of Scientific Revolutions*, 2nd ed. (Chicago, IL: University of Chicago Press, 1970). For a discussion of twenty-one different ways in which the paradigm concept is employed, see Margaret Masterman, "The Nature of a Paradigm," in Imre Lakatos and Alan Musgrave (eds.), *Criticism and the Growth of Knowledge* (Cambridge: Cambridge University Press, 1970), pp. 61–5.

5 Robert W. Cox, "Critical Political Economy," in Bjorn Hettne (ed.), *International Political Economy: Understanding Global Disorder* (London: Zed Books, 1995), p. 35.

6 *Ibid.*, p. 34.

7 For examples of how regimes are conceived to consist primarily of national governments, see most of the essays in Stephen D. Krasner (ed.), *International Regimes* (Ithaca, NY: Cornell University Press, 1983), and Volker Rittberger (ed.), *Regime Theory and International Relations* (Oxford: Clarendon Press, 1993), as well as Robert O. Keohane, *After Hegemony: Cooperation and Discord in the World Political Economy* (Princeton, NJ: Princeton University Press, 1984), pp. 98–106.

8 For an exception in this regard, see Virginia Haufler, "Crossing the Boundary between Public and Private: International Regimes and Non-State Actors," in Rittberger (ed.), *Regime Theory and International Relations*, pp. 94–111.

9 For written expressions of this ambivalent perspective, see Robert Gilpin, *War and Change in World Politics* (New York: Cambridge University Press, 1981), p. 7; Alan James and Robert H. Jackson, "The Character of Independent Statehood," in A. James and R. H. Jackson (eds.), *States in a Changing World: A Contemporary Analysis* (Oxford: Clarendon Press, 1993), pp. 5–8; Stephen D. Krasner, "Sovereignty: An Institutional Perspective," in James A. Caporaso (ed.), *The Elusive State: International and Comparative Perspectives* (Newbury Park, CA: Sage, 1989), Chap. 4; Eugene B. Skolnikoff, *The Elusive Transformation: Science, Technology, and the Evolution of International Politics* (Princeton, NJ: Princeton University Press, 1993), p. 7; and Kenneth N. Waltz, *Theory of International Politics* (Reading, MA: Addison-Wesley, 1979), p. 94.

10 Seyom Brown, *New Forces, Old Forces, and the Future of World Politics* (New York: HarperCollins, Post-Cold War Edition, 1995), Chap. 8.

11 James P. Sewell and Mark B. Salter, "Panarchy and Other Norms for Global Governance," *Global Governance*, Vol. 1 (September–December 1995), pp. 373–82.

12 Andrew Dunsire, "Modes of Governance," in J. Kooiman, *Modern Governance*, p. 31.

13 For a cogent discussion of the dynamics driving change in globalizing directions, see Philip G. Cerny, "Globalization and the Changing Logic of Collective Action," *International Organization*, Vol. 49 (Autumn 1995), pp. 595–625.

14 For a useful discussion of the nature of authority and the forms it can take, see Bruce Lincoln, *Authority: Construction and Corrosion* (Chicago, IL: University of Chicago Press, 1994).

15 Timothy J. Sinclair, "Investment, Knowledge and Governance: Credit Rating Processes and the Global Political Economy" (Toronto: Ph.D. Dissertation, York University, 1995).

16 James N. Rosenau, "Governance in the 21st Century," *Global Governance*, Vol I (Winter 1995), p. 14.

17 I am indebted to Ken Conca for this listing.

18 Jan Kooiman, "Social-Political Governance: Introduction," in J. Kooiman (ed.), *Modern Governance*, p. 1.

19 Quoted from the back flap of B. Marin and R. Mayntz, *Policy Networks*, in Jan Jooiman,

"Findings, Speculations and Recommendations," in J. Kooiman (ed.), *Modern Governance*, p. 258 (italics in the original).
20 J. Kooiman, "Social-Political Governance: Introduction," p. 1.

14 Governance in the twenty-first century

1 This chapter is reprinted from *Global Governance: A Review of Multilateralism and International Organizations*, Vol. 1, #1. Copyright © 1995 by Lynne Rienner Publishers Inc. Used with permission.
2 Alexander King and Bertrand Schneider, *The First Global Revolution: A Report of the Council of Rome* (New York: Pantheon Books, 1991), pp. 181–2 (italics added). For other inquiries that support the inclusion of small, seemingly local systems of rule in a broad analytic framework, see John Friedmann, *Empowerment; The Politics of Alternative Development* (Cambridge, MA: Blackwell, 1992), and Robert Huckfeldt, Eric Plutzer, and John Sprague, "Alternative Contexts of Political Behavior: Churches, Neighborhoods, and Individuals," *Journal of Politics*, Vol. 55 (May 1993), pp. 365–81.
3 Steven A. Rosell *et al.*, *Governing in an Information Society* (Montreal: Institute for Research on Public Policy, 1992), p. 21.
4 Rule systems have much in common with what has come to be called the "new institutionalism." See, for example, Robert O. Keohane, "International Institutions: Two Approaches," *International Studies Quarterly*, Vol. 32 (December 1988), pp. 379–96; James G. March and Johan P. Olsen, "The New Institutionalism: Organizational Factors in Political Life," *American Political Science Review*, Vol. 78 (September 1984), pp. 734–49; and Oran R. Young, "International Regimes: Toward a New Theory of Institutions," *World Politics*, Vol. 39 (October 1986), pp. 104–22. For an extended discussion of how the concept of control is especially suitable to the analysis of both formal and informal political phenomena, see James N. Rosenau, *Calculated Control as a Unifying Concept in the Study of International Politics and Foreign Policy* (Princeton, NJ: Research Mongraph No. 15, Center of International Studies, Princeton University, 1963).
5 Cf. James N. Rosenau and Ernst-Otto Czempiel (eds.), *Governance Without Government: Order and Change in World Politics* (Cambridge: Cambridge University Press, 1992). Also see the formulations in Peter Mayer, Volker Rittberger, and Michael Zurn, "Regime Theory: State of the Art and Perspectives," in V. Rittberger (ed.), *Regime Theory and International Relations* (Oxford: Oxford University Press, 1993), and Timothy J. Sinclair, "Financial Knowledge as Governance," a paper presented at the Annual Meeting of the International Studies Association, Acapulco, March 23–27, 1993.
6 For a discussion of the breadth and depth of the world's authority crises, see James N. Rosenau, "The Relocation of Authority in a Shrinking World: From Tiananmen Square in Beijing to the Soccer Stadium in Soweto via Parliament Square in Budapest and Wencelas Square in Prague," *Comparative Politics*, Vol. 24 (April 1992), pp. 253–72.
7 A vivid picture of the organizational explosion in the nongovernmental world is presented in Lester M. Salamon, *The Global Associational Revolution: The Rise of the Third Sector on the World Scene* (Baltimore, MD: Institute for Policy Studies, Occasional Paper #15, 1993). As for the world of governments, in addition to the new states that have recently swollen the ranks of the international system, a measure of the extraordinary organizational density that has evolved can be extrapolated – assuming the pattern is global in scale – from the following description of the United States some three decades ago: "It has been estimated that there are over 8,000 multifunctional and autonomous local governments, including over 3,000 counties and more than that number of urban governments for the thousands of incorporated municipalities which speckle the map. The mesh is made still finer by the number of special-purpose districts which have been mushrooming over the past decades, particularly in the major metropolitan regions. From 1942 to 1962 the number of special districts (excluding school districts) grew from 8,300 to over 18,000. When school districts are added, the result in 1962

was an astonishing total of over 63,000 local governments with some autonomous authority over specific parcels of US space. . . . Emerging from this complex geopolitical web are thousands of discrete units of territorial identity and exclusion – cities and suburbs, townships and counties, school districts and whole metropolitan regions – which instill a sense of community and apartness usually surpassed only at the national and family levels." Edward W. Soja, *The Political Organization of Space* (Washington, DC: Association of American Geographers, Resource Paper No. 8, 1971), p. 45.

8 Anthony G. McGrew, "Global Politics in a Transitional Era," in Anthony G. McGrew *et al.*, *Global Politics: Globalization and the Nation-State* (Cambridge: Polity Press, 1992), p. 318.

9 Martin Hewson, "The Media of Political Globalization," a paper presented at the Annual Meeting of the International Studies Association, Washington DC, March 1994, p. 2.

10 For a cogent analysis of the territorial bases of political organization, see Soja, *The Political Organization of Space*.

11 The skill revolution is outlined in James N. Rosenau, *Turbulence in World Politics: A Theory of Change and Continuity* (Princeton, NJ: Princeton University Press, 1990), Chap. 13. An analysis of how the skill revolution has empowered people to engage more effectively in collective action can be found in Rosenau, "The Relocation of Authority in a Shrinking World," pp. 253–72.

12 The dynamics of subgroupism are set forth in Rosenau, *Turbulence in World Politics*, pp. 133–6, 396–8.

13 See, for example, Peter F. Drucker, *Post-Capitalist Society* (New York: HarperCollins, 1993).

14 A discussion of the impact of new interdependence issues is offered in Rosenau, *Turbulence in World Politics*, pp. 429–30. The emergent role of new social movements is assessed in R. B. J. Walker, *One World, Many Worlds: Struggles for a Just World Peace* (Boulder, CO: Lynne Rienner Publishers, 1988), and Leslie Paul Thiele, "Making Democracy Safe for the World: Social Movements and Global Politics," *Alternatives*, Vol. 18 (1993), pp. 273–305.

15 For analyses of these contradictory trends, see James N. Rosenau, "The Person, The Household, The Comunity, and The Globe: Notes for a Theory of Multilateralism in a Turbulent World," a paper presented at the UNU Symposium on Theoretical Perspectives on Multilateralism and Images of World Order, Florence: European University Institute, September 1992.

16 None of this is to imply, of course, that the shifts in the loci of authority occur easily, with a minimum of commotion and a maximum of clarity. Far from it: the shifts derive from delicate bargaining, and usually they must overcome extensive opposition, with the result that the "[t]ransfer of authority is a complicated process and it seems there no longer is one single identifiable sovereign, but a multitude of authorities at different levels of aggregation and several centres with differing degrees of coercive power (not all of them public and governmental!). . . . [I]t becomes increasingly difficult to differentiate between public and private institutions, the State and Civil Society, domestic and international." Kaisa Lahteenmaki and Jyrki Kakonen, "Regionalization and Its Impact on the Theory of International Relations," a paper presented at the Annual Meeting of the International Studies Association, Washington, DC, March 1994, pp. 32–3.

17 John Vogler, "Regimes and the Global Commons: Space, Atmosphere and Oceans," in McGrew *et al.*, *Global Politics*, p.118.

18 For a conception of political adaptation in which adaptive systems are posited as being able to keep fluctuations in their essential structures within acceptable limits, see James N. Rosenau, *The Study of Political Adaptation* (London: Frances Pinter Publishers, 1981).

19 For a cogent analysis in which this bottom-up process is posited as passing through five distinct stages, see Bjorn Hettne, "The New Regionalism: Implications for Development and Peace," in Bjorn Hettne and Andras Inotai, *The New Regionalism: Implications for Global Development and International Security* (Helsinki: UNU World Institute for Development Economics Research, 1994), pp. 7–8.

20 Diana Jean Schemo, "Rebuilding of Suburban Dreams," *New York Times*, May 4, 1994, p. A11.

21 Steven Greenhouse, "Kissinger Will Help Mediate Dispute Over Zulu Homeland," *New York Times*, April 12, 1994, p. A8.

22 Peter B. Evans, "Building an Integrative Approach to International and Domestic Politics: Reflections and Projections," in Peter B. Evans, Harold K. Jacobson, and Robert D. Putnam (eds.), *Double-Edged Diplomacy: International Bargaining and Domestic Politics* (Berkeley, CA: University of California Press, 1993), p. 419. For interesting accounts of how multinational corporations are increasingly inclined to form transnational alliances, see "The Global Firm: R.I.P.," *The Economist*, February 6, 1993, p. 69, and "The Fall of Big Business," *The Economist*, April 17, 1993, p. 13.

23 Jan Aart Scholte, *International Relations of Social Change* (Philadelphia, PA: Open University Press, 1993), pp. 44–5.

24 Roberto C. Goizueta, "The Challenges of Getting What You Wished For," remarks presented to the Arthur Page Society, Amelia Island, Florida, September 21, 1992.

25 Camilleri, "Rethinking Sovereignty in a Shrinking, Fragmented World," p. 35.

26 Kathryn Sikkink, "Codes of Conduct for Transnational Corporations: The Case of the UWH/UNICEF Code," *International Organization*, Vol. 40 (Autumn 1986), pp. 815–40.

27 Janie Leatherman, Ron Pagnucco, and Jackie Smith, "International Institutions and Transnational Social Movement Organizations: Challenging the State in a Three-Level Game of Global Transformation," a paper presented at the Annual Meeting of the International Studies Association, Washington, DC, March 1994.

28 Leatherman, Pagnucco, and Smith, "International Institutions and Transnational Social Movement Organizations," p. 20.

29 Robert W. Cox, "Global Perestroika," in Ralph Milband and Leo Panitch (eds.), *Socialist Register* (London: Merlin Press, 1992), p. 34.

30 Hettne, "The New Regionalism," p. 2.

31 *Ibid.*, p. 6.

32 William Drozdiak, "Revving Up Europe's 'Four Moters,' " *Washington Post*, March 27, 1994, p. C3.

33 For an analysis which conceives of these "four motors" of Europe in terms of micro regions rather than as cities – the Rhone Alps instead of Lyon, Lombardy instead of Milan, Baden-Wurttemberg instead of Stuttgart, and Catalonia instead of Barcelona – see Lahteenmaki and Kakonen, "Regionalization and Its Impact on the Theory of International Relations," p. 15.

34 Drozdiak, "Revving Up Europe's 'Four Moters,' " p. C3.

35 Pascal Maragall, quoted in Drozdiak, "Revving Up Europe's 'Four Moters,' " p. C3. For extensive inquiries that posit the transnational roles of cities as increasingly central to the processes of global governance, see Saskia Sassen, *The Global City: New York, London, Tokyo* (Princeton, NJ: Princeton University Press, 1991), and Earl H. Fry, Lee H. Radebaugh, and Panayotis Soldatos (eds.), *The New International Cities Era: The Global Activities of North American Municipal Governments* (Provo, UT: Brigham Young University Press, 1989).

36 Thomas P. Rohlem, "Cosmopolitan Cities and Nation States: A 'Mediterranean' Model for Asian Regionalism," a paper presented at the Conference on Asian Regionalism, Maui, December 17–19, 1993, pp. 1–2.

37 Ricardo Petrilla, as quoted in Drozdiak, "Revving Up Europe's 'Four Moters,' " p. C3. For an analysis by the same author which indicates concern over the trend to city-like

states, see Riccardo Petrella, "Techno-racism: The City-States of the Global Market Will Create a 'New Apartheid,' " *Toronto Star*, August 9, 1992.

38 Kenichi Ohmae, "The Rise of the Region State," *Foreign Affairs*, Vol. 72 (Spring 1993), p. 78.

39 *Ibid.*, pp. 78–9.

40 *Ibid.*, p. 80.

41 Michael Clough and David Doerge, *Global Changes and Domestic Transformations: New Possibilities for American Foreign Policy: Report of a Vantage Conference* (Muscatine, IA: Stanley Foundation, 1992), p. 9. For indicators that a similar process is occurring in the Southwest without the approval of Washington, DC, or Mexico City, see Cathryn L. Thorup, *Redefining Governance in North America: The Impact of Cross-Border Networks and Coalitions on Mexican Immigration into the United States* (Santa Monica, CA: Rand Corporation, 1993). Although using a different label ("tribes"), a broader discussion of regional states can be found in Joel Kotkin, *Tribes: How Race, Religion and Identity Determine Success in the New Global Economy* (New York: Random House, 1993).

42 Ohmae, "The Rise of the Region State," p. 83.

43 *Ibid.*, pp. 84–85.

44 Hettne, "The New Regionalism," p. 7.

45 *Ibid.*, pp. 2–3. For another formulation that also differentiates between the old and new regionalism, see Lahteenmaki and Kakonen, "Regionalization and Its Impact on the Theory of International Relations," p. 9. For a contrary perspective, see Stephen D. Krasner, "Regional Economic Blocs and the End of the Cold War," paper presented at the International Colloqium on Regional Economic Integration, University of San Paulo, December 1991.

46 See, for example, the remarkable developments cited in James Brooke, "The New South Americans: Friends and Partners," *New York Times*, April 8, 1994, p. A3.

47 An extended application of the concept of regionness to the various regions of the present-day world can be found in Hettne, "The New Regionalism," pp. 7–8, 12–34.

48 *Ibid.*, p. 11.

49 This is the central point advanced in James N. Rosenau, "Distant Proximities: The Dynamics and Dialectics of Globalization," a paper presented as the Morgen Lecture, Dickinson College, Carlyle, October 27, 1993.

50 Arthur Stein, "Coordination and Collaboration: Regimes in an Anarchic World," in David A. Baldwin (ed.), *Neorealism and Neoliberalism: The Contemporary Debate* (New York: Columbia University Press, 1993), p. 29.

51 Vogler, "Regimes and the Global Commons," p. 123.

52 Stein, "Coordination and Collaboration," p. 31.

53 Cathryn L. Thorup, "Redefining Governance in North America: Citizen Diplomacy and Cross-Border Coalitions," *Enfoque*, (Spring 1993), pp. 1, 12.

54 For a valuable attempt to explore this concept theoretically and empirically, see Cathryn L. Thorup, "The Politics of Free Trade and the Dynamics of Cross-Border Coalitions in US–Mexican Relations," *Columbia Journal of World Business*, Vol. 26 (Summer 1991), pp. 12–26.

55 David Ronfeldt and Cathryn L. Thorup, "North America in the Era of Citizen Networks: State, Society, and Security," RAND Corporation (Santa Monica, CA: 1993), p. 22.

56 Ivo D. Duchachek, "The International Dimension of Subnational Government," *Publius*, Vol. 14 (Fall 1984), p. 25.

57 Ronfeldt and Thorup, "North American in the Era of Citizen Networks," p. 24.

58 This brief discussion of the credit-rating agencies in the private sector is based on Timothy J. Sinclair, "The Mobility of Capital and the Dynamics of Global Governance: Credit Risk Assessment in the Emerging World Order," a paper presented at the Annual Meeting of the International Studies Association, Washington, DC, March 1994, and Timothy J. Sinclair, "Passing Judgment: Credit Rating Processes as

Regulatory Mechanisms of Governance in the Emerging World Order," *Review of International Political Economy*, Vol. 1, No. 1 (April 1994), pp. 133–59.

59 For a cogent discussion of how knowledge serves as a form of authority and govern-ance, see Susan Strange, *States and Markets: An Introduction to International Political Economy* (New York: Basil Blackwell, 1988).

60 Sinclair, "The Mobility of Capital and the Dynamics of Global Governance," p. 16.

61 It is noteworthy, though hardly surprising, that the more pervasive violations of widely shared norms become, the more do they provoke the evolution of new transnational rule systems which seek to contain, if not to end, the activities of TCOs. Cf. Ethan A. Nadelman, "Global Prohibition Regimes: The Evolution of Norms in International Society," *International Organization*, Vol. 44 (Autumn 1990), pp. 479–526.

62 Phil Williams, "Transnational Criminal Organizations and International Security," *Survival*, Vol. 36 (Spring 1994), p. 97. See also Phil Williams, "International Drug Trafficking: An Industry Analysis," *Low Intensity Conflict and Law Enforcement*, Vol. 2 (Winter 1993), pp. 397–420. For another dimension of transnational criminality, see Victor T. Levine, "Transnational Aspects of Political Corruption," in Arnold J. Heidenheimer, Michael Johnston, and Victor T. Levine (eds.), *Political Corruption: A Handbook* (New Brunswick, NJ: Transaction Publishers, 1989), pp. 685–99.

63 Williams, "Transnational Criminal Organizations and International Security," p. 100.

64 Rensselaer W. Lee III, "Post-Soviet Organized Crime and Western Security Interests," Testimony submitted to the Subcommittee on Terrorism, Narcotics and International Operations, Senate Committee on Foreign Relations, Washington, DC, April 21, 1994.

65 Williams, "Transnational Criminal Organizations and International Security," p. 106.

66 *Ibid.*, p. 105.

67 See, for example, Elaine Sciolini, "New US Peacekeeping Policy De-emphasizes Role of the UN," *New York Times*, May 6, 1994, p. 1.

68 Thomas Risse-Kappen, "Faint-Hearted Multilateralism: The Re-Emergence of the United Nations in World Politics," a paper presented at the Annual Meeting of the International Studies Association, Washington, DC, March 1994.

69 For a cogent and recent assessment of the UN's strengths and weaknesses, see Gene M. Lyons, "A New Collective Security: The United Nations and International Peace," *The Washington Quarterly*, Vol 17, No. 2, (1994), pp. 173–99.

70 As a point of departure for breaking into the vast literature on the EU, one might well begin with the items in the extensive listing to be found in the bibliography and three appendices included in Alberta Sbragia, "The Community as Polity: The Political Economy of Regulation" (Pittsburgh, PA: West European Studies Program, University of Pittsburgh, photocopy, n.d.).

71 Alberta Sbragia, "From 'Nation-State' to 'Member-State': The Evolution of the European Community," a paper presented at the Europe After Maastrict Symposium, Washington University, St. Louis, October 1–3, 1993, pp. 1–2.

72 Christopher Brewin, "The European Community: A Union of States Without Unity of Government," in Friedrich Kratochwil and Edward D. Mansfield (eds.), *International Organization: A Reader* (New York: HarperCollins, 1994), p. 301–2.

73 *Ibid.*, p. 302.

74 For an extensive exploration of the history and practices through which external moni-toring of domestic elections has evolved as a form of transnational governance, see James N. Rosenau and Michael Fagen, "Domestic Elections as International Events," in Carl Kaysen, Robert A. Pastor, and Laura W. Reed (eds.), *Collective Responses to Regional Problems: The Case of Latin America and the Caribbean* (Cambridge, MA: American Academy of Arts & Sciences, 1994).

75 See, for example, Larry Garber, *Guidelines for International Election Observing* (Washington, DC: International Human Rights Law Group, 1984).

76 Of these, 278 organizations were present on election day, with 435 observers fielded by the OAS visiting 3,064 voting sites (some 70 percent of the total) and 237 UN monitors visiting 2,155 sites. In addition, some 1,500 members of the international press corps were on the scene. Cf. Pastor, "Nicaragua's Choice," p. 18, 21.

77 Rosenau, "Distant Proximities: The Dynamics and Dialectics of Globalization."

78 An effort to break into the growing literature on ethnic groups and their transnational ties can usefully begin with Michael E. Brown (ed.), *Ethnic Conflict and International Security* (Princeton, NJ: Princeton University Press, 1993). For a creative solution to the problem that posits a form of transnational governance, see Gidon Gottlieb, "Nations Without States," *Foreign Affairs*, Vol. 73 (May/June 1994), pp. 100–12.

15 Global governance as disaggregated complexity

1 Alice D. Ba and Matthew J. Hoffmann (eds.), *Contending Perspectives on Global Governance: Coherence, Contestation and World Order* (London: Routledge, 2005, pp. 131–53).

2 Wolfgang Sachs *et al.*, *The Jo'burg Memo: Fairness in a Fragile World* (Berlin: Heinrich Boll Foundation, 2002).

3 James N. Rosenau, *Turbulence in World Politics: A Theory of Change and Continuity* (Princeton, NJ: Princeton University Press, 1990).

4 Cf. Hilary French, *Vanishing Borders: Protecting the Planet in the Age of Globalization* (New York: W. W. Norton, 2000), p. 159, and Sachs *et al.*, *The Jo'burg Memo*, p. 65.

5 Alexander Wendt, *Social Theory of International Politics* (Cambridge: Cambridge University Press, 1999), p. 308.

6 Jan Aart Scholte, *Globalization: A Critical Introduction* (London: Macmillan Press, 2000), pp. 56–8.

7 James N. Rosenau, *Along the Domestic–Foreign Frontier: Exploring Governance in a Turbulent World* (Cambridge: Cambridge University Press, 1997), Chap. 7.

8 Wolfgang H. Reinicke, "The Other World Wide Web: Global Public Policy Networks," *Foreign Policy* (Winter 1999–2000), p. 45.

9 Raimo Väyrynen (ed.), *Globalization and Global Governance* (Lanham, MD: Rowman and Littlefield, 1999), p. 25.

10 James N. Rosenau, "Governance in the 21st Century," *Global Governance*, Vol. 1 (1995), pp. 13–43.

11 James N. Rosenau, "Governance, Order, and Change in World Politics," in J. N. Rosenau and E. O. Czempiel (eds.), *Governance without Government: Order and Change in World Politics* (Cambridge: Cambridge University Press, 1992), Chap. 1.

12 Seán Ó Siochrú and Bruce Girard, *Global Media Governance: A Beginner's Guide* (Lanham, MD: Rowman & Littlefield, 2002).

13 For a typological formulation that attempts to account for the diversity of governance forms, see the previous chapter, especially Table 13.1.

14 A formulation that elaborates on "mobius-web" governance is set forth in Chapter 16.

15 Timothy J. Sinclair, *The New Masters of Capital: American Bond Rating Agencies and the Politics of Creditworthiness* (Ithaca and London: Cornell University Press, 2005).

16 Sverker Carlsson and Johannes Stripple, "Climate Governance beyond the State – Contributions from the Insurance Industry," a paper presented at the International Political Science Association, Quebec City, August 1–5, 2000.

17 For a host of other examples of effective governance in the multi-centric world, see A. Claire Cutler, Virginia Haufler, and Tony Porter (eds.), *Private Authority in International Affairs* (Albany, NY: State University of New York Press, 1999).

18 Mark Zacher, "Uniting Nations: Global Regimes and the United Nations Systems," in R. Väyrynen (ed.), *Globalization and Global Governance* (Lanham, MD: Rowman and Littlefield, 1999).

19 A penetrating discussion of the distinction between science and indigenous knowledge can be found in Sheila Jasanoff and Marybeth Long Martello (eds.), *Earthly*

Politics: Local and Global in Environmental Governance (Cambridge, MA: MIT Press, 2004), pp. 1–30.

20 Sachs *et al.*, *The Jo'burg Memo*, p. 14.

21 James N. Rosenau, *Distant Proximities: Dynamics Beyond Globalization* (Princeton, NJ: Princeton University Press, 2003).

22 Walter Truett Anderson, *All Connected Now: Life in the First Global Civilization* (Boulder, CO: Westview Press, 2001), p. 117.

23 James Gustave Speth, "Recycling Environmentalism," *Foreign Policy*, No. 131 (July/ August 2002), p. 76.

24 Anthony Giddens and Christopher Pierson, *Conversations with Anthony Giddens: Making Sense of Modernity* (Cambridge: Polity Press, 1998), pp. 115–17.

16 Change, complexity, and governance in globalizing space

1 This chapter was originally published in Jan Pierre (ed.), *Debating Governance* (Oxford: OUP, 2000), pp. 167–200, and is reprinted here by permission of Oxford University Press, www.oup.com.

2 Adam Przeworski, "Democratization Revisited," *Items*, Vol. 51 (March 1997), p. 11.

3 For an analysis of the sources of one of these theoretical gaps, see Mary Durfee and James N. Rosenau, "Playing Catch-Up: IR Theory and Poverty," *Millennium*, Vol. 25, No. 3 (1996), pp. 521–45.

4 And even when the underpinnings of change in world affairs do seem worthy of investigation, such inquiries tend to focus exclusively on states and to ignore the complexities of globalization. Indeed, in one recent case "globalization" is not an entry in the index and the author's concern with global change turns out to be a preoccupation with changes in the international system. Cf. Zeev Maoz, *Domestic Sources of Global Change* (Ann Arbor, MI: University of Michigan Press, 1996).

5 Lately, however, there are signs of movement in this direction. In addition to conferences such as the one for which this paper was prepared, a new journal, *Global Governance*, was founded in 1995 and several books organized around the concept of governance on a global scale are now available. See, for example, the sources listed in Note 1 of Chapter 12, as well as Paul F. Diehl (ed.), *The Politics of Global Governance: International Organizations in an Interdependent World* (Boulder, CO: Lynne Rienner Publishers, 1997); Richard Falk, *On Humane Governance: Toward a New Global Politics* (University Park, PA: Pennsylvania State University Press, 1995); and David Held, *Democracy and the Global Order: From the Modern State to Cosmopolitan Governance* (Stanford, CA: Stanford University Press, 1995). Still, this literature is not yet so voluminous that clarity on the obstacles to such forms of governance has been achieved. There remains plenty of room for what the above epigraph calls this "sort of thing we are going to be thinking about."

6 Nor are those who scoff at such formulations confined to scholars who perceive constancy as the central tendency of world affairs. Calling them "semantic euphemisms," for example, a vigorous advocate of looking "seriously at the power exercised by authorities other than states," Susan Strange, derisively dismisses such concepts as globalization, interdependence, and global governance as deceptive means for depicting and analyzing the dynamics of change and the advent of political and economic processes that extend beyond the competence of states. Even those outside the IR mainstream, in other words, are having difficulty moving beyond the long-established terminology. Or at least the dismissal of these newer labels seems in conflict with Strange's ensuing comment that, "I have at last reached the final parting of the ways from the discipline of international relations. . . . I can no longer profess a special concern with international politics if that is defined as a study different from other kinds of politics and which takes the state as the unit of analysis and the international society of states as the main problematic." Susan Strange, *The Retreat of the State: The Diffusion of Power in the World Economy* (Cambridge: Cambridge University Press, 1996),

pp. xiii, xv. For a cogent discussion of the terminological problems that follow from the dynamics of change, see Czeslaw Mesjasz, "Stability, Turbulence or Chaos? System Analogies and Metaphors in the Language of Theory and Practice of International Security," a paper presented at the Annual Meeting of the International Studies Association, Toronto, March 18–22, 1997.

7 The conception of governance as systems of rule that embrace mechanisms of control is developed in Chapter 13. So as to insure a focus on nongovernmental as well as governmental rule systems, I use the label "collectivity" to refer to any group of people – be it a state, a corporation, a nonprofit organization, a social movement, etc. – who have a common affiliation but who are so numerous that they cannot interact on a face-to-face basis.

8 See, for example, the essays in James N. Rosenau and Ernst-Otto Czempiel (eds.), *Governance Without Government: Order and Change in World Politics* (Cambridge: Cambridge University Press, 1992).

9 These diverse "scapes" are the formulation of Arjun Appadurai, in *Modernity at Large: Cultural Dimensions of Globalization* (Minneapolis, MN: University of Minnesota Press, 1996), p. 33. One observer characterizes financescapes as a "space without rules" wherein a "several trillion-dollar pool . . . sloshes around in what is effectively a supranational cyberspace." Jessica Mathews, "We Live in a Dangerous Neighborhood," *Washington Post*, April 24, 1995, p. A19.

10 For an analysis of the bifurcation that resulted in the multi- and state-centric worlds, see James N. Rosenau, *Turbulence in World Politics: A Theory of Change and Continuity* (Princeton, NJ: Princeton University Press, 1990), Chap. 10.

11 John Mueller, "Democracy, Capitalism, and the End of Transition," in Michael Mandelbaum (ed.), *Postcommunism: Four Perspectives* (New York: Council on Foreign Relations, 1996), p. 103.

12 Harvey Schacter, "Simplicity," *Globe and Mail*, March 8, 1997, sec. D, pp. D1, D3.

13 For an extensive formulation of the change concept, see Rosenau, *Turbulence in World Politics*, Chap. 4. The notion that change and stasis are linked dialectically through the process of globalization and localization is advanced in James N. Rosenau, "New Dimensions of Security: The Interaction of Globalizing and Localizing Dynamics," *Security Dialogue*, Vol. 25, No. 3 (September 1994), pp. 255–81.

14 It should be noted that I do not take the measurement problems associated with the differences in kind and degree lightly even though I assume they are solvable. Here, however, my concern is analytic clarity rather than empirical precision and thus no attempt is made to elaborate on how the differences might be measured.

15 David Held, "Democracy and the New International Order," in Daniele Archibugi and David Held (eds.), *Cosmopolitan Democracy: An Agenda for a New World Order* (Cambridge: Polity Press, 1995), p. 101.

16 Stephen J. Kobrin, "The Architecture of Globalization: State Sovereignty in a Networked Global Economy," in John H. Dunning (ed.), *Globalization, Governments and Competition* (Oxford: Oxford University Press, 1996), pp. 3–4 in typescript version (italics in the original).

17 For an amusing fantasy that captures these differences by imagining King George III in 1776 tuned into CNN and possessing fiber optic phone lines, a pocket beeper, and access to the World Wide Web as he copes with a rebellious colony in America – with the result that "had the communications miracle been granted us earlier, there would be no Washington, DC for our politicians to blame for everything that annoys their constituents" – see Russell Baker, "Beep Beep King," *New York Times*, July 2, 1996, p. A15.

18 For diverse indicators pointing to the skill revolution, see James N. Rosenau, *Turbulence in World Politics: A Theory of Change and Continuity* (Princeton, NJ: Princeton University Press, 1990), Chap. 13. An effort to more directly and systematically test the skill revolution hypothesis can be found in James N. Rosenau and W. Michael Fagen, "A

New Dynamism in World Politics: Increasingly Skillful Citizens?" *International Studies Quarterly*, Vol. 41 (December 1997), pp. 655–86. See also Chapter 19 of Volume I of this collection.

19 For cogent analyses of complexity theory, see Roger Lewin, *Complexity: Life at the Edge of Chaos* (New York: Macmillan, 1992), and M. Mitchell Waldrop, *Complexity: The Emerging Science at the Edge of Order and Chaos* (New York: Simon and Schuster, 1992).

20 As one complexity theorist put it, referring to self-organization as a natural property of complex genetic systems, "There is 'order for free' out there." Stuart Kauffman, quoted in Lewin, *Complexity*, p. 25.

21 It should be noted, moreover, that the characteristics of complex adaptive systems pose substantial methodological problems. A major implication of the distortive potential of initial conditions, for instance, is that situations are content-dependent, thus rendering it extremely difficult to generalize from one situation to another. This is not the place, however, to address the methodological challenges that attend the presumption of complexity.

22 Howard W. French, "Ending a Chapter, Mobotu Cremates Rwanda Ally," *New York Times*, May 16, 1997, p. A4.

23 See, for example, the various essays in Thomas Princen and Matthew Finger, *Environmental NGOs in World Politics* (London: Routledge, 1994), and Peter Willetts (ed.), *The Conscience of the World: The Influence of Non-Governmental Organizations in the UN System* (Washington, DC: Brookings Institution, 1996).

24 By the Union of International Associations, which for more than three decades has published a series of annual compilations – known as the *Yearbook of International Organizations* – of established governmental and nongovernmental organizations active in the global arena.

25 The difference between NGOs and PVOs is that the former may be partially or fully funded by governments, whereas the latter rely exclusively on private sources for funding.

26 The 1992/1993 edition of its *Yearbook of International Organizations* has no fewer than thirty-two pages of appendices (all with two columns of fine print) that elaborate the definitions and classification rules used to generate, compile, and classify the thousands of diverse organizations it identifies. For a summary of the main outlines of the data presented in the 1992/1993 edition of the *Yearbook* (Munich: K. G. Saur Verlag, 1992) as well as for a discussion of the methodological problems that attach to gathering materials on a variety of types of NGOs, see James N. Rosenau, "Organizational Proliferation in a Changing World," in Commission on Global Governance, *Issues in Global Governance* (London: Kluwer Law International, 1995), pp. 265–94.

27 Cf. Joel Bleeke and David Ernst (eds.), *Collaborating to Compete: Using Strategic Alliances and Acquisitions in the Global Marketplace* (New York: Wiley, 1993).

28 These processes are amply described in Ronnie D. Lipschutz with Judith Mayer, *Global Civil Society and Global Environmental Governance* (Albany, NY: State University of New York Press, 1996); Kathryn Sikkink, "Human Rights, Principled Issue-Networks, and Sovereignty in Latin America," *International Organization*, Vol. 47 (Summer 1993), pp. 411–42; Bron Raymond Taylor (ed.), *Ecological Resistance Movements: The Global Emergence of Radical and Popular Environmentalism* (Albany, NY: State University of New York Press, 1995); and Paul Wapner, *Environmentalism Activism and World Civic Politics* (Albany, NY: State University of New York Press, 1996).

29 See, for example, Celestine Bohlen, "First Troops in Peace Force Get a Fanfare From Albania," *New York Times*, April 16, 1997, p. A7; Taylor B. Seybolt, *Coordination in Rwanda: The Humanitarian Response to Genocide and Civil War* (Cambridge, MA: Working Paper Series, Conflict Management Group, February 1997); and Christine M. Cervenak, *Learning on the Job: Organizational Interaction in El Salvador, 1991–1995*

(Cambridge, MA: Working Paper Series, Conflict Management Group, February 1997).

30 See, for example, Karen T. Litfin, *Ozone Discourses: Science and Politics in Global Environmental Cooperation* (New York: Columbia University Press, 1994), and Timothy J. Sinclair, "Passing Judgment: Credit Rating Processes as Regulatory Mechanisms of Governance in the Emerging World Order," *Review of International Political Economy,*" Vol. 1, No. 1 (April 1994), pp. 133–59.

31 Thomas L. Friedman, "Don't Mess With Moody's," *New York Times*, February 22, 1995, p. A19.

32 See the various essays in Thomas G. Weiss, *Humanitarian Emergencies and Military Help in Africa* (London: Macmillan Press, 1990).

33 See, for example, Ron Eyerman and Andrew Jamison, *Social Movements: A Cognitive Approach* (Cambridge: Polity Press, 1991); Enrique Laraña, Hank Johnston, and Joseph R. Gusfield (eds.), *New Social Movements: From Ideology to Identity* (Philadelphia, PA: Temple University Press, 1994); Sidney Tarrow, *Power in Movement: Social Movements, Collective Action and Politics* (Cambridge: Cambridge University Press, 1994); and Peter Willetts (ed.), *"The Conscience of the World": The Influence of Non-Governmental Organizations in the UN System* (Washington, DC: The Brookings Institution, 1996).

34 Dee W. Hock, "Institutions in the Age of Mindcrafting," a paper presented at the Bionomics Annual Conference, San Francisco, October 22, 1994.

35 W. Mitchell Waldrop, "The Trillion-Dollar Vision of Dee Hocks," *Fast Company* (October–November 1996), pp. 75–86.

36 Alan Webber, "The Best Organization Is No Organization," *USA Today*, March 6, 1997. p. 13a.

37 *Ibid.*

38 Lester M. Salamon, "The Global Associational Revolution: The Rise of the Third Sector on the World Scene," *Foreign Affairs*, Vol. 73 (July/August 1994), p. 109.

39 A good place to begin this rethinking process is Walter W. Powell, "Neither Market Nor Hierarchy: Network Forms of Organization," in Barry M. Staw and L. L. Cummings (eds.), *Research in Organizational Behavior*, Vol. 2 (Greenwich, CT: JAI Press, 1990), pp. 295–336.

40 For a cogent example of the understanding that can be developed if a conceptual adjustment to a networking perspective is accomplished, see Cathryn L. Thorup, *Redefining Governance in North America: The Impact of Cross-Border Networks and the Coalitions on Mexican Immigration into the United States* (Santa Monica, CA: Rand Corporation, 1993). See also Kathryn Sikkink, "Human Rights, Principled Issue-Networks, and Sovereignty in Latin America," *International Organization*, Vol. 47 (Summer 1993), pp. 411–42.

41 Cf. *Sharpening the Responses Against Global Corruption: Transparency International (TI Report 1996)* (Berlin, March 1996).

42 For an elaboration of the notion that world politics may mimic the global martket place, see John Agnew and Stuart Corbridge, *Mastering Space: Hegemony, Territory and International Political Economy* (New York: Routledge, 1995), p. 207.

43 The role of corporations is essayed in Claire Cutler, Virginia Haufler, and Tony Porter, "Private Authority and International Regimes," draft of a paper for a workshop at the Annual Meeting of the International Studies Association, San Diego, April 16, 1996, and David C. Korten, *When Corporations Rule the World* (West Hartford, CT: Kumarian Press, 1995).

44 Robert Boyer and Daniel Drache, "Introduction," in R. Boyer and D. Drache (eds.), *States Against Markets: The Limits of Globalization* (London: Routledge, 1996), p. 7.

45 See, for example, Kathryn Sikkink, "Codes of Conduct: The WHO/UNICEF Case," *International Organization*, Vol. 40 (Autumn 1986), pp. 815–40.

46 William Minter, "South Africa: Straight Talk on Sanctions," *Foreign Policy*, No. 65 (Winter 1986–1987), pp. 43–63.

47 Michael Edwards and David Hulme, "NGO Performance and Accountability," in M.

Edwards and D. Hulme (eds.), *Beyond the Magic Bullet: NGO Performance and Accountability in the Post-Cold War World* (West Hartford, CT: Kumanrian Press, 1996), p. 8.

48 John Markoff, "If Medium Is the Message, the Message Is the Web," *New York Times*, November 20, 1995, p. A1.

49 James K. Glassman, "Brave New Cyberworld," *Washington Post*, August 29, 1995, p. A19.

50 *Ibid.* (italics in the original).

51 *Ibid.*

52 *Ibid.*

53 Elizabeth Corcoran, "How the 'Butter Fund' Spread the Internet to Mongolia," *Washington Post*, March 1, 1996, p. A1.

54 "Internet Thrives in Nation Starved of Information," *Eastern Express* (Hong Kong), April 6, 1995, p. 9.

55 Zygmunt Bauman, "A Sociological Theory of Postmodernity," in Peter Beilharz, Gillian Robinson, and John Rundell (eds.), *Between Totalitarianism and Postmodernity: A Thesis Eleven Reader* (Cambridge, MA: MIT Press, 1992), p. 160.

17 Strong demand, huge supply: governance in an emergent epoch

1 This chapter was originally published in Ian Bache and Matthew Flinders (eds.), *Multi-Level Governance* (New York: Oxford University Press, 2004), pp. 31–48, and is reprinted here by permission of Oxford University Press, www.oup.com.

2 Jan M. Grell and Gary Gappert, "The Future of Governance in the United States: 1992–2002," *The Annals*, Vol. 522 (July 1992), p. 68. For reasons that are indicated below, I have altered this definition by treating "a membership or constituency" as the focus of governance rather than (as Grell and Gappert put it) "a culturally diverse society."

3 Viewing the government–governance distinction in this way, and influenced by the example of the European Union, my qualification of the concept of multi-level governance is to regard it as referring exclusively to governmental levels. Such a conception precludes treating multi-level governance as a form or precursor of transnational civil society.

4 The concept of SOAs is elaborated in James N. Rosenau, *Distant Proximities: Dynamics Beyond Globalization* (Princeton, NJ: Princeton University Press, 1990), Chap. 13.

5 The bifurcation of world affairs is amplified in James N. Rosenau, *Turbulence in World Politics: A Theory of Change and Continuity* (Princeton, NJ: Princeton University Press, 1990), Chap. 10.

6 Peter Evans, "The Eclipse of the State? Reflections on Stateness in an Era of Globalization," *World Politics*, Vol. 50 (October 1997), p. 65.

7 Floyd Norris, "Fewer Borders for Global Accounting," *New York Times*, January 26, 2001, p. C1.

8 David Ignatius, "Think Globally, Build Networks," *Washington Post*, January 28, 2001, p. B7.

9 Alexander Wendt, *Social Theory of International Politics* (Cambridge: Cambridge University Press, 1999), p. 308. For a similar and more encompassing critique along these lines, see Craig Murphy, "Global Governance: Poorly Done and Poorly Understood," *International Affairs*, Vol. 76, No. 4 (2000), pp. 789–803.

10 James N. Rosenau, *Along the Domestic–Foreign Frontier: Exploring Governance in a Turbulent World* (Cambridge: Cambridge University Press, 1997), Chap. 6.

11 Michael Schrage, "The Relationship Revolution," Merrill Lynch Forum (http://www.ml.com/woml/forum/relation.htm).

12 For an elaboration of forms of governance that are "non-spatial in essence . . . and populated by people who share a strong affinity with each other," see Bruce

E. Tonn and David Feldman, "Non-Spatial Government," *Futures*, Vol. 27, No. 1 (1995), pp. 11–38.

13 David Bornstein, "A Force Now in the World, Citizens Flex Social Muscle," *New York Times*, July 10, 1999, p. B7.

14 John Arquilla and David Ronfeldt, "A New Epoch – and Spectrum – of Conflict," in J. Arquilla and D. Ronfeldt (eds.), *In Athena's Camp: Preparing for Conflict in the Information Age* (Santa Monica, CA: RAND Corporation, 1997), p. 5.

15 For an elaborate and convincing account of the potential of authority exercised horizontally, see Dee Hock, *Birth of the Chaordic Age* (San Francisco, CA: Berrett-Koehler Publishers, 1999), esp. Chap. 8.

16 Jan Aart Scholte, *Globalization: A Critical Introduction* (London: Macmillan Press, 2000), pp. 56–8.

17 This is the central theme of Rosenau, *Along the Domestic–Foreign Frontier*.

18 Wolfgang H. Reinicke, "The Other World Wide Web: Global Public Policy Networks," *Foreign Policy* (Winter 1999–2000), p. 45.

19 For an elaboration of these prime fragmegrative dynamics, see Rosenau, *Distant Proximities*, Chap. 8.

20 For an incisive discussion praising the utility of the multi-level approach, see Thomas J. Courchene, "Celebrating Flexibility: An Interpretive Essay on the Evolution of Canadian Federalism," Benefactors Lecture (Montreal: C. D. Howe Institute, October 16, 1995).

21 John Boli, "Conclusion: World Authority Structures and Legitimations," in J. Boli and G. M. Thomas (eds.), *Constructing World Culture: International Nongovernmental Organizations Since 1875* Stanford, CA: Stanford University Press, 1999), p. 273.

22 For example, the levels-of-government typology – "called the ladder of governance" – traces the movement of issues onto and around the various rungs of the ladder as they arrest the attention of officials and publics, thereby highlighting the prospect that multi-level governance will prevail in the future. This scheme has been developed by the Workshop on Globalization and the Comprehensive Governance of Water, sponsored by the Commission on Economic, Environmental, and Social Policy of the World Conservation Union (Gland, Switzerland). Similarly, another state-based typology seeks "to capture a rather complex reality" through five models that "constitute a continuum ranging from the [societies] most dominated by the State and those in which the State plays the least role and indeed one in which there is argued to be governance without government" (B. Guy Peters and Jon Pierre, "Is There a Governance Theory?" a paper presented at the International Political Science Association, Quebec City, August 1–5, 2000, pp. 4, 5).

23 For example, see Thomas A. Loya and John Boli, "Standardization in the World Polity: Technical Rationality over Power," in J. Boli and G. M. Thomas (eds.), *Constructing World Culture: International Nongovernmental Organizations Since 1875*, Chap. 7.

24 David John Frank, Ann Hironaka, John W. Meyer, Evan Schofer, and Nancy Brandon Tuma, "The Rationalization and Organization of Nature in World Culture," in Boli and Thomas (eds.), *Constructing World Culture: International Nongovernmental Organizations Since 1875*, Chap. 3.

25 Hongying Wang and James N. Rosenau, "Transparency International and Corruption as an Issue of Global Governance," *Global Governance*, Vol. 7 (January 2001), pp. 25–49.

26 See, for example, "The Emergence and Transformation of the International Women's Movement," in Boli and Thomas (eds.), *Constructing World Culture: International Nongovernmental Organizations Since 1875*, Chap. 4.

27 One analyst estimates, however, that in the course of these complex sequences the governance of issues will become more formalized under IGOs and states, thereby "eating into the realms of the INGOs/NGOs." John Boli, personal correspondence (April 30, 1999).

28 Anthony Giddens and Christopher Pierson, *Conversations with Anthony Giddens: Making Sense of Modernity* (Cambridge: Polity Press, 1998), pp. 115–17.
29 See Chapter 8.
30 Ignatius, "Think Globally, Build Networks," p. B7.

Appendix
Publications of James N. Rosenau

Two-act play

Kwangju: An Escalatory Spree (produced at the Odyssey Theater, Los Angeles, Fall 1991).

Books and monographs

(with David Earnest, Yale Ferguson, and Oli R. Holsti), *On the Cutting Edge of Globalization: An Inquiry into American Elites* (Lanham, MD: Rowman & Littlefield, 2005).

Editor (with Ersel Aydinli), *Globalization, Security and the Nation State: Paradigms in Transition* (Albany, NY: State University of New York Press, 2005).

Distant Proximities: Dynamics Beyond Globalization (Princeton: Princeton University Press, 2003).

Editor (with J. P. Singh), *Information Technologies and Global Politics: The Changing Scope of Power and Governance* (Albany, NY: State University of New York Press, 2002).

Stability, Stasis and Security: Reflections on Superpower Leadership (Washington, DC: National Defense University Press, Global Forum, Vol. 1, No. 1, June 2000).

Editor (with Thomas C. Lawton and Amy C. Verdun), *Strange Power: Shaping the Parameters of International Relations and International Political Economy* (Brookfield, VT: Ashgate, 2000).

(with Mary Durfee), *Thinking Theory Thoroughly: Coherent Approaches to an Incoherent World* (Boulder, CO: Westview Press, 1995); revised edition (2000).

Along the Domestic–Foreign Frontier: Exploring Governance in a Turbulent World (Cambridge: Cambridge University Press, 1997).

Editor and contributor, *Global Voices: Dialogues in International Relations* (Boulder, CO: Westview Press, 1993).

The United Nations in a Turbulent World: Engulfed or Enlarged? (Boulder, CO: Lynne Rienner Publishers, 1992; translated into Japanese and published in Japan, 1995).

Editor (with Ernst-Otto Czempiel), *Governance Without Government: Order and Change in World Politics* (Cambridge: Cambridge University Press, 1992); translated into Portuguese and published by Editora UNB in Brazil (2000); translated into Chinese and published by Jianxi People's Publishing (forthcoming).

Turbulence in World Politics: A Theory of Change and Continuity (Princeton: Princeton University Press, 1990; Chapter 1 reproduced in P. R. Viotti and M. V. Kauppi (eds.), *International Relations Theory: Realism, Pluralism, Globalism, and Beyond* (Boston: Allyn and Bacon, 3rd ed., 1999), pp. 459–67, and also in R. W. Mansbach and E. Rhodes (eds.), *Global Politics in a Changing World: A Reader* (Boston: Houghton Mifflin, 2000), pp. 20–5; translated into Romanian and published by Editura Academiei Romane (Bucharest, 1994).

Editor (with Joseph Kruzel), *Journeys Through World Politics: Autobiographic Reflections of Thirty-Four Academic Travelers* (Lexington, MA: Lexington Books, 1989).

Editor (with Ernst-Otto Czempiel), *Global Changes and Theoretical Challenges: Approaches to World Politics for the 1990s* (Lexington, MA: Lexington Books, 1989).

Editor (with Hylke Tromp), *Interdependence and Conflict in World Politics* (Aldershot, UK: Gower Publications, 1989).

Editor (with Charles F. Hermann and Charles W. Kegley, Jr.), *New Directions in the Study of Foreign Policy* (Boston, MA: George Allen & Unwin, 1987).

Beyond Imagery: The Long-Run Adaptation of Two Chinas (Washington, DC: Washington Institute for Values in Public Policy, 1985).

(with Ole R. Holsti), *American Leadership in World Affairs: Vietnam and the Breakdown of Consensus* (Boston, MA: George Allen & Unwin, 1984).

Editor (with W. Ladd Hollist), *World Systems Structure: Continuity and Change* (Beverly Hills, CA: Sage Publications, 1981).

The Study of Political Adaptation (London: Frances Pinter Publishers, Ltd., 1981).

The Scientific Study of Foreign Policy (New York: Free Press, 1971; revised and enlarged edition, Frances Pinter Publishers, Ltd., 1980).

The Study of Global Interdependence (London: Frances Pinter Publishers, Ltd., 1980).

The Dramas of Political Life: An Introduction to the Problems of Governance (Duxbury, MA: Duxbury Press, 1980).

Editor (with Gavin Boyd and Kenneth Thompson), *World Politics* (New York: Free Press, 1976).

Editor, *In Search of Global Patterns* (New York: Free Press, 1976).

Citizenship Between Elections: An Inquiry Into the Mobilizable American (New York: Free Press, 1974).

Editor, *Comparing Foreign Policies: Theories, Findings and Methods* (Beverly Hills, CA: Sage Publications, 1974).

International Studies and the Social Sciences (Beverly Hills, CA: Sage Publications, 1973).

The Dramas of Politics: An Introduction to the Joys of Inquiry (Boston, MA: Little, Brown, 1973).

The Attentive Public in an Interdependent World: A Survey of Theoretical Perspectives and Empirical Findings (Columbus, OH: Mershon Center, Ohio State University, 1972).

Editor (with Vincent Davis and Maurice East), *The Analysis of International Politics* (New York: Free Press, 1972).

The Adaptation of National Societies: A Theory of Political Behavior and Its Transformation (New York: McCaleb-Seiler, 1970).

Race in International Politics: A Dialogue in Five Parts (Monograph Series in World Affairs, University of Denver, Vol. 7, No. 2, 1969–1970).

Editor, *Linkage Politics: Essays on the Convergence of National and International Systems* (New York: Free Press, 1969).

Editor (with Klaus Knorr), *Contending Approaches to International Politics* (Princeton, NJ: Princeton University Press, 1969).

The Attentive Public and Foreign Policy: A Theory of Growth and Some New Evidence (Research Monograph No. 31, Center of International Studies, Princeton University, 1968).

Of Boundaries and Bridges (Research Monograph No. 27, Center of International Studies, Princeton University, 1967).

Editor, *Domestic Sources of Foreign Policy* (New York, NJ: Free Press, 1967).

Editor, *International Aspects of Civil Strife* (Princeton, NJ: Princeton University Press, 1964).

National Leadership and Foreign Policy: A Case Study in the Mobilization of Public Support (Princeton, NJ: Princeton University Press, 1963).

Calculated Control as a Unifying Concept in the Study of International Politics and Foreign Policy (Research Monograph No. 15, Center of International Studies, Princeton University, 1963).

Public Opinion and Foreign Policy: An Operational Formulation (New York: Random House, 1961).

Editor, *International Politics and Foreign Policy: A Reader in Research and Theory* (New York: Free Press, 1961; revised edition, 1969).

The Nomination of "Chip" Bohlen (New York: Henry Holt, 1958).

Editor, *The Roosevelt Treasury* (New York: Doubleday, 1951).

Editor, *F.D.R. – His Personal Letters, 1905–1928* (New York: Duell, Sloan & Pearce, 1949).

Articles and papers

"Think Globally, Pray Locally," *World Order*, Vol. 37, Nos. 2–3 (2005–06).

"People and the Internet as Agents of Change," a paper presented at the Workshop on Governance Regulations and Powers on the Internet, Paris, May 27–28, 2005.

(with Thomas Olesen), "The Reduction of Distance and the Construction of Proximity: Solidarity Movements in World Politics," a paper presented at the 46th Annual Meeting of the International Studies Association, Honolulu, March 1–5, 2005.

"Declaration of Interdependence," *International Studies Perspectives*, Vol. 6 (February 2005), p. 155.

"Fairness and Globalization," in Richard Pratt (ed.), *Fairness, Globalization and Public Institutions* (Honolulu: University of Hawaii Press, 2005), Chap. 6.

(with Yale Ferguson), "Superpowerdom Before and After September 11, 2001: A Postinternational Perspective," translated into French and published in *Études Internationales*, Vol. XXXV (December 2004), pp. 623–39.

"Understanding World Affairs: The Potential of Collaboration," *Globalizations*, Vol. 1, No. 2 (December 2004), pp. 326–39.

(with Ersel Aydinli), "Courage versus Caution: A Dialogue on Entering and Prospering in IR," *International Studies Review*, Vol. 6 (Fall 2004), pp. 511–26.

"Partisanship and the Dynamics of Globalization," in Henry R. Nau and David Shambaugh (eds.), *Divided Diplomacy and the Next Administration: Conservative and Liberal Alternatives* (Washington, DC: The Elliott School of International Affairs, George Washington University, 2004), pp. 97–101.

"Governing the Ungovernable: The Challenge of a Global Disaggregation of Authority," a paper prepared for presentation at the Annual Conference of the International Society for New Institutional Economics, Tucson, September 30–October 3, 2004.

"Turbulence and Terrorism: Reframing or Readjusting the Model?" in Ersel Aydinli and James N. Rosenau (eds.), *Globalization, Security and the Nation State: Paradigms in Transition* (Albany, NY: State University of New York Press, 2005), pp. 221–9.

"Territorial Affiliations and Emergent Roles: The Shifting Nature of Identity in a Globalizing World," a paper prepared for presentation at the 5th Pan-European International Relations Conference, The Hague: September 11, 2004.

"The Skill Revolution as a Dynamic Process," a paper presented at the Annual Conference of the Future Society, Washington, July 30, 2004.

(with David Earnest), "On the Cutting Edge of Globalization Before and After 9/11," a paper presented at the Annual Meeting of the International Studies Association, Montreal, March 2004.

"Building Blocks of a New Paradigm for Studying World Politics," a paper prepared for presentation at the International Symposium on "Non-State Actors and New International Realities," Pantelon University, Athens, Greece, January 30, 2004.

"Strong Demand, Huge Supply: Governance in an Emergent Epoch," in Ian Bache and Matthew Flinders (eds.), *Multi-Level Governance* (Oxford: Oxford University Press, 2004), pp. 31–48.

"Emergent Spaces, New Places, and Old Faces: Proliferating Identities in a Globalizing World," in Jonathan Friedman and Shalini Randeria (eds.), *Worlds on the Move: Globalization, Migration, and Cultural Security* (London: I.B. Tauris, 2004), pp. 29–68.

"Many Globalizations, One International Relations," *Globalizations*, Vol. 1, No. 1 (September 2004), pp. 1–8.

"Followership and Discretion: Assessing the Dynamics of Modern Leadership," *Harvard International Review*, Vol. XXVI, No. 3 (Fall 2004).

"The Theoretical Imperative: Unavoidable Explication," *Asian Journal of Political Science*, Vol. 11 (December 2003), pp. 7–20.

(in French) Entretien avec James Rosenau, "Mondialisation: le pouvoir deviant flou," *Alternatives Internationales* (Juillet–août 2003), pp. 46–50.

(with David Earnest), "Signifying Nothing? The Perils for International Relations Theory of the Complexity Sciences," in Neil E. Harrison (ed.), *Global Complexity: Agent-Based Models in Global and International Studies* (Albany, NY: SUNY Press, forthcoming).

(with Diane Wildsmith), "Jakarta and the Zone of Fragmegration," in Ryan Bishop, John Phillips and Wei Wei Yeo (eds.), *Postcolonial Urbanism: The Southeast Asia Cities and Global Processes* (New York and London: Routledge, 2003), pp. 187–202.

"Global Governance as Disaggregated Complexity," a paper presented at the Conference on Contending Perspectives on Global Governance, University of Delaware, October 18, 2002.

"Globalization and Governance: Bleak Prospects for Sustainability," *International Politics and Society*, No. 3 (2003), pp. 11–29; reproduced in Alfred Pfaller and Marika Lerch (eds.), *New Trends in International Politics and Society* (Somerset, NJ: Transaction Publishers, 2005).

"NGOs and Fragmented Authority in Globalizing Space," in Yale Ferguson and R. Barry Jones (eds.), *Political Space: Frontiers of Change and Governance in a Globalizing World* (Albany, NY: State University of New York Press, 2002), pp. 261–79.

"The Globalization of Globalization," in Michael Brecher and Frank Harvey (eds.), *Millennium Reflections in International Studies* (Ann Arbor,: University of Michigan Press, 2002), pp. 271–90.

"Generational Change and Internet Literacy," a paper prepared for presentation at the Annual Meeting of the American Political Science Association, Boston, August 29, 2002.

"Global–Local Tensions in the Asia Pacific Region," a paper presented at the Biennial Conference on Enhancing Regional Security Cooperation, sponsored by the Asia-Pacific Center for Security Studies, Honolulu, July 16, 2002.

"Ominous Tensions in a Globalizing World," a paper presented at the 10th International Summer Seminar on The New International Crisis: Implications for International Politics, Hydra, Greece, July 1, 2002, and again at the Conference on International Relations, Middle East Technological University, Ankara, Turkey, July 3, 2002.

"Unfulfilled Potential: Sociology and International Relations," *International Review of Sociology*, Vol. 12, No. 3 (November 2002), pp. 543–47.

"Transnational Accountability and the Politics of Shame," *ILSA Journal of International & Comparative Law*, Vol. 8 (Spring 2002), pp. 353–56.

"Globalization and Domestic Conflict," a paper presented at the Conference on Colombian

Political, Social and Economic Conditions, sponsored by Los Andes University, Bogota, April 12, 2002.

"Big Judgments, Elusive Phenomena, and Nuanced Analysis: Assessing Where the World is Heading," a paper prepared for the Workshop on Global Governance: Towards a New Grand Compromise?, sponsored by the Department of Political Science at the University of Toronto in conjunction with the Canadian Political Science Association Annual Meeting, May 29, 2002.

"Rigid Boundaries: States, Societies, and International Relations," a paper presented at the Annual Meeting of the International Studies Association, New Orleans, March 26, 2002.

"Fairness and Globalization," a paper presented at the Dialogic Conference on Globalization, Public Institutions and Fairness, University of Hawaii, Honolulu, January 8, 2002.

"Human Rights in a Turbulent and Globalizing World," in Alison Brysk (ed.), *Globalization and Human Rights* (Berkeley, CA: University of California Press, 2002), pp. 148–67.

(with Peter Koehn), "Transnational Competence in an Emergent Epoch," *International Studies Perspectives*, Vol. 3 (2002), pp. 105–27.

(with David Johnson), "Information Technologies and Turbulence in World Politics," in Juliann Allison (ed.), *Technology, Development, and Democracy Conflict, Cooperation and Information* (Albany, NY: State University of New York Press, 2002), pp. 55–78.

"The Governance of Fragmegration: Neither a World Republic Nor a Global Interstate System," *Studia Diplomatica*, Vol. LIII, No. 5 (2000), pp. 15–39.

"Aging Agendas and Ambiguous Anomalies: Tensions and Contradictions of an Emergent Epoch," in Stephanie Lawson (ed.), *The New Agenda for International Relations* (Cambridge: Polity Press, 2002), pp. 19–34.

"The Challenges and Tensions of Global Life," in Donald Lamberton (ed.), *Managing the Global: Globalization, Employment and Quality of Life* (London and New York: I.B. Tauris, 2002), pp. 105–17.

"Information Technologies and the Skills, Networks, and Structures that Sustain World Affairs," in James N. Rosenau and J. P. Singh (eds.), *Information Technologies and Global Politics: The Changing Scope of Power and Governance* (Albany, NY: State University of New York Press, 2002), pp. 275–85.

"Governance in a New Global Order," in David Held and Anthony McGrew (eds.), *Governing Globalization: Power, Authority and Global Governance* (Cambridge: Polity Press, 2002), pp. 70–86.

"Change as Concept and Conversation-Stopper," a paper presented at the Annual Meeting of the American Political Science Association, San Francisco, August 30, 2001.

"Pre-Theorizing About Foreign Policy in a Globalized World," a paper prepared for presentation at the Meeting of the International Studies Association, Hong Kong, July 2001.

"Stability, Stasis, and Change: A Fragmegrating World," in Richard L. Kugler and Ellen L. Frost (eds.), *The Global Century: Globalization and National Security*, (Washington, DC: National Defense University, 2001), Vol. 1, pp. 127–53.

"Political Science and Political Processes: Narrowing the Gap?" in Frank H. Fu (ed.), *The Development of Social Sciences in the 21st Century* (Hong Kong: Faculty of Social Sciences, Hong Kong Baptist University, 2001), pp. 32–47.

"Supraterritoriality and Interdisciplinarity," *International Studies Review*, Vol. 3 (Spring 2001), pp. 115–18.

"Three Overlapping Revolutions: One Neutral, All Powerful," a paper presented at the Annual Meeting of the International Studies Association, Chicago, February 22, 2001.

(with Hongying Wang), "Transparency International and Corruption as an Issue of Global Governance," *Global Governance*, Vol. 7 (January 2001), pp. 25–49.

"Boundaries as Bumps in the Road of a Fragmegrated World," a paper presented at the Conference on the Canada–US Border, Vancouver, Waterfront Centre Hotel, October 24, 2000.

"Confessions of a Pre-Postmodernist: Or Can an Old-Timer Change Course?" in Neil L. Waters (ed.), *Beyond the Area Studies War: Toward a New International Studies* (Hanover: University Press of New England, 2000), pp. 181–9.

"Diplomacy, Proof, and Authority in the Information Age," in Bernard I. Finel and Kristin Lord (eds.), *Power and Conflict in the Age of Transparency* (New York: St. Martin's Press, 2000), pp. 315–38.

"R. I. S. Interview with Jim Rosenau," *Review of International Studies*, Vol. 26 (2000), pp. 465–75.

"Disaggregated Order and Disorder in Globalized Space," in Birthe Hansen and Bertel Heurlin (eds.), *The New World Order: Contrasting Theories* (London: Macmillan Press, 2000), pp. 18–45.

(with David C. Earnest), "The Spy Who Loved Globalization," *Foreign Policy*, (September/October 2000), pp. 88–90.

"The Challenges and Tensions of a Globalized World," *American Studies International*, Vol. XXXVIII, No. 2 (2000), pp. 8–22.

"The Information Revolution: Both Powerful and Neutral," in Thomas E. Copeland (ed.), *The Information Revolution and National Security* (Carlisle, PA: Strategic Studies Institute, 2000), pp. 9–27.

(with Thomas C. Lawton and Amy C. Verdun) "Introduction: Looking Beyond the Confines," in T. C. Lawton, J. N. Rosenau, and A. C. Verdun (eds.), *Strange Power: Shaping the Parameters of International Relations and International Political Economy* (Brookfield, VT: Ashgate, 2000), pp. 3–18.

(with David C. Earnest, Louis W. Pauly, T. C. Lawton, and A. C. Verdun), "Reflections: Blurring the Boundaries and Shaping the Agenda," in Lawton, Rosenau, and Verdun (eds.), *Strange Power*, pp. 409–20.

"Strategic Links in an Emergent Epoch: From People to Collectivities and Back Again," a paper prepared for the Conference on the New Strategic Discourse, sponsored by the Jaffee Center for Strategic Studies and the Cummings Center for Russian and East European Studies at Tel Aviv University, in collaboration with the IDF Doctrine Division of the General Staff, May 28–June 3, 2000.

"Normative and Complexity Theories: Complementary Approaches to World Affairs," in Paul Wapner and Lester Edwin J. Ruiz (eds.), *Principled World Politics: The Challenge of Normative International Relations* (Lanham, MD: Rowman & Littlefield, 2000), pp. 35–49.

"Governance in a Globalizing World," in David Held and Anthony McGrew (eds.), *The Global Transformations Reader* (Cambridge, UK: Polity Press, 2000), pp. 181–90; revised edition (2003), pp. 223–33.

"States, Sovereignty, and Diplomacy in the Information Age," United States Institute of Peace, *Virtual Diplomacy Series*, No. 5 (Washington, D.C.: February 2000), pp. 1–16.

"Authority in Crisis: A Global Process and a Hong Kong Reality," *Asian Journal of Political Science*, Vol. 7 (December 1999), pp. 1–20.

(with David C. Earnest), "No One's Disciple: The American Academy's Reaction to the Works of Susan Strange," a paper prepared for presentation at the Annual Meeting of the International Studies Association, Los Angeles, March 16, 2000.

"Change, Complexity, and Governance in Globalized Space," in Jan Pierre (ed.), *Debating Governance* (Oxford: Oxford University Press, 2000), pp. 167–200.

"Beyond Postinternationalism," in Heidi Hobbs (ed.), *Pondering Postinternationalism: A Paradigm for the 21st Century?* (Albany, NY: State University of New York Press, 2000), pp. 219–37.

"A Transformed Observer in a Transforming World," *Studia Diplomatica*, Vol. LII, No. 1–2 (1999), pp. 5–14.

"Many Damn Things Simultaneously – At Least for Awhile: Complexity Theory and World Affairs," *Theoria*, No. 94 (December 1999), pp. 48–66.

"The Future of Politics," *Futures*, Vol. 31 (November/December 1999), pp. 1005–16.

"People, Nations, and Credit Cards: Major Variables in an Emergent Epoch," *International Politics*, Vol. 36 (September 1999), pp. 291–320.

(with James H. Liu) "The Psychology of Fragmegration: On the Uses of a Simultaneity of Consciousness in the 'New World Order,' ' a paper presented at the Third Conference of the Asian Association of Social Psychology, Taipei, Taiwan, August 4–7, 1999.

"Toward an Ontology for Global Governance," in Martin Hewson and Timothy J. Sinclair (eds.), *Approaches to Global Governance Theory* (Albany, NY: State University of New York Press, 1999), pp. 287–301.

"The Challenge of Systemic Hatred: Rebuilding The State in War-torn Societies," a paper presented at a summer workshop sponsored by the Academic Council for the United Nations System, New Haven, July 29, 1999.

"Relocated Politics in a Reorganized World," a paper presented at the Managing Global Issues Seminar, Carnegie Endowment for International Peace, Washington, June 21, 1999.

"In Search of Institutional Contexts," a paper presented at the Conference on International Institutions: Global Processes-Domestic Consequences, Duke University, April 9–11, 1999.

"The Skill Revolution and Restless Publics in Globalized Space," in Michel Girard (ed.), *Individualism and World Politics* (New York: St. Martin's Press, 1999), pp. 44–68; also translated into Chinese.

"The Future of Governance," a paper prepared for the Roundtable of the Renewing Governance Project, Toronto, Parliamentary Centre, February 9, 1999.

(with Ole R. Holsti), "Linkages Between Domestic and Foreign Policy Beliefs Among American Opinion Leaders: Partisan and Ideological Foundations," in E. R. Wittkopf and James M. McCormick (eds.), *The Domestic Sources of American Foreign Policy: Insights and Evidence*, 3rd ed. (Lanham, MD: Rowman and Littlefield, 1999), pp. 33–50.

(with Ole R. Holsti), "US Internationalism: Intact or In Trouble?" in E. R. Wittkopf and Christopher M. Jones (eds.), *The Future of American Foreign Policy*, 3rd ed. (New York: St. Martin's Press, 1999), pp. 124–39.

"Preface," Joshua S. Goldstein (ed.), *Longman Atlas of War and Peace* (New York: Longman, 1999), pp. 1–2.

"The United States in a Turbulent World," in Robert L. Hutchings (ed.), *At the End of the American Century: America's Role in the Post-Cold War World* (Washington, DC: Woodrow Wilson Center Press, 1998), pp. 98–109.

"Governance and Democracy in a Globalizing World," in Daniele Archibugi, David Held, and Martin Köhler (eds.), *Citizenship, Sovereignty and Cosmopolitanism: Studies in Cosmopolitan Democracy* (Cambridge: Polity Press, 1998), pp. 28–57.

"Powerful Tendencies, Enduring Tensions, and Glaring Contradictions: The United Nations in a Turbulent Era," in Albert J. Paolini, Anthony P. Jarvis, and Christian

Reus-Smit (eds.), *Between Sovereignty and Global Governance: The United Nations, the State and Civil Society* (New York: St. Martin's Press, 1998), pp. 252–73.

"The Intermestics of the US Policy-Making Process," translated as "La Interméstica del Proceso Estadounidense de Formulación de Políticas," in Juan Gabriel Tokatlian (ed.), *Colombia y Estados Unidos: Problemas y Perspectivas* (Bogotá: TM Editores, 1998), pp. 297–312.

"Hurricanes Are Not the Only Intruders: The Caribbean in an Era of Global Turbulence," in M. C. Desch and J. I. Domínguez (eds.), *From Pirates to Drug Lords: The Post-Cold War Caribbean Security Environment* (Albany, NY: State University of New York Press, 1998), pp. 11–32.

"States and Sovereignty in a Globalizing World," in J. Eatwell, E. Jelin, A. McGrew, and J. Rosenau, *Understanding Globalization: The Nation-State, Democracy and Economic Policies in the New Epoch* (Stockholm: Swedish Ministry for Foreign Affairs, 1998), pp. 31–55.

"Global Environmental Governance: Delicate Balances, Subtle Nuances, and Multiple Challenges," in Mats Rolén, Helen Sjöberg, and Uno Svedin (eds.), *International Governance on Environmental Issues* (Dordrecht, The Netherlands: Kluwer Academic Publishers, 1997), pp. 19–56.

"Beyond Latin America: Change and Complexity in Globalized Space," a paper prepared for presentation at the I Brazilian Congress of International Relations, sponsored by the Graduate Program in International Relations of the Universidade de Brasilia, Brasilia, March 24, 1998.

"Global Affairs in an Epochal Transformation," in Edward Peartree and Ryan Henry (eds.), *The Information Revolution and International Security* (Washington, DC: CISS Press, 1998), pp. 31–57.

"The Dynamism of a Turbulent World," in Michael Klare and Yogesh Chandrani (eds.), *World Security: Challenges for a New Century*, 3rd ed. (New York: St. Martin's Press, 1998), pp. 18–35.

"Foreword," in C. Richard Nelson and Kenneth Weisbrode (eds.), *Reversing Relations with Former Adversaries: US Foreign Policy After the Cold War* (Gainesville, FL: University Press of Florida, 1998), pp. vii–x.

"Disorder and Order in a Turbulent World: The Emergence of Globalized Space," in C. W. Kegley and E. R. Wittkopf (eds.), *The Global Agenda*, 5th ed. (New York: McGraw Hill, 1998), pp. 145–69.

(with W. Michael Fagen), "Increasingly Skillful Citizens: A New Dynamism in World Politics?" *International Studies Quarterly*, Vol. 41 (December 1997), pp. 655–86; abridged and translated into Japanese, Kenichiro Hirano (ed.), *Japan, Asia and the Global System: Toward the Twenty-First Century* (Tokyo: Kokusai Shoin, Co., Ltd., 1998), Chap. 7.

"The Complexities and Contradictions of Globalization," *Current History* (November 1997), pp. 360–4; reprinted in H. E. Purkitt (ed.), *World Politics 98/99*, 19th ed. (Guilford, CT: Dushkin/McGraw-Hill, 1998), pp. 15–19.

"Symbols of Sovereignty and Realities of Globalization: A Context for Mexican Affairs," a paper prepared for a cancelled seminar on Globalization: Effects on Mexican Foreign Policy, sponsored by the Universidad Iberoamericana and the Georgetown University Mexico Project, Mexico City, February 27–28, 1998.

"Daring to Probe: Change, Contradiction, and Complexity in Globalized Space," a paper prepared for presentation at the Seminar on International Studies in the Americas: Reflections at fin de siècle, sponsored by the Venezuelan Center of International and Global Relations, Caracas, November 13, 1997.

"Material and Imagined Communities in Globalized Space," in Donald H. McMillen (ed.),

Globalization and Regional Communities: Geoeconomic, Sociocultural and Security Implications for Australia (Toowomba, Australia: USQ Press, 1997), pp. 24–40.

"Change and Complexity: Challenges to Understanding in World Affairs," a paper presented at the Inaugural Ceremonies for the new Master's Program in World Politics, Universidad National de Colombia, Bogota, August 29, 1997; translated into Spanish and published in *Analisis Politico*, No. 12 (September 1997), pp. 106–19.

"Citizenship Without Moorings: Individual Responses to a Turbulent World," in T. K. Oommen (ed.), *Citizenship and National Identity: From Colonialism to Globalism* (New Delhi: Sage, 1997), pp. 227–59.

"Imposing Global Order: A Synthesized Ontology for a Turbulent Era," in Stephen Gill and James H. Mittelman (eds.), *Innovation and Transformation in International Studies* (Cambridge: Cambridge University Press, 1997), pp. 220–35.

"The Person, The Household, The Community, and The Globe: Notes for a Theory of Multilateralism in a Turbulent World," in Robert W. Cox (ed.), *The New Realism: Perspectives on Multilateralism and World Order* (Basingstoke: Macmillan, 1997), pp. 57–80.

"Enlarged Citizen Skills and Enclosed Coastal Seas: Notes on the Delicacies of Governance and the Complexities of the Environment," in L. Anathea Brooks and Stacy D. VanDeveer (eds.), *Saving the Seas: Values, Scientists and International Governance* (College Park, MD: Maryland Sea Grant College, 1997), pp. 329–559.

(with Mary Durfee), "Playing Catch-Up: IR Theory and Poverty," *Millennium*, Vol. 25, No. 3 (1996), pp. 521–45.

(with Vincent Davis and Maurice A. East), "Harold and Margaret Sprout," in Patricia H. Marks (ed.), *Luminaries: Princeton Faculty Remembered* (Princeton, NJ: Association of Princeton Graduate Alumni, 1996), pp. 285–96.

"From the Laboratory to the Bully Pulpit: Science in a Turbulent World," a paper presented at the Seminar Series on New Science and Technology Issues and Their Impact on the International System, sponsored by the Rand Corporation, Washington, DC, November 21, 1996.

"Many Damn Things Simultaneously: Complexity Theory and World Affairs," in David S. Alberts and Thomas J. Czerwinski (eds.), *Complexity, Global Politics, and National Security* (Washington, D.C.: National Defense University, 1997), pp. 73–100; translated into Spanish and published in *Nueva Sociedad*, No. 148 (March/April 1997), pp. 70–83.

"Along the Domestic–Foreign Frontier: An Ontology for a World with Shifting and Porous Boundaries," a paper presented at the Nobel Institute Research Seminar, Oslo, Norway, June 6, 1996: revised for the Annual Meeting of the American Political Science Association, San Francisco, August 31, 1996.

"The Dynamics of Globalization: Toward an Operational Formulation," *Security Dialogue*, Vol. 27 (September 1996), pp. 247–62; reprinted in Richard Higgott and Anthony Payne (eds.), *The New Political Economy of Globalization* (Cheltenham: Edward Elgar, 2000).

"Complexity, Sovereignty, and Humanitarian Interventions: Obstacles to the Quest for Vision," a paper presented at the Conference on Sovereignty, Responsibility, and Accountability: A Challenge for Africa, sponsored by the Brookings Institution, Washington, DC, June 24, 1996.

"Powerful Tendencies, Startling Discrepancies, and Elusive Dynamics: The Challenge of Studying World Politics in a Turbulent Era," *Australian Journal of International Affairs*, Vol. 50 (April 1996), pp. 23–30; translated into Farsi and published in the *Middle East Quarterly*, Vol. 2 (Summer 1995), pp. 329–40.

"Complex Humanitarian Emergencies: Toward an Integrated Understanding," a paper presented at the Panel Discussion on Humanitarian Intervention, Globalization Trends, and the Changing State-Centric Paradigm of the Post-Cold War Era, sponsored by the Common Security Forum, Center for Population and Development Studies, Harvard University, Cambridge, April 1, 1996.

"The Adaptation of the United Nations in a Turbulent World," in Ramesh Thakur (ed.), *The United Nations at Fifty: Retrospect and Prospect* (Dunedin: University of Otago Press, 1996), pp. 229–40; reprinted in R. Thakur (ed.), *Past Imperfect, Future Uncertain: The United Nations at Fifty* (New York: St Martin's Press, 1998), pp. 176–88.

"Moral Concerns, National Interests, and Humanitarian Interventions," a paper presented at the Festival of Ideas '96: Innovative Ideas and Solutions for the Twenty-first Century, West Virginia University, Morgantown, February 7, 1996.

(with Ole R. Holsti), "Liberals, Populists, Libertarians, and Conservatives: The Link Between Domestic and International Affairs," *International Political Science Review*, Vol. 17 (January 1996), pp. 29–54.

"Distant Proximities: The Dynamics and Dialectics of Globalization," in Bjorn Hettne (ed.), *International Political Economy: Understanding Global Disorder* (London: Zed Books, 1995), pp. 46–64.

"Multilateral Governance and the Nation-State System: A Post-Cold War Assessment," (Washington, DC: Occasional Papers in Western Hemisphere Governance, No. 1, Inter-American Dialogue, September 1995).

"Changing Capacities of Citizens, 1945–1995," in Commission on Global Governance, *Issues in Global Governance* (London: Kluwer Law International, 1995), pp. 1–58.

"Changing States in a Changing World, 1945–1995," in Commission on Global Governance, *Issues in Global Governance* (London: Kluwer Law International, 1995), pp. 265–94.

"Organizational Proliferation in a Changing World," in Commission on Global Governance, *Issues in Global Governance* (London: Kluwer Law International, 1995), pp. 371–403.

"Security in a Turbulent World," *Current History*, Vol. 94 (May 1995), pp. 193–200.

"Governance in the 21st Century," *Global Governance*, Vol. 1 (1995), pp. 13–43; reprinted in Richard Higgott and Anthony Payne (eds.), *The New Political Economy of Globalization* (Cheltenham: Edward Elgar, 2000).

(with Ole R. Holsti), "Gender and Political Beliefs of American Opinion Leaders," in F. D'Amico and P. R. Beckman (eds.), *Women and World Politics* (Westport, CT: Bergin and Garvey, 1995), pp. 113–42.

"Sovereignty in a Turbulent World," in Michael Mastanduno and Gene Lyons (eds.), *Beyond Westphalia? State Sovereignty and International Intervention* (Baltimore, MD: Johns Hopkins University Press, 1995), pp. 191–227.

"Signals, Signposts, and Symptoms: Interpreting Change and Anomalies in World Politics," *European Journal of International Relations*, Vol. 1 (March 1995), pp. 113–22.

"Multilateralism and the United Nations," a paper presented at United Nations University Global Seminar '94, Shonan Village, Japan, September 6, 1994.

(with Burton M. Sapin), "Theory and Practice in Foreign Policy-Making: Academics and Practitioners – the American Experience," in Michel Girard, Wolf-Dieter Eberwein, and Keith Webb (eds.), *Theory and Practice in Foreign Policy-Making: National Perspectives on Academics and Professionals in International Relations* (London: Pinter Publishers, 1994), pp. 126–35.

"New Dimensions of Security: The Interaction of Globalizing and Localizing Dynamics," *Security Dialogue*, Vol. 25, No. 3 (September 1994), pp. 255–81; translated into Spanish and reprinted in *Dialogo Y Seguridad*, No. 2 (November 1995), pp. 21–52.

(with Michael Fagen), "Domestic Elections as International Events," in Carl Kaysen, Robert A. Pastor, and Laura W. Reed (eds.), *Collective Responses to Regional Problems: The*

Case of Latin America and the Caribbean (Cambridge, MA: American Academy of Arts and Sciences, 1994), pp. 29–68, 167–76.

"China in a Bifurcated World: Competing Theoretical Perspectives," in Thomas W. Robinson and David Shambaugh (eds.), *Chinese Foreign Policy: Theory and Practice* (Oxford: Oxford University Press, 1994) pp. 524–51.

"Restless Publics as Sources of Global Turbulence," a paper presented at the Table-Ronde on Individuals in World Politics, Congress of the Association Francaise de Science Politique, Paris, September 24, 1992; translated and reproduced as "Les Individus en Mouvement Comme Source de Turbulence Globale," in Michel Girard (ed.), *Les Individus Dans La Politique Internationale* (Paris: Economica, 1994), pp. 81–106; also translated into Russian and Chinese.

"A Wherewithal for Revulsion: Notes on the Obsolescence of Interstate War," a paper presented at the Annual Meeting of the American Political Science Association, Washington, DC, August 30, 1991; translated and reproduced as "Neue Perspektiven in der Weltpolitik: Anmerkungen zur Antiquiertheit zwischenstaatlicher Kriege," in G. Krell and H. Müller (eds.), *Frieden und Konflikt in den Internationalen Beziehungen: Festschrift für Ernst-Otto Czempiel* (Frankfurt: Campus Verlag, 1994), pp. 116–32.

"Armed Force and Armed Forces in a Turbulent World," in James Burk (ed.) *The Military in New Times: Adapting Armed Forces to a Turbulent World* (Boulder, CO: Westview Press, 1993), pp. 25–60; reproduced in James Burk (ed.), *The Adaptive Military: Armed Forces to a Turbulent World*, 2nd ed. (New Brunswick, NJ: Transaction Publishers, 1998), pp. 49–85.

(with Eileen Crum), "From Superpower Deadlock to Ordinary Relationship: Materials for a Theory of US–Soviet Relations," in Manus I. Midlarsky, John A. Vasquez, and Peter V. Gladkov (eds.), *From Rivalry to Cooperation: Russian and American Perspectives on the Post-Cold War Era* (New York: HarperCollins, 1994), pp. 126–44.

(with Ole R. Holsti), "The Foreign Policy Beliefs of American Leaders After the Cold War: The Persistence or Abatement of Partisan Cleavages?" in Eugene R. Wittkopf (ed.), *The Future of American Foreign Policy* (New York: St. Martin's Press, 1994), pp. 127–47.

(with Ole R. Holsti), "The Structure of Foreign Policy Beliefs Among American Opinion Leaders – After the Cold War," *Millennium*, Vol. 22 (Summer 1993), pp. 235–78.

"The Global Context: Change, Turbulence, and Order," in E. J. Kirk, B. D. Smith, and W. T. Wander (eds.), *Trends and Implications for Arms Control, Proliferation, and International Security in the Changing Global Environment* (Washington, DC: American Association for the Advancement of Science, 1993), pp. 1–24.

"The Processes of Globalization: Substantive Spillovers, Elusive Exchanges, and Subtle Symbols," *Etudes Internationales*, Vol. XXIV (September 1993), pp. 497–512.

"Integrating and Disintegrating Forces in International Affairs," *Moral Education III* (New York: Carnegie Council on Ethics and International Affairs, 1993), pp. 1–8.

(with Paul R. Viotti), "Military Establishments in the Aftermath of the Cold War: A Theoretical and Comparative Analysis," a paper presented at the Annual Meeting of the American Political Science Association, Washington, DC, September 3, 1993.

"Notes on the Servicing of Triumphant Subgroupism," *International Sociology*, Vol. 8 (March 1993), pp. 77–90.

"Coherent Connection or Commonplace Contiguity? Theorizing About the California–Mexican Overlap," in Katrina Burgess and Abraham F. Lowenthal (eds.), *The California–Mexico Connection* (Stanford: Stanford University Press, 1993), pp. 3–33.

"Environmental Challenges in a Turbulent World," in Ronnie D. Lipschutz and Ken Conca (eds.), *The State and Social Power in Global Environmental Politics* (New York: Columbia University Press, 1993), pp. 71–93.

"International Theory and Policy: Toward a Convergence," *International Affairs Review*, Vol. 2 (Spring 1993), pp. 3–10.

"International Relations," in Joel Krieger (ed.), *The Oxford Companion to Politics of the World* (New York: Oxford University Press, 1993), pp. 455–60; 2nd ed. (2001), pp. 424–27.

"Environmental Challenges in a Global Context," in Sheldon Kamieniecki (ed.) *Environmental Politics in the International Arena: Movements, Parties, Organizations, and Policy* (Albany, NY: SUNY Press, 1993), pp. 257–74.

"The New Global Order: Underpinnings and Outcomes," in Armand Clesse, Richard Cooper, and Yoshikazu Sakamoto (eds.), *The International System After the Collapse of the East–West Order* (Dordrecht, The Netherlands: Martinus Nijhoff Publishers, 1994). pp. 106–26; translated and reproduced as "Le Nouvel Ordre Mondial: Forces Sous-Jacentes et Resultats," *Etudes Internationales*, Vol. XXIII (March 1992), pp. 9–36.

(with R. B. A. DiMuccio), "Turbulence and Sovereignty in World Politics: Explaining the Relocation of Legitimacy in the 1990s and Beyond," in Z. Mlinar (ed.), *Globalization and Territorial Identities* (London: Avesbury-Gower Publishing, 1992), pp. 60–76.

"Foreword," in Dmitri C. Constas and Athanassios G. Platias (eds.) *Diasporas in World Politics: The Greeks in Comparative Perspective* (London: Macmillan, 1993), pp. xv–xxi.

"Foreword," in Alex Roberto Hybel, *Power Over Rationality: The Bush Administration and the Gulf Crisis* (Albany, NY: State University of New York, 1993), pp. ix–xi.

"Preface," in Mark V. Kauppi and Paul R. Viotti, *The Global Philosophers: World Politics in Western Thought* (New York: Lexington, 1992), pp. xi–xiii.

"Individual Aspirations and Collective Outcomes: Notes for a Micro–Macro Theory of World Politics," a paper presented at the Annual Meeting of the American Political Science Association, Chicago, September 4, 1992.

"Normative Challenges in a Turbulent World," *Ethics & International Affairs*, Vol. 6 (1992), pp. 1–19.

"Constitutions in a Turbulent World," a paper presented at the Conference on Unification of Multi-System Nations, Taipei, Taiwan, September 27, 1991; translated and reproduced as "Les Constitutions dans un Monde en Proie aux Turbulences," *Cultures & Conflicts*, No. 8 (Winter 1992–1993), pp. 164–88.

"The Relocation of Authority in a Shrinking World: From Tiananmen Square in Beijing to the Soccer Stadium in Soweto via Parliament Square in Budapest and Wencelas Square in Prague," *Comparative Politics*, Vol. 24 (April 1992), pp. 253–72; reproduced in William C. Olson with James R. Lee (eds.), *The Theory and Practice of International Relations*, 9th ed. (Engelwood Cliffs, NJ: Prentice Hall, 1994), pp. 34–53.

"Governance, Order, and Change in World Politics," in J. N. Rosenau and E. O. Czempiel (eds.), *Governance without Government: Order and Change in World Politics* (Cambridge: Cambridge University Press, 1992), Chap. 1.

"Citizenship in a Changing Global Order," in J. N. Rosenau and E. O. Czempiel (eds.), *Governance without Government: Order and Change in World Politics* (Cambridge: Cambridge University Press, 1992), Chap. 10.

"Interdependence and the Simultaneity Puzzle: Notes on the Outbreak of Peace," in C. W. Kegley, Jr. (ed.), *The Long Postwar Peace: Contending Explanations and Projections* (New York: HarperCollins, 1991), pp. 307–28.

"Peripheral International Relationships in a More Benign World: Reflections on American Orientations Toward ANZUS," in Richard W. Baker (ed.), *Australia, New Zealand, and the United States: Internal Change and Alliance Relations in the ANZUS States* (New York: Praeger, 1991), Chap. 10.

(with Mary Durfee), "Global Order and Disorder: An Exploration of Chaos Theory" (October 1990), photocopy.

"Beyond Yalta and Malta," a paper prepared for the Conference on the Yalta System and After: Stability and Change in Northeast Asia, sponsored by the Korean Institute of International Studies, September 3–4, 1990.

(with Ole R. Holsti), "The Foreign Policy Beliefs of American Leaders: Prospects for a Post-Cold War Consensus," *ORBIS*, Vol. 34 (Fall 1990), pp. 579–97.

"Conceptualizing the Micro–Macro Dimension in World Politics," a paper prepared for the Steering Committee of the 4th World Assembly of International Studies, Buenos Aires, August, 1991.

"Superpower Scholars: Sensitive, Submissive, or Self-Deceptive," in Longin Pastusiak (ed.), *National Context of International Relations Studies* (Warsaw: Polish Institute of International Affairs, 1990), pp. 7–37.

(with Ole R. Holsti), "The Structure of Foreign Policy Attitudes Among American Leaders," *Journal of Politics*, Vol. 52 (February 1990), pp. 94–125.

"Authority in a Shrinking World: The Lessons of Tiananmen Square," a paper presented at the 31st Annual Conference of the American Association for Chinese Studies, Laramie, Wyoming, August 24, 1989.

"Global Transformations: Notes for a Workshop on Change in the International System," *Emerging Issues*, Occasional Paper #1 (Cambridge, MA: American Academy of Arts and Sciences, November 1989).

"Toward a Post-International Politics," prepared for presentation at the Annual Meeting of the International Studies Association, London, March 31, 1989.

"Change, Peace, and Scholarship: Notes for Five Papers in Search of a Program," prepared for presentation at the Center of International Affairs, Harvard University, November 10, 1988, and the University of Massachusetts at Amherst, November 22, 1988.

"Global Changes and Theoretical Challenges: Toward a Postinternational Politics for the 1990s," in E. O. Czempiel and J. N. Rosenau (eds.), *Global Changes and Theoretical Challenges* (Lexington, MA: Lexington Books, 1989), pp. 1–20.

"The Scholar as an Adaptive System," in J. Kruzel and J. N. Rosenau (eds.), *Journeys Through World Politics: Autobiographic Reflections of Thirty-Four Academic Travelers* (Lexington, MA: Lexington Books, 1989), pp. 53–68.

(with Ole R. Holsti), "Foreign and Domestic Policy Belief Systems Among American Leaders," *Journal of Conflict Resolution*, Vol. 32 (June 1988), pp. 248–94.

"Subtle Sources of Global Interdependence: Changing Criteria of Evidence, Legitimacy, and Patriotism," in J. N. Rosenau and H. Tromp (eds.), *Interdependence and Conflict in World Politics* (Aldershot: Gower, 1989), pp. 31–47.

"Patterned Chaos in Global Life: Structure and Process in the Two Worlds of World Politics," *International Political Science Review*, Vol. 9 (October 1988), pp. 357–94.

"Post-International Politics: The Micro Dimension," a paper presented at the 14th World Congress of the International Political Science Association, Washington, DC, September 1, 1988.

"Governance Without Government" a paper presented at the Annual Meeting of the American Political Science Association, Washington, DC, September 3, 1988.

"American Belief Systems and Consensus in a More Benign World" (Los Angeles: Institute for Transnational Studies, University of Southern California, 1988).

(with Ole R. Holsti), "A Leadership Divided: The Foreign Policy Beliefs of American Leaders, 1976–1984," in C. W. Kegley and E. R. Wittkopf (eds.), *The Domestic Sources of American Foreign Policy: Insights and Evidence* (New York: St. Martin's Press, 1988), pp. 30–44.

"The State in an Era of Cascading Politics: Wavering Concept, Widening Competence, Withering Colossus, or Weathering Change?" *Comparative Political Studies*, Vol. 21 (April 1988), pp. 13–44; reproduced in James A. Caporaso (ed.), *The Elusive State: International and Comparative Perspectives* (Newbury Park, CA: Sage, 1989), pp. 17–48.

"Toward Single-Country Theories of Foreign Policy: The Case of the USSR," in C. F. Hermann, C. W. Kegley, Jr., and J. N. Rosenau (eds.), *New Directions in the Study of Foreign Policy* (Boston, MA: Allen & Unwin, 1987), pp. 53–74.

(with James A. Caporaso, Charles F. Hermann, Charles W. Kegley, Jr., and Dina A. Zinnes), "The Comparative Study of Foreign Policy: Perspectives on the Future," *International Studies Notes*, Vol. 13, No. 2 (Spring 1987), pp. 32–46.

"CFP and IPE: The Anomaly of Mutual Boredom," *International Interactions*, Vol. 14, No. 1 (1988), pp. 17–26.

"Learning in East–West Relations: The Superpowers as Habit-Driven Actors," *Australian Outlook*, Vol. 41 (December 1987), pp. 141–50; abridged and reproduced in M. D. Intriligator and H. A. Jacobsen (eds.), *East–West Conflict: Elite Perceptions and Political Options* (Boulder, CO: Westview Press, 1988), pp. 19–44.

"Roles and Role Scenarios in Foreign Policy," in S. Walker (ed.), *Role Theory and Foreign Policy Analysis* (Durham, NC: Duke University Press, 1987), pp. 44–65.

"The Micro-Electronic Revolution and the Conduct of Foreign Policy," in S. J. Cimbala (ed.), *Artificial Intelligence and National Security* (Lexington, MA: Lexington Books, 1987), pp. 1–18.

(with Ole R. Holsti), "Consensus Lost. Consensus Regained? Foreign Policy Beliefs of American Leaders, 1976–1980+," *International Studies Quarterly*, Vol. 30 (December 1986), pp. 375–409.

(with Ole R. Holsti), "The Foreign Policy Beliefs of American Leaders: Some Further Thoughts on Theory and Method," *International Studies Quarterly*, Vol. 30 (December 1986), pp. 473–84.

"Before Cooperation: Hegemons, Regimes, and Habit-Driven Actors in World Politics," *International Organization*, Vol. 40 (Autumn 1986), pp. 849–94.

"Learning and Living World Politics: Involvement Through Detachment," *International Studies Notes*, Vol. 12 (Spring 1986), pp. 25–27.

"Micro Sources of Macro Global Change," (Los Angeles: Institute for Transnational Studies, University of Southern California, August 1986).

"Proof in World Politics" (Occasional Papers Series C, Center for Economic and Political Studies, University of Amsterdam, May 1987).

"Authority Structures in North–South Relations: A Search for Conceptual Uniformity," a paper presented at the Annual Meeting of the American Political Science Association, New Orleans, August 30, 1985.

"A Pre-Theory Revisited: World Politics in an Era of Cascading Interdependence," *International Studies Quarterly*, Vol. 28 (September 1984), pp. 245–306.

"On the Multiplicity of Actors, Levels, and Systems: Empirical-Pluralist Versus Grand-Theoretical Approaches to World Affairs," a paper presented at the Seminar on the Political Foundations of World Economic Trends, Chongqing, China, October 18, 1984; translated into Spanish and published as "El Pluralista Empirico vs. Los Puntos de Vista de las Grandes Teorias Sobre Relaciones Internacionales," *Foro Internacional*, Vol. 25 (April–June 1985), pp. 301–10; also translated into Japanese.

"Academe's Two Cultures: The Buddy System and the Jury System," (Los Angeles: Institute for Transnational Studies, University of Southern California, April 1984).

"New Non-Land Resources as Global Issues," in C. W. Kegley, Jr., and E. R. Wittkopf (eds.), *The Global Agenda: Issues and Perspectives* (New York: Random House, 1984), pp. 390–97.

"Breakpoints in History: Nuclear Weapons, Oil Embargos, and Public Skills as Parametric Shifts" (Los Angeles: Institute for Transnational Studies, University of Southern California, November 1983).

"Teaching and Learning in a Transnational World," *Educational Research Quarterly*, Vol. 8, (1983), pp. 29–35.

"The Adaptation of Small States," in B. A. Ince, A. T. Bryan, H. Addo, and R. Ramsaran (eds.), *Issues in Caribbean International Relations* (Lanham, MD: University Press of America, 1983), pp. 3–28.

" 'Fragmegrative' Challenges to National Security," in Terry L. Heyns (ed.), *Understanding US Strategy: A Reader* (Washington, D.C.: National Defense University, 1983), pp. 65–82.

"Provocation and Proof in World-System Analysis," *Comparative Political Studies*, Vol. 15 (October 1982), pp. 357–63.

(with Ole R. Holsti), "A Leadership Divided: The Foreign Policy Beliefs of American Leaders, 1966–1980," in C. W. Kegley and E. R. Wittkopf (eds.), *Perspectives on American Foreign Policy* (New York: St. Martin's Press, 1983), pp. 196–212.

(with Ole R. Holsti), "American Leadership in a Shrinking World: The Breakdown of Consensuses and the Emergence of Conflicting Belief Systems," *World Politics*. Vol. XXXV (April 1983), pp. 368–92; reproduced in G. J. Ikenberry (ed.), *American Foreign Policy: Theoretical Essays* (Glenview, IL: Scott, Foresman and Co., 1989), pp. 539–60.

(with Ole R. Holsti), "End of 'The Vietnam Syndrome'?: Continuity and Change in American Leadership Beliefs, 1976–1980," a paper prepared for the XIIth World Congress of the International Political Science Association, Rio de Janeiro, Brazil, August 14, 1982.

"Order and Disorder in the Study of World Politics: A Foreword to Ten Essays in Search of Perspective," in R. Maghroori and B. Ramberg (eds.), *International Relations' Third Debate: Globalism vs. Realism* (Boulder, CO: Westview Press, 1982), pp. 1–8.

"The Civic Self in a Transnational World," in Judith Gillespie and Dina Zinnes (eds.), *Missing Elements in Political Inquiry* (Beverly Hills, CA: Sage, 1982), pp. 157–76.

"National (and Factional) Adaptation in Central America," in Richard Feinberg (ed.), *Central America: International Dimensions of the Crisis* (New York: Holmes & Meier, 1982), pp. 239–69.

"The Elusiveness of Third World Demands: Conceptual and Empirical Issues," in W. L. Hollist and J. N. Rosenau (eds.), *World System Structure: Continuity and Change* (Beverly Hills, CA: Sage, 1981), pp. 262–88.

(with Ole R. Holsti), "The Foreign Policy Beliefs of Women in Leadership Positions," *Journal of Politics*, Vol. 43 (May 1981), pp. 326–47; reproduced in E. Boneparth (ed.), *Women, Power, and Policy* (New York: Pergammon Press, 1982), pp. 238–62.

(with W. Ladd Hollist), "World System Debates," *International Studies Quarterly*, Vol. 25 (March 1981), pp. 5–18.

(with Ole R. Holsti), "The Three-Headed Eagle Revisited: Who Are the Cold War Internationalists, Post-Cold War Internationalists, and Isolationists?" a paper presented at the Annual Meeting of the International Studies Association, Philadelphia, March, 1981.

"Toward a New Civics: Teaching and Learning in an Era of Fragmenting Loyalties and Multiplying Responsibilities," a paper presented at the Annual Meeting of the American Political Science Association, Washington, DC, September 1, 1979; translated into French and published in J. Sevrin (ed.), *La Democratie Pluraliste* (Paris: Economica, 1981), pp. 269–91.

(with Ole R. Holsti), "Cold War Axioms in the Post-Vietnam Era," in Alexander George, Ole R. Holsti, and Randolph M. Siverson (eds.), *Change in the International System* (Boulder, CO: Westview Press, 1980), pp. 263–301.

"Thinking Theory Thoroughly," in K. P. Misra and Richard Smith Beal (eds.), *International Relations Theory: Western and Non-Western Perspectives* (New Dehli: Vikas Publishing House, 1980), pp. 14–28; reproduced in P. R. Viotti and M. V. Kauppi (eds.), *International Relations Theory: Realism, Pluralism, Globalism, and Beyond*, 3rd ed. (Boston, MA: Allyn and Bacon, 1999), pp. 29–37.

(with Ole R. Holsti), "Does Where You Stand Depend on When You Were Born? The Impact of Generation on Post-Vietnam Foreign Policy Beliefs," *Public Opinion Quarterly*, Vol. 44 (Spring 1980), pp. 1–22.

(with Ole R. Holsti), "The United States in (and out of) Vietnam: An Adaptive Transformation?" *Yearbook of World Affairs* (1980), pp. 186–204.

(with Ole R. Holsti), "Public Opinion and Soviet Foreign Policy: Competing Belief Systems in the Policy-Making Process," *Naval War College Review*, Vol. XXXII, No. 4 (July–August 1979), pp. 4–14.

"Muddling, Meddling, and Modelling: Alternative Approaches to the Study of World Politics in an Era of Rapid Change," *Millennium*, Vol. 8 (Autumn 1979), pp. 130–44.

"The Terrorist and the Tourist: Two Extremes on the Same Transnational Continuum," a paper presented at the Annual Meeting of the International Studies Association, Washington DC, February 22, 1978; translated into French and published in *Etudes Internationales*, Vol. X (June 1979), pp. 219–52.

(with Ole R. Holsti), "America's Foreign Policy Agenda: The Post-Vietnam Beliefs of American Leaders," in Charles W. Kegley, Jr. and Patrick J. McGowan (ed.), *Challenges to America: United States Foreign Policy in the 1980s* (Beverly Hills, CA: Sage, 1979), pp. 231–68.

(with Robert R. Kaufman), "Comparative Politics," in D. M. Freeman (ed.), *Political Science: History, Scope and Methods* (New York: Free Press, 1977), pp. 45–83.

(with Ole R. Holsti), "Problem Recognition: Belief Systems of American Leaders," a paper presented at the Annual Conference of the International Studies Association, South Columbia, SC, October 27–29, 1977.

(with Ole R. Holsti), "Vietnam, Consensus, and the Belief Systems of American Leaders," a paper presented at the Hendricks Symposium on American Politics and the World Order, University of Nebraska, Lincoln, October 6–7, 1977; abridged and published in *World Politics*, Vol. XXXII (October 1979), pp. 1–56.

"Decision-Making Approaches and Theories," in A. de Conde (ed.), *Dictionary of the History of American Foreign Policy* (New York: Charles Scribner's Sons, 1978), Vol. I, pp. 219–28.

(with Ole R. Holsti), "The Meaning of Vietnam: Belief Systems of American Leaders," *International Journal*, Vol. XXXII (Summer 1977), pp. 452–74.

(with five graduate students), "Of Syllabi, Texts, Students, and Scholarship in International Relations: Some Data and Interpretations on the State of a Burgeoning Field," *World Politics*, Vol. XXIX, No. 2 (January 1977), pp. 263–342.

"Capabilities and Control in an Interdependent World," *International Security*, Vol. 1, No. 2 (October 1976), pp. 32–49; reprinted in R. O. Matthews, A. R. G. Rubinoff, and J. Stein (eds.), *International Conflict and Conflict Management* (Scarborough, Ontario: Prentice Hall of Canada, 1984), pp. 215–26.

"Puzzlement in Foreign Policy," *Jerusalem Journal of International Relations*, Vol. I, No. 4 (Summer 1976), pp. 1–10.

"The Restless Quest," in J. N. Rosenau (ed.), *In Search of Global Patterns*, pp. 1–9.

"Restlessness, Change and Foreign Policy Analysis," in J. N. Rosenau (ed.), *In Search of Global Patterns*, pp. 369–76.

(with Ole R. Holsti), "The 'Lessons' of Vietnam: A Study of American Leadership," a paper presented at the 17th Annual Meeting of the International Studies Association, Toronto, Canada, February 25–29, 1976.

(with Ole R. Holsti), "Vietnam Revisited: A Comparison of the Recollections of Foreign Service and Military Officers of the Lessons, Sources, and Consequences of the War," a paper presented at the Xth Congress of the International Political Science Association, Edinburgh, Scotland, August 16–19, 1976.

"International Studies in a Transnational World," *Millenium*, Vol. 5, No. 1 (Spring 1976), pp. 1–20.

"Intellectual Identity and the Study of International Relations, or Coming to Terms With Mathematics as a Tool of Inquiry," in D. A. Zinnes and J. V. Gillespie (eds.), *Mathematical Models in International Relations* (New York: Praeger, 1976), pp. 3–9.

"Comparison is a State of Mind," *Studies in Comparative Communism*, Vol. III (Spring/Summer 1975), pp. 57–61.

"Problembereich und National-Internationale Vermimttlungsprozesse," in Helga Haftendorn (ed.), *Theorie der Internationalen Politik: Gengenstand und Methode der Internationalen Beziehungen* (Hamburg: Hoffman und Campe Verlag, 1975), pp. 318–36.

"Changing Foreign Policy Orientations in Two Ohio Communities" (Los Angeles: Institute for Transnational Studies, University of Southern California, 1975).

"In Search of Global Patterns," *Society*, Vol. 13 (July/August 1975), pp. 29–33.

"Perspectives on World Politics," in J. N. Rosenau, K. W. Thompson, and G. Boyd (eds.), *World Politics*, pp. 1–11.

"The Study of Foreign Policy," *ibid.*, pp. 15–35.

"The Transnationalization of Urban Communities: Some Data on Elites in a Midwestern City" (Los Angeles: Institute for Transnational Studies, University of Southern California, 1974).

"Comparative Foreign Policy: One-Time Fad, Realized Fantasy, and Normal Field," in C. W. Kegley, Jr., A. G. Raymond, R. M. Rood, and R. A. Skinner (eds.), *International Events and the Comparative Analysis of Foreign Policy* (Columbia, SC: University of South Carolina Press, 1975), pp. 3–38.

(with George R. Ramsey, Jr.), "External vs. Internal Typologies of Foreign Policy Behavior: Testing the Stability of an Intriguing Set of Findings," in P. J. McGowan (ed.), *Sage International Yearbook of Foreign Policy Studies*, Vol. III (Beverly Hills, CA: Sage, 1975), pp. 251–68.

"The Final Examination as a Group Process," *Teaching Political Science*, Vol. 2 (October 1974), pp. 65–77.

"The Coming Transformation of America: Resistance or Accommodation?" *World Studies*, Vol. I (Spring 1974), pp. 1–26.

"Assessment in International Studies: Ego Trip or Feedback?" *International Studies Quarterly*, Vol. 18 (September 1974), pp. 339–67.

"Foreign Intervention as Adaptive Behavior," in J. N. Moore (ed.), *Law and Civil War in the Modern World* (Baltimore: Johns Hopkins University Press, 1974), pp. 129–41.

"Paradigm Lost: Five Actors in Search of the Interactive Effects of Domestic and Foreign Affairs," *Policy Sciences*, Vol. 4 (December 1973), pp. 415–36.

"Comparing Foreign Policies: Why, What, How?" in J. N. Rosenau (ed.), *Comparing Foreign Policies*, pp. 3–22.

"Theorizing Across Systems: Linkage Politics Revisited," in J. Wilkenfeld (ed.), *Conflict Behavior and Linkage Politics* (New York: David McKay, 1973), pp. 25–56.

"Mobilizing the Attentive Citizen: A Model and Some Data on a Neglected Dimension of Political Participation," a paper presented at the Annual Meeting of the American Political Science Association, New Orleans, LA, September 6, 1973.

"International Studies in the United States: Some Problems and Issues for the 1970s," *Yearbook of World Affairs* (1973), pp. 401–16.

(with Philip M. Burgess and Charles F. Hermann), "The Adaptation of Foreign Policy Research: A Case Study of an Anti-Case Study Project," *International Studies Quarterly*, Vol. 17 (March 1973), pp. 119–44.

(with Gary D. Hoggard), "Foreign Policy Behavior in Dyadic Relationships: Testing a Pre-Theoretical Extension," in J. N. Rosenau (ed.), *Comparing Foreign Policies*, pp. 117–50.

"Dissent and Political Leadership," *Dialogue*, Vol. 5 (1972), pp. 36–45.

"Foreword," in Davis B. Bobrow, *International Relations: New Approaches* (New York: Free Press, 1972).

"Adaptive Politics in an Interdependent World," *Orbis*, Vol. XVI (Spring 1972), pp. 153–73.

"The Domestic Sources of Foreign Policy," in R. Romani (ed.), *The International Political System* (New York: Wiley, 1972), pp. 403–07.

"Public Opinion, Foreign Policy, and the Adaptation of National Societies," *Societas*, Vol. 1 (Spring 1971), pp. 85–100.

(with Raymond Tanter), "Field and Environmental Approaches to World Politics: Implications for Data Archives," *Journal of Conflict Resolution*, Vol. XIV (December 1970), pp. 513–26.

"Public Protest, Political Leadership, and Diplomatic Strategy," *Orbis*, Vol. XIV (Fall 1970), pp. 557–71.

"Foreign Policy as Adaptive Behavior: Some Preliminary Notes for a Theoretical Model," *Comparative Politics*, Vol. 2 (April 1970), pp. 365–89.

"Adaptive Strategies for Research and Practice in Foreign Policy," in F. W. Riggs (ed.), *A Design for International Studies: Scope, Objectives, and Methods* (Philadelphia, PA: American Academy of Political and Social Science), pp. 218–45.

"The External Environment as a Variable in Foreign Policy Analysis," in J. N. Rosenau, V. Davis, and M. East (eds.), *The Analysis of International Politics*, pp. 145–65.

"The Politics of National Adaptation," a paper presented to the Round Table on the Comparative Study of Foreign Policy at the 65th Annual Meeting of the American Political Science Association, September 1969.

"Intervention as a Scientific Concept," *Journal of Conflict Resolution*, Vol. XII (June 1969), pp. 149–71; reprinted in Richard A. Falk (ed.), *The Vietnam War and International Law*, Vol. 2 (Princeton: Princeton University Press, 1969), pp. 979–1009.

"Toward the Study of National-International Linkages," in J. N. Rosenau (ed.), *Linkage Politics*, pp. 44–63.

(with Klaus Knorr), "Tradition and Science in the Study of International Politics," in K. Knorr and J. N. Rosenau (eds), *Contending Approaches to International Politics*, Chap. 1.

"The Concept of Intervention," *Journal of International Affairs*, Vol. XXII (Summer 1968), pp. 165–76.

"Political Science 221: Douglass College," in V. Davis and A. N. Gilbert (eds.), *Basic Courses in International Relations: An Anthology of Syllabi* (Beverly Hills, CA: Sage, 1968), pp. 84–90.

"Moral Fervor, Systematic Analysis, and Scientific Consciousness in Foreign Policy Research," in A. Ranney (ed.), *Political Science and Public Policy* (Chicago, IL: Markham, 1968), pp. 197–236.

"Comparative Foreign Policy: Fad, Fantasy, or Field," *International Studies Quarterly*, Vol. 12 (September 1968), pp. 296–329.

(with Neil McDonald), "Political Theory as Academic Field and Intellectual Activity," *Journal of Politics*, Vol. 30 (May 1968), pp. 311–44; reprinted in M. Irish (ed.), *Political Science: Advance of the Discipline* (Englewood Cliffs, NJ: Prentice Hall, 1968), pp. 21–54.

"The National Interest," *International Encyclopedia of the Social Sciences* (New York: Crowell-Collier, 1968), Vol. II, pp. 34–40.

"Private Preferences and Political Responsibilities: The Relative Potency of Individual and Role Variables in the Behavior of US Senators," in J. D. Singer (ed.), *Quantitative International Politics: Insights and Evidence* (New York: Free Press, 1968), pp. 17–50.

"Compatibility, Consensus and an Emerging Political Science of Adaptation," *American Political Science Review*, Vol. LXI (December 1967), pp. 938–88.

"Games International Relations Scholars Play," *Journal of International Affairs*, Vol. XXI (Summer 1967), pp. 293–303.

"Foreign Policy as an Issue Area," in J. N. Rosenau (ed.), *Domestic Sources of Foreign Policy*, pp. 11–50.

"The Premises and Promises of Decision-Making Analysis," in J. C. Charlesworth (ed.), *Contemporary Political Analysis* (New York: Free Press, 1967), pp. 189–211.

"Pre-Theories and Theories of Foreign Policy," in R. B. Farrell (ed.), *Approaches to Comparative and International Politics* (Evanston, IL: Northwestern University Press, 1966), pp. 27–92; partially reprinted in W. D. Coplin and C. W. Kegley, Jr. (eds.), *Analyzing International Relations: A Multimethod Introduction* (New York: Praeger, 1975), pp. 37–47, and in J. A. Vasquez (ed.), *Classics of International Relations* (Englewood Cliffs, NJ: Prentice Hall, 1986), pp. 148–62.

"Transforming the International System: Small Increments Along a Vast Periphery," *World Politics*, Vol. XVIII (April 1966), pp. 525–45; partially reprinted in H. S. Kariel (ed.), *The Political Order: A Reader in Political Science* (New York: Basic Books, 1970), pp. 356–59.

"Behavioral Science, Behavioral Scientists, and the Study of International Phenomena," *Journal of Conflict Resolution*, Vol. IX (December 1965), pp. 509–20.

"Internal War as an International Event," in J. N. Rosenau (ed.), *International Aspects of Civil Strife*, pp. 45–91; reprinted in G. A. Kelly and C. W. Brown, Jr. (eds.), *Struggles in the State: Sources and Patterns of World Revolution* (New York: Wiley, 1970), pp. 196–222.

"Meticulousness as a Factor in the Response to Mail Questionnaires," *Public Opinion Quarterly*, Vol. XXVIII (Summer 1964), pp. 312–14.

"The Functioning of International Systems," *Background*, Vol. 7 (November 1963), pp. 111–17.

"Convergence and Cleavage in the Study of International Politics and Foreign Policy," *Journal of Conflict Resolution*, Vol. VI (December 1962), pp. 359–67.

"Consensus-Building in the American National Community: Some Hypotheses and Some Supporting Data" *Journal of Politics*, Vol. 24 (November 1962), pp. 639–61; reprinted in J. E. Mueller (ed.), *Approaches to Measurement in International Relations: A Non-Evangelical Survey* (New York: Appleton-Century, 1969), pp. 68–87.

"Consensus, Leadership and Foreign Policy," *SAIS Review*, Vol. 6 (Winter 1962), pp. 3–10.

"The Birth of a Political Scientist," *PROD*, Vol. 3 (January 1960), pp. 19–21.

"Senate Attitudes Toward a Secretary of State," in J. C. Wahlke and H. Eulau (eds.), *Legislative Behavior* (New York: Free Press, 1959), pp. 333–46.

Index of subjects

Index of authors

For Product Safety Concerns and Information please contact our EU
representative GPSR@taylorandfrancis.com
Taylor & Francis Verlag GmbH, Kaufingerstraße 24, 80331 München, Germany

www.ingramcontent.com/pod-product-compliance
Lightning Source LLC
Chambersburg PA
CBHW050343270326
41926CB00016B/3582

9 780415 385480